MINERALS OF THE WORLD

Second Edition

Walter Schumann

MINERALS OF THE WORLD

Second Edition

STERLING

New York / London
www.sterlingpublishing.com

Translated by Elisabeth E. Reinersmann and Daniel Shea

STERLING and the distinctive Sterling logo are registered trademarks of
Sterling Publishing Co., Inc.

Library of Congress Cataloging-in-Publication Data

Schumann, Walter
  [Mineralien aus aller Welt. English]
  Minerals of the World / Walter Schumann; translated by Elizabeth E. Reinersman.
—2nd. ed.
    p. cm.
  Includes index.
  ISBN-13 978-1-4027-5339-8
  1. Minerals—Handbooks, manuals, etc. 2. Minerals—Identification—Handbooks,
manuals, etc. I. Title.

QE366.8.S3813 2008
549—dc22   2007045241

10 9 8 7 6 5 4 3 2 1

Published by Sterling Publishing Co., Inc
387 Park Avenue South, New York, N.Y. 10016
English translation © 2008 by Sterling Publishing Co., Inc.
Original Edition published in German under
the title *Mineralien aus aller Welt*
© 2007 by BLV Verlagsgesellschaft mbH, München 19
Distributed in Canada by Sterling Publishing
c/o Canadian Manda Group, 165 Dufferin Street
Toronto, Ontario, Canada M6K 3H6
Distributed in the United Kingdom by GMC Distribution Services
Castle Place, 166 High Street, Lewes, East Sussex, England BN7 1XU
Distributed in Australia by Capricorn Link (Australia) Pty. Ltd.
P.O. Box 704, Windsor, NSW 2756, Australia

Printed in China
All rights reserved

Sterling ISBN 978-1-4027-5339-8

For information about custom editions, special sales, premium
and corporate purchases, please contact Sterling Special Sales
Department at 800-805-5489 or specialsales@sterlingpublishing.com.

Contents

Preface

This field guide with its rapid-identification system represents something entirely new. The minerals are organized into categories based on three easily measurable properties: the streak, Mohs' hardness, and specific gravity. The properties are displayed in a multicolored bar on the left margin of the descriptive pages. Identifying individual minerals is made much easier by using the left margin bar.

Countless minerals that were previously difficult to recognize can now be identified or can—up to a point at least—be classified as belonging to a particular group.

The book covers the three main areas. The first part of the introduction explains how to use the rapid-identification system. Next, the many forms and properties of minerals are discussed. And lastly, the reader can use the guide for identification, learning how to apply the properties that can be determined.

The main section, the actual guide for identification, has the multicolored margin bar of properties along the left page. For collectors, this is the heart of the book.

Following the guide for identification, there is an extensive glossary. Combined with the extensive index, this makes the book not only a field guide but also a good reference work.

The glossary carries terms that are not explained in the text. Other concepts are listed in the index.

Many of my friends and colleagues have contributed to the success of this field guide with much enthusiasm. Countless people and several institutes supplied charts and photos. And to all of them, I give my heartfelt thanks.

Walter Schumann

 Permanently or strongly radioactive minerals

 Occasionally or more weakly radioactive minerals

Important Note

The advice and recommendations made in this book are based on the long-time experience of the author and have proven themselves in practice. However, in the interest of the reader, it is recommended to always proceed prudently and to take all necessary precautions especially when dealing with poisonous and radioactive substances. Neither the author nor the publication house and its employees can be held liable for personal, material, and property damage.

Organization

Recognizing Minerals From the approximately 3,000 known minerals in the world and their several thousand varieties, well over 500 entries have been carefully chosen.

The choices are not free from subjective judgment. Criteria governing them are how common they are, their degree of popularity as well as their availability on the international market. In fact, only a few hundred minerals in the world are found in abundance, are in a condition worthwhile for collecting, and, therefore, are of interest to mineral collectors.

Text The text for the guide is brief, often in a telegraphic style, and tailored to the interested collector, novice, or expert. The glossary further explains terminology. Primary emphasis is placed on information that is helpful to the user who wants to identify minerals. Included are notations of where an individual mineral is found, to which category it belongs, and what minerals are similar to the one in question. The multicolored bar of properties along the outside margin of the left page—opposite the photos of minerals—corresponds to the group of minerals discussed in the text.

With the text organized on the left and photos on the right, the user can easily compare the written information with the visual example.

Photographs The samples used for the photographs are not one-of-a-kind museum pieces but rather minerals and aggregates that any typical collector could find or buy. The specimens were photographed in such a way that the reader will be able to recognize many distinctive features with the naked eye. Some photographs have been enlarged either to clarify certain information or whenever technical reasons made it necessary to do so. The degree of enlargement is given in the form of a ratio. For instance, 1:3 means the photo is three times larger than the actual size; 1:½ means the photo represents one-half the actual size. For larger than actual size, only whole numbers are used, eliminating decimal points for simplicity. If the difference between the photo and the actual size is small, no ratio is given.

Drawings of Crystals These drawings are typical, though somewhat idealized. They are meant to give a general impression of the form of a particular crystal. The drawings were taken from scientific literature.

Localities The places where a particular mineral has been found in nature are listed generally either as a region or a country. To find specific localities, other sources must be consulted. When searching for a locality for a particular mineral, it is advisable to investigate several regions or countries of known occurrence as well as places that are of mineralogical, historic, or economic importance.

How to Find a Particular Mineral

The Rapid-Identification System

To identify a mineral, which means distinguishing it from any other, the collector has to make certain determinations. The identification system of this guide is based on three properties determined in the following order:

1. The streak
2. The Mohs' hardness
3. The specific gravity of the particular mineral

Additional characteristics must be carefully noted, including the luster, transparency, and cleavage.

With this information, it is possible to determine the mineral group to which a particular specimen belongs. The text, drawings, and photographs in the guide allow an even closer identification. Categories of minerals with similar characteristics are kept small enough so that it is often possible to make a positive identification after inspecting only one or two pages of photographs. Sometimes three pages may need to be consulted, but seldom more than four.

If a specimen displays a streak shading that might fall into more than one category, or if its degree of hardness or specific gravity points to another group, other possibilities are suggested in a boxed footnote on the page where the first group is discussed.

First Determination: What Is the Streak?

A simple method for the rough identification of a mineral is to look at its streak, also called powder color. Because, even if a mineral appears to have more than one color, or shows differing shades of color, its inherent color—or streak—is always the same.

The guide distinguishes among six streak categories, namely, white and colorless, green, gray and black, red and orange, gold and brown, and blue.

Along the outside margin of each left page of the guide is a bar of properties including the streak at the top. The bar corresponds to the group of minerals whose particular properties are discussed on the page.

Streak	Streak	Streak	Streak	Streak	Streak
White and colorless	Green	Gray and black	Red and orange	Gold and brown	Blue

If a mineral has a streak shading that might fall under two or more of the guide's streak categories, the mineral is discussed under one group and references in the box at the bottom of the page point the reader to the pages for the second category. A mineral, for instance, with a blue-green streak might be described in the green group (with photo and identifying characteristics), and cross-referenced in a boxed footnote in the blue group. If there is any doubt, check all the likely streak categories.

Light gray is used in the margin bar for the white and colorless group. Minerals with a definite gray streak are discussed in the gray and black group. A more detailed discussion of streak can be found on page 17.

Second Determination: What Is the Mohs' Hardness?

The degree of scratch hardness can be determined by observing the resistance of the mineral when scratched with a sharp-edged testing device (see also page 20). In developing the rapid-identification system, four hardness groups have been established based on the ten-point Mohs' hardness scale:

Mohs' hardness 1–2 ½
Mohs' hardness 3–4 ½
Mohs' hardness 5–6 ½
Mohs' hardness 7–10

If a particular streak category has only a few minerals in a specific hardness group, then two hardness groups have been combined.

The multicolored margin bar along the left page displays the relative Mohs' hardness scale in the middle section. One glance will tell the reader if the determined scratch hardness of the specimen corresponds to the range given in the scale—of course within the appropriate streak category; if not, continue within the streak category until the hardness is correctly identified. Each streak category progresses through the hardness groups from hardness 1 through 10.

Third Determination: What Is the Specific Gravity?

This characteristic—also called "relative density"—is often the one that will make a positive identification of a specimen possible. Specific gravity is the weight of a specific material compared with the weight of the same volume of water. This characteristic and its determination are discussed on pages 22 and 23.

Several ranges of specific gravity are again defined as groups for the lower section of the multicolored margin bar. As many minerals as possible are included in each group.

The lower section of the margin bar is fitted with a scale displaying values from 1 to 7. Values beyond 7 are indicated by an arrow pointing downward at the bottom of the scale.

Additional Determinations (If Necessary)

Most of the time these three basic properties—streak, Mohs' hardness, and specific gravity—are sufficient for the identification of an unknown mineral. If not, refer to the guide, checking the additional characteristics mentioned for minerals in that group. Perhaps some typical characteristics of a mineral are not well represented in the photograph or are not detectable in the specimen. Another property such as color, luster, or transparency may give the needed clue; or maybe the shape of the crystal or the discussion of the aggregates will clarify the determination.

The three basic properties and other ways of testing a specimen are discussed on pages 17 through 26. The additional characteristics may help narrow the field of possibilities among several minerals with similar streak, Mohs' hardness, and specific gravity.

Example—Fluorite

Rapid identification of a specimen is often possible by matching the information in the multicolored margin bar along the left page.

Determination	Result	Marking on left margin bar	Appropriate Pages
Streak?	White	Streak White and colorless	30–132 = 52 pages of photographs
Mohs' hardness?	4 belongs to hardness group 3–4½	Mohs' h. 1 2 3 4	56–80 = 13 pages of photographs
Specific gravity?	3.18 belongs to group 3.1–4.0	S. gravity 1 2 3 4	72–76 = 3 pages of photographs

Examining the remaining three pages usually makes it possible to quickly identify the specimen. Additional properties helpful in the decision-making process include the color (here: brownish), transparency (here: clear), shape of the crystal (here: cubic), and additional characteristics mentioned in the text.

External Shapes of Minerals

Structure of Minerals

Minerals are naturally occurring, self-contained components of celestial bodies, whether in the Earth or in the solid parts of other celestial bodies in the universe. They have a definite chemical composition with very definite physical and optical properties, and nearly all have an ordered atomic arrangement. Minerals are usually expressed in chemical formulas, excluding impurities even when they may cause part or all of the mineral's color.

We differentiate between 10 minerals:

Elements
Sulfides and related compounds
Halides
Oxides and hydroxides
Nitrates, carbonate
Borates
Sulfates, chromates, molybdates, and wolframate
Phosphates, arsenates, and vanadates
Silicates
Organic compounds

Synthetic products with the same composition and structure as a naturally occurring mineral are, nevertheless, not considered to be minerals.

There are minerals, however, that have the same chemical composition, but each mineral is its own distinct entity. The reason they are separate minerals is the difference in the crystal form. Such minerals are called polymorphic crystals with modified internal structures. For instance, carbon is a polymorph of graphite and diamond. The minerals quartz, cristobalite, citrine, amethyst, and tridymite, as well as opal, are polymorphs of silica.

Most minerals occur in crystalline form—whether they appear to be shapeless, display crystal faces, or are found in well-rounded pebbles. Each possesses its own internal geometric structure, which may be similar to other mineral crystals of differing compositions. The inner structure determines the physical and optical properties: the outer shape (faces), as well as the hardness, cleavage, type of fracture, specific gravity, refractive index, and optical axes. When this inner structure, the arrangement of atoms, ions, and molecules, appears in a regular, recurring pattern, it is called the spatial or crystal lattice.

Minerals with such a lattice are called crystalline; those without a definite inner arrangement are termed amorphous. Another category is crystals which are isomorphous—components of the lattice can be substituted by other substances without changing their basic crystalline and chemical structure. When such an exchange takes place to a large degree, the isomorphous crystals form a so-called solid solution such as for the calcium sodium feldspars—plagioclase.

It is common to find within a group of monomineralic crystals distinct varieties that, nevertheless, have the same properties. The basic chemical and crystalline structure within each

Geometrical crystal lattice of halite (large circles: chlorine; small circles: sodium).

Crystal Systems

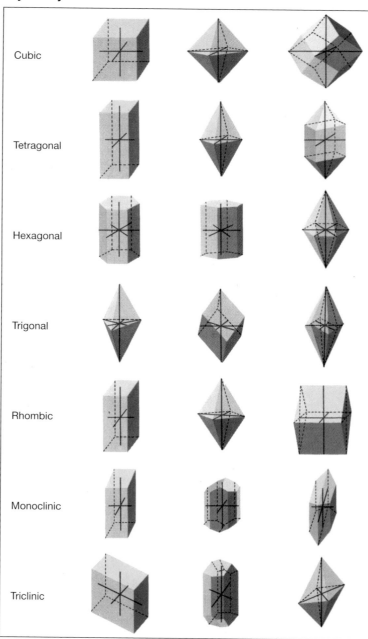

Cubic

Tetragonal

Hexagonal

Trigonal

Rhombic

Monoclinic

Triclinic

such apparent variety remains essentially fixed, given the conditions for crystal growth in the normal development of the mineral. Some minerals with a certain hardness and variations in color are used as gemstones for jewels.

Crystal Systems

Most minerals develop orderly geometrical atomic structures that are specific to the particular mineral crystal. The atomic structure controls the symmetry and overall shape of the crystals. In crystallography, crystals are divided into seven such symmetry systems. The difference between them is determined by crystal axes and angles. On the opposite page are diagrams of the seven crystal systems and some typical crystal forms.

Cubic System (Isometric and Regular) All three axes have the same length and intersect at right angles. Typical crystal shapes are the cube and octahedron (8 faces), rhombic dodecahedron (12 square faces), pentagon dodecahedron (12 pentagonal faces), icosi-tetrahedron (24 faces), and hexoctahedron (48 faces).

Tetragonal System All three axes intersect at right angles; two are of the same length and are in the same plane while the third (main axis) is either shorter or longer. Typical crystal shapes are four-sided prisms and pyramids, trapezohedrons and eight-sided pyramids as well as double pyramids.

Hexagonal System Three of four axes are in the same plane, are of equal length and intersect at an angle of 120° (respectively 60°). The fourth axis of differing length is at right angles to the others. Typical crystal shapes are hexagonal prisms and dipyramids as well as dihexagonal dipyramids and double pyramids.

Trigonal System (Rhombohedral) Axes and angles are similar to the preceding system and often the two systems are combined as the hexagonal. The difference is one of symmetry. In the hexagonal system, the cross section of the prism base is six-sided; in the trigonal system, it is three-sided. The hexagonal shape is formed when the corners of the triangles are beveled. Typical crystal forms are three-sided prisms and pyramids, rhombodehra, and scalenohedra.

Rhombic System (Orthorhombic) Three axes of unequal length are at right angles. Typical crystal shapes are basal pinacoids, rhombic prisms, and pyramids as well as rhombic double pyramids.

Monoclinic System Two of the three axes—all unequal in length—are at right angles to each other; the third is inclined. Typical crystal forms are basal pinacoids and prisms with inclined end faces.

Triclinic System All three axes are of different length and inclined toward each other. Typical crystal forms are paired faces.

The Law of Constant Angles

Each crystal, even of the same type of mineral, looks slightly different. You will find crystals that are large and small, narrow and wide, straight and angled. The ideal shape (ideal crystal) is rarely ever achieved. In nature, the grown crystal (as a real crystal) is usually somewhat misshapen; we say that it is distorted.

Despite the differences in appearance, there nevertheless exists a universally valid law among each type of crystal that can be recognized with the bare eye, the so-called constant angle. The angles between the edges, that is, those angles created by two corresponding faces always remain constant among minerals belonging to the same group (see ill. below regarding distortions with quartz crystals).

This law of constant angles is a significant supportive theory in crystallography. Experts use it to construct the ideal shape (ideal crystal) from the real crystal shape of the mineral crystal.

The law of constant angles is also a classification aid when identifying unknown minerals. With protractor instruments such as a goniometer, the crystal angles can be determined and minerals of similar appearance can be differentiated. With a calcite rhombohedron, for example, the contact angle is 75°; the rhombohedron of siderite is 73°; and the rhombohedron of magnesite is 72½°.

For the amateur collector, there is the easy-to-handle contact goniometer (see ill. below). The precision of measurement is here ½°.

The contact goniometer consists of a disc with a straight baseline, a semi-circle marked on it, and a movable arm that is centered on the semi-circle. Both the inner angles of the crystals and the complementary angles can be read with the help of the semi-circle.

The contact goniometer is only suitable for larger crystals or larger pieces.

In mineralogical science, researchers employ very exact measuring optical instruments, so-called reflecting goniometers. These instruments can be employed with even the smallest crystals.

Angle measurement on a rock crystal with a contact goniometer.

Possible distortions with various quartz crystals.

Twinning in Crystals

Where two or more crystals of the same group and the same shape are intergrown according to certain laws, it is called twinning. Depending on whether the individual crystals simply grow together or are intergrown, it is either contact twinning or penetration twinning. Depending on the number of individual members, it is also referred to as tripling, quadrupling, etc. Twinning of many individual crystals is often called multiple twinning.

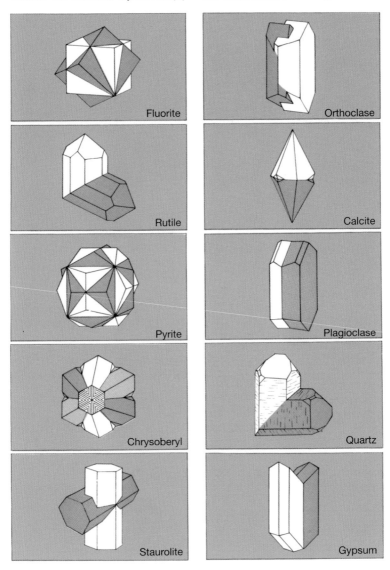

Fluorite

Orthoclase

Rutile

Calcite

Pyrite

Plagioclase

Chrysoberyl

Quartz

Staurolite

Gypsum

Mineral Aggregates

When several minerals—in sizes anywhere from millimeters to many meters—are irregularly intergrown, they are called aggregates. The individual minerals need not belong to the same group. Large units of aggregate are called rocks. An aggregate with several well-defined surface crystals is called a terrace.

The photographs above show some typical examples of mineral aggregates.

1 **skeletal** bearing some resemblance to dendrites, moss, branching trees, wire, knitting (copper);
2 **flaky** foliated, bearing some resemblance to scales, rose petals, rosettes (gypsum rose);
3 **radial** bearing some resemblance to radial filaments or striae (pyrite—so-called marcasite tubers);
4 **granular** recognizable with the naked eye, grainy-textured aggregate (olivine);
5 **crusty** bearing some resemblance to bark, thin coating of a cavity (pyromorphite);
6 **glass bead–like** reniform, botryoidal, wart-like, mammillary (red hematite);
7 **parallel fibrous** bearing some resemblance to tufts, bundles (amianthus/actinolite);
8 **disordered fibrous** bearing some resemblance to a tangled radiating texture, matted (actinolite);
9 **oolitic** pisolitic (pea-shaped concretions), bearing some resemblance to roe, shells (aragonite).

Mineral Characteristics

Color of Minerals and Streak

Only a very few minerals come in a single, characteristic color such as green malachite, red cinnabar, blue azurite, or yellow phosphor. Most minerals exhibit many different colors; some even have all the colors of the spectrum. Color alone is seldom a useful characteristic by which to identify an unknown specimen.

The streak, also called powder color, on the other hand, is a good, objective means for identification. The inherent color—or streak—can be seen whenever a mineral is pulverized. While the apparent coloring of a mineral variety is produced by impurities or the result of a disturbed crystal structure (thereby not the inherent color), the streak is always a distinct and constant color for a particular mineral. It is inherent—i.e., characteristic. The finely ground powder acts

Streak   Top, left to right: orpiment, pyrite, cinnabar
Bottom, left to right: hematite, azurite, malachite

Streak test on a porcelain streak plate. Brass-yellow pyrite produces a grayish-black streak.

like thin, transparent platelets. The streak color of fluorite (see page 10) is white, even if the mineral appears to be yellow, green, blue, violet, or black.

The inherent color can be determined by streaking the mineral on an unglazed porcelain tile, the streak plate. In the absence of an actual streak plate, the unglazed portion on the underside of a porcelain bowl or vase, the surface of an electrical fuse, or back of a glazed wall tile will do just fine.

Pulverizing the mineral by rubbing it across the plate will produce the streak. If no streak is detectable, the mineral's streak is said to be white or colorless.

Sometimes—for more accurate identification—it is advisable to compare a visible streak on the streak plate with the "streak" of the edge of another streak plate. Such hints are mentioned in the description of minerals in the guide for identication.

When the hardness of the specimen is greater than that of the streak plate (above Mohs' hardness 6), a small portion must first be pulverized. The powder is then rubbed onto the tile.

Use only fresh fractures when performing the streak test; avoid those parts that have been oxidized or discolored.

Pleochroism

Some transparent minerals appear to show a different color or depth of color when viewed from different angles. The reason is that light is absorbed differently depending on the direction it travels through the mineral. Pleochroism is the collective term for any such phenomena.

If two main colors can be observed, it is often called dichroism; three colors, trichroism. Dichroism is possible only in tetragonal, hexagonal, and trigonal crystal systems; trichroism only in rhombic, monoclinic, and triclinic systems. Amorphous minerals and those belonging to the cubic crystal system do not show pleochroism. The presence of pleochroism can be either weak, distinct, vivid, or very strong.

Light Effects and Surface Luster

With some minerals, specific striated light effects and surface color effects (luster) can only be observed after the mineral has been shaped or polished. These effects are not related to the mineral's color or streak and are not caused by impurities or chemical composition, but are caused by the reflection, interference, and refraction of light.

Adularescence: When cut en cabochon, some varieties of adularia reveal a milky or bluish sheen that glides across the surface as the stone is moved. It is caused by intergrowths due to its lamellar structure. Moonstone shown.

Asterism (Star Effect) Appearance of star-shaped figure of light that intersect in one spot. Arises through reflection of light on parallel fibers, needles or channels. Diopside (left) and rose quartz (right) shown.

Aventurescence Leaf-like inclusions create play of color of metallic reflections. Aventurine contains fuchsite mica or hematite plates; sunstone has plates of hematite or goethite. Sunstone shown.

Chatoyancy (Cat's Eye Effect) Light effect resembling the slit of a cat's eye. Results when light rays are reflected on parallel fibers, needles, or channels. Ulexite shown.

Labradorescence A play of color in metallic hues, particularly in labradorite. Blue and green effects are often found. Results from interferences within the finest lamellae. Spectrolite, a variety of labradorite, is shown.

Opalization A speckled play of color of some opal varieties that changes according to the angle of observation. It is caused by light reflection and interference of tiny inclusions. Black noble opal shown.

Mohs' Hardness

When a mineral collector speaks of hardness, the reference is usually to scratch hardness. In essence, this is a practical determination of the ability of the specimen to resist scratches that the collector is trying to make using a sharp-edged test mineral.

The scratch hardness test was invented by the Viennese mineralogist Friedrich Mohs (1773–1839). He developed a scale of ten minerals of increasing hardness. Mohs' scale is still a standard tool in use throughout the world. Scratch hardness 1 represents the softest mineral, 10 the hardest.

Some minerals show different hardness on different faces or in different directions. In general, however, the differences are so small that a collector need not be concerned.

Only in a few cases where the differences are very great must they be taken into consideration. Kyanite, for instance, has a Mohs' hardness of 4 to 4½ in the long direction of the crystal, while across it is 6 or 7.

Mohs' scratch hardness is a relative scale. It only shows which mineral scratches another. An absolute value of increasing hardness within the scale is not possible with Mohs' scale.

Each mineral in the series of ten scratches the previous one, and can be scratched by the following one. Minerals with equal hardness cannot scratch each other. By comparative application of Mohs' hardness scale, every mineral can be assigned a hardness. In the course of time half degrees of hardness have been added to the scale; but they are always written as ½ and not as 0.5.

Every book dealing with minerals uses Mohs' scale to designate the hardness of a mineral. Minerals with a scratch hardness of 1 and 2 are considered soft, 3 to 6 medium hard, over 6 hard.

Mohs' scale is only a relative measurement and lacks the necessary accuracy for strict scientific evaluation. A technically involved process has been established for determining "absolute" hardness. In the table above, the absolute values are compared to the relative Mohs' hardness. It is easy to see substantial differences between the two descriptions. However, the Mohs' hardness scale is indispensable to the collector—if only because it is so practical. Determining an absolute value of hardness is intractable for the layperson and not necessary for the identification of minerals.

Relative and Absolute Hardness Scale

Mohs' Hardness	Mineral	Simple Testing Devices	Absolute Hardness
1	Talc	Fingernail; rubbing	0.03
2	Gypsum	Fingernail: scratching possible	1.25
3	Calcite	Copper coin: scratching possible	4.5
4	Fluorite	Knife: scratching easily possible	5.0
5	Apatite	Knife: scratching still possible	6.5
6	Orthoclase	Steel file: scratching possible	37
7	Quartz	Will scratch window glass	120
8	Topaz		175
9	Corundum		1,000
10	Diamond		140,000

Tools for Testing the Scratch Hardness

Implements to test the Mohs' hardness of specimens are readily available such as kits of mineral samples or handy metal holders in which mineral chips are set. In the absence of such kits, a few simple devices can be used for a rough determination: A fingernail will scratch up to hardness 2; a copper coin to 3; a good steel pocketknife to as high as 5½. Steel files are even harder and will scratch to hardness 6. Quartz, Mohs' hardness 7, will visibly scratch window glass. Quite easily and simply a rough evaluation can be made in the field.

When a scratch test is made, it is important to make sure that only a sharp-edged test piece is used on an unbroken mineral face. Uneven formation, foliated or chipped crystals, and weathered surfaces can give a false lower hardness.

After the test scratch, a powder-like residue will remain on the surface of the unknown mineral. This residue might be either the test mineral or the mineral being tested. Therefore, wipe the dust off with a finger. If the dust can be removed revealing no scratch

Metal holders in which mineral chips are set for testing scratch hardness

mark, the test mineral is softer than the unknown mineral. If a scratch mark is revealed, the test mineral is harder. If no clear result can be detected with the naked eye, suggesting that the test mineral and the unknown mineral may have the same hardness, a magnifying glass may help decide the issue.

Mohs' hardness test kit of sample minerals, steel file, and knife.

Specific Gravity

Specific gravity—also called "relative density"—is the weight of a specific material compared with the weight of the same volume of water. For instance, quartz with a density of 2.65 is 2.65 as heavy as the same volume of water.

The specific gravity of minerals varies between 1 and 20. Values under 2 are considered light (amber 1.1); those from 2 to 4 normal (calcite 2.7); and those above 4 are heavy (lead 7.5). In mining practice, mineral with a value above 2.9 are called heavy.

Precious stones and precious metals have a specific gravity that is clearly higher than the ordinary rock-forming minerals that make up sand such as quartz and feldspar. This is the principle of panning and explains why they settle—in moderately moving waters—before the lighter sand minerals in river and coastal deposits.

Specific gravity is established according to the following formula:

$$\text{Specific Gravity} = \frac{\text{Weight of the Mineral}}{\text{Volume of the Mineral}}$$

The weight of the mineral is established on a scale. The more accurate the weight the more accurate will be the identification of the specimen. Experts work with $\frac{1}{100}$ gram precision.

Volume can be determined in several different ways: water displacement measured in a graduated cylinder or weight determined with a hydrostatic balance.

The first method requires the following procedure: The specimen is placed in a graduated cylinder that is halfway filled with water. The narrower the cylinder the more accurate the volume measurement. The amount of water displacement (the difference in the level of the water surface before and after the mineral is placed in the cylinder) is the volume of the object.

This method is not very good for small specimens since water displacement is minimal. In addition, reading the difference is made more difficult by a capillary effect; the surface of the water is higher at the edge of the cylinder than it is in the center (see illustration below). Always try to read from the lowest point of the water's surface.

Best results are obtained with a hydrostatic balance. It is based on Archimedes' Principle: The rise in the water level is equal to the volume of the water that has been displaced by the mineral. First weigh the specimen in air and then in water.

Method of determining volume by water displacement.

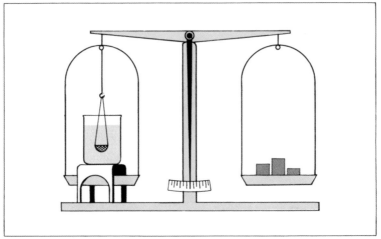

Method of determining volume with a hydrostatic balance.

The difference is equal to the weight of the displaced water and therefore also to the volume of the mineral.

Example:

Weight in air	5.2g
Weight in water	3.3g
Difference = Volume	1.9g

$$\text{Specific Gravity} = \frac{\text{Weight}}{\text{Volume}} = \frac{5.2}{1.9} = 2.7$$

The specific gravity of the specimen is 2.7. Based on this value, the specimen could be calcite.

It is important that the mineral—when weighed in air—is dry and free of any foreign substances. Some minerals, however, are naturally "contaminated"—if only slightly—or are subject to variation in the combination of their components. Either would mean that the specific gravity would be variable depending on the particular specimen.

In gemology, in addition to the hydrostatic balance, a so-called heavy liquid, or suspension, method is used to determine the specific gravity of a precious stone. It rests on the idea that by definition an object will remain suspended in a liquid of the same specific gravity; it will neither sink to the bottom nor float to the surface. The specimen is put into a liquid with a high specific gravity. The liquid is diluted—and the degree of dilution is recorded—until the specimen is suspended. Control indicators of known specific gravity, such as pieces of glass or minerals, can also be used to match the specific gravity of the diluted liquid. In either case, the result is the specific gravity of the specimen.

The suspension method is recommended when certain precious stones have to be separated from a group of unknown stones, or where synthetic stones or imitations have to be identified.

Cleavage

In mineralogy cleavage refers to the quality of a crystallized substance of splitting along definite planes. The crystal lattice of a mineral—the cohesive property of the atoms—determines if cleavage is possible. If the

Crystal lattice of halite. Due to the straight alignment of atoms, such a mineral can be split easily.

Crystal lattice of quartz. Due to the "turbid" alignment in the crystal lattice, no cleavage is possible.

components of the lattice are arranged in such a way that (theoretically) a flat object could pass through without touching any, cleavage is possible; if not, the attempt would result in fractures which create irregular surfaces.

The ease with which a crystal can be cleaved depends on the cohesive strength of the atoms as well as their arrangement. In the guide for identification, degrees of cleavability are differentiated as

perfect
complete
incomplete
none

Some minerals can only be split along one plane; others allow separation along two or more. Miners in the past would call minerals with very good cleavability spar. Examples include feldspars, river spar (sapphire), spar calcite or Iceland spar, and heavy spar (barite).

A cleavage plane of a mineral is unrelated to its external shape (e.g., crystal growth faces) and depends only on the structure of the crystal lattice. Different minerals that possess the same crystal symmetry may produce very similar cleavage forms—even if the original shapes were very different. Cleavage of galena and halite will always produce cubes; rhombohedra; fluorite: octahedral. The cleavage angle (the angle between two edges of a cleavage plane) is a characteristic property of a mineral.

Crystal growth faces usually do not have the same luster and are seldom as smooth as cleavage planes. Crystal faces typically show tiny flaws, patterns, and indentations.

Fracture

Whenever a mineral is accidentally broken (due to pressure or a blow) producing irregular surfaces, it is called fracture; however, if the resulting pieces have flat, smooth surfaces, it is called cleavage. The loosening of contact twins is not cleavage but separation. A fracture may be conchoidal (resembling the impression left by a seashell), uneven, smooth, fibrous, dendritic, hook-shaped, splintery, or crumbly (like crumbled earth).

Conchoidal fracture with well-expressed shell-like depressions (obsidian).

Tenacity and Toughness

Less known among collectors is the so-called tenacity for the classification of minerals. Tenacity refers to the reaction of a mineral when mechanically deformed, particularly the characteristic of ductility and elasticity. A mineral's tenacity can be described by the following terms: brittleness, flexibility, elasticity, and ductility.

Brittle: The brittleness of a mineral is tested with a steel needle scratching the surface of the mineral.

By using a scratching needle, one can test whether a mineral is brittle (1), malleable (2), or sectile (3).

If small mineral splinters jump off, then the mineral is brittle (ill. left, 1), if mineral powder collects next to the carving groove, then the mineral is considered malleable (ill. left, 2). In case the steel needle only leaves the carved scratching line without showing any powdered material, then we say that the mineral is sectile (ill. left, 3).

Some examples of brittle minerals are calcite, sulfur, and zinc-blende. Stibnite, galena, molybdenite are counted among the malleable minerals. Examples of minerals that can be cut and shaped include pure gold, argentite, and pure bismuth.

Malleable: Minerals that can be expanded and shaped when being pounded on, are called malleable (or forgeable). Examples are pure gold, silver as well as argentite.

Flexible: Small sections of fibrous and acicular minerals can sometimes be bent.

If the manually bent pieces spring back to their original position, the minerals are considered flexible and elastic. Asbestos, biotite, and muscovite belong to this group.

If the bent sections remain in their new position after being bent, then these minerals are flexible but inelastic, such as, for example, antimony and gypsum.

Toughness (in the more narrow sense of the word): Minerals that do not bend, cannot be shattered with a hammer, or shattered only with great difficulty (such as nephrite and jadeite), we call tough.

Magnetism

Magnetic behavior varies for different minerals. For instance, some minerals (such as magnetite) have magnetic properties of their own, while others

Some minerals (e.g., magnetite) act like a magnet, they attract metal parts.

(such as magnesite) are attracted by a magnet. The balance of minerals is magnetically neutral. Inherent magnetism and being attracted to a magnet are mineral properties that are easily determined with a directional compass.

The suspended magnetized needle in a compass is sensitive to even slight magnetic influence. Position the specimen at rest next to the compass needle and observe any changes. Small specimens and those with weaker magnetic forces are tested by moving them back and forth over the compass—as close as possible. For some minerals the degree of magnetism varies according to the locality as well as their iron content.

Transparency

Transparency is the ability of light to penetrate a mineral. There are transparent, semi-transparent, and opaque minerals. In very thin sections, many opaque minerals are transparent or semi-transparent. All metals are opaque, regardless of how thin the sample might be. Granular, fibrous, or dendritic minerals, as well as all aggregates, are always opaque.

Luster

Many minerals have their own characteristic luster. It is the result of light reflected back from the surface and is dependant on the refractive index and the nature of the surface, but not on the color.

When describing minerals, one speaks of vitreous (glassy), waxy, and resinous as well as silky, mother-of-pearl, adamantine (diamond), greasy, and metallic.

Minerals without luster are described as dull.

Vitreous luster is the most common among minerals—accounting for about two-thirds of all minerals. Metallic luster is only found in opaque minerals, particularly those of the pure metals, sulfides, and oxides. Silky luster is found in fibrous minerals as well as mineral aggregates. Mother-of-pearl and greasy luster are mostly found of the plane of cleavage.

Tarnish, discolorations, and weathering are all able to detract from the luster of a mineral. Therefore, only examine a specimen that has not been otherwise altered, and only in bright light.

Refraction of Light and Double Refraction

Apart from optical characteristics, such as color, luster, and transparency, the refraction of light and double refraction are also valuable means to determine transparent and translucent minerals.

Refraction of light The refraction of light (alteration of light rays when entering the crystal) belongs to the most important tools when it comes to identifying polished gems.

The refractometer measures the refractive index. The exact measurements can be read on a scale.

Double refraction Double refraction occurs when a ray of light enters the crystal and separates into two rays. All transparent minerals, except those that are cubic and amorphous, show some degree of double refraction. Calcite found in Iceland shows double refraction especially clearly. It is also easily seen in zircon and sphene, where double refraction at the lower edge of the crystal can be observed with the naked eye. In general, however, a special instrument is needed in order to detect double refraction.

For the mineral collector, the double refraction is an even more important tool when it comes to identifying minerals. It occurs with all transparent minerals, except amorphous ones and those of the cubic system. Here, a single ray of light is split into two rays when entering the crystal.

The double refraction needs to be measured and represents a constant of mineral characteristics.

With the Iceland spar, the double refraction can be seen most distinctly. An underlaid graphic, for example, appears with its lines doubled (see ill. below). This calcite is, therefore, also called optical calcite.

Double refraction in calcite from Iceland.

Radioactivity

The characteristic of sending out rays without energy supply is called radioactivity.

We differentiate between three types of rays: alpha rays (α-rays), beta rays (β-rays), and gamma rays (γ-rays).

Alpha radiation is the most insignificant one. Beta radiation is slightly stronger; however, its reach and penetrating power are still pretty weak. Gamma radiation is the most intensive one. It has the ability to penetrate iron and thick walls. Due to this strong penetrating power, gamma radiation is also called hard radiation.

Attention!
Radioactive radiation is dangerous!

Never store radioactive minerals (not even in small amounts) in your living room, bedroom, or workrooms. Keep food and film away.

Place minerals that you are not currently examining several feet away.

If you take radioactive material into your hands, make sure that you wash them thoroughly afterward.

Change any clothing that has come into contact with radioactive stones or dust and wash them.

Mark any radiating minerals clearly as radioactive.

In the present texts, continually or strongly radiating minerals are marked with a strong radiation protection logo, the remaining radioactive minerals with a weakly depicted logo.

Always keep radioactive material out of reach of children.

It is advisable for collectors to only keep few mineral specimens, if possible, in order to minimize the radiation hazard.

Radioactive radiation can be life-threatening!

Fluorescent minerals under white light (left) and under ultraviolet light (right); barium, calcium, potassium, sodium, strontium.

Fluorescence

Fluorescence is the ability of a substance to glow (luminesce) when exposed to ultraviolet light. Many minerals will only give off a white light; others produce a color in one of many hues. The name fluorescence comes from the mineral fluorite, which was the substance in which this phenomenon was first observed. If the object continues to glow after the ultraviolet light has been turned off, the effect is called phosphorescence—after the well-known glow of phosphorous.

Luminescence is the collective term for the phenomenon of substances glowing regardless of the physical or chemical reaction or rays that are illuminating them, with the exception of heat radiation. The cause of these phenomena is the incorporation of impurities and other structural discrepancies within the crystal. Some minerals will react only to short waves (2,800–2,000 Å), others only to long waves (4,000–3,150 Å). Some minerals will react to both long wave (designated 3,650 Å) and short wave (designated 2,537 Å) ultraviolet light.

For identification purposes, fluorescence is only of limited use, because specimens of the same mineral group can produce entirely different shades of color, while others do not react at all. At times fluorescence might be a helpful characteristic when a particular locality from which a mineral originated needs to be identified. Some localities yield very distinct fluorescent colors for a particular mineral.

Fluorescence is very useful in recognizing synthetic and imitation specimens. The glue used to join mineral pieces, for instance, has a different fluorescence than the mineral itself.

Flame-Test Color

Since some elements have the ability to change the color of a flame, a flame test can be useful in determining the chemical components of an unknown mineral. A gas flame is preferred over a candle flame because the gas is easily regulated so that the flame's own color is not visible. It is best to darken the room when conducting a flame test. Strontium produces a purplish red flame, lithium a carmine red, calcium a brick red, sodium a yellow,

Flame color as a method of identifying minerals.

| Barium | Calcium | Kalium | Natrium | Strontium |

barium a yellowish green, boron a green, copper a blue, and potassium a violet flame.

Only a small sliver of the material is necessary for a flame test. Hold the sliver—with a pair of tweezers or a platinum loop—in the flame until the sliver begins to glow. It is important to make sure that the piece to be tested is not contaminated.

Other Characteristics

Sometimes the identification process can be greatly assisted by very simple tests, such as smelling (sulfurous, earthy), tasting (salty, bitter), or touching (greasy, cold—which means that it is a good conductor of heat). Water solubility and reactions to acid or base can also be helpful.

Experts must sometimes undertake very specific tests under particular circumstances, such as when dealing with precious stones or when a potentially economic mineral vein has been located. Among the properties that can be tested are the optical dispersion of white light into its spectral colors, absorption and absorption spectra, microscopic studies of reflection as well as incident and penetrating light, fusibility and radioactivity.

Imitations

Always be critical and even skeptical when it comes to identifying minerals since there are many ingenious imitations!

Sometimes crystals are pasted onto the mother rock or are embellished through coloring as well as irradiating.

Since all minerals can be produced synthetically as well, one should pay special attention to individual crystals, particularly with minerals that are intended as gemstones and are purchased in a foreign country.

Borax

Na$_2$[B$_4$O$_5$(OH)$_4$] · 8 H$_2$O

① Boron, California/USA
② Boron, California/USA

Streak white. **Mohs' hardness** 2–2$\frac{1}{2}$. **Specific gravity** 1.7–1.8. **Characteristics**: white, yellowish, seldom bluish, greenish. Weathered surface: gray. Luster: greasy, vitreous, resinous, weathered surface dull; transparent to opaque. Cleavage: perfect. Fracture: conchoidal; brittle; easily soluble in water. Taste: bitter-sweet. Crystals: (monoclinic) short-prismatic, thick columned, also tabular. **Aggregates**: rough, grainy, fibrous, crumbly, powdery, as crust; present in salt lake beds, hot spring deposits, and volcanic vents. **Accompanied by**: halite, soda, gypsum, calcite, colemanite, kernite, ulexite. **Found in**: Nevada/USA; Tibet/China; Kashmir/Pakistan/India; Kazakhstan; Iran. **Similar to**: kernite, colemanite, sassolite, soda, trona.

Sassolite boric acid

B(OH)$_3$

③ Death Valley, California/USA

Streak white. **Mohs' hardness** 1. **Specific gravity** 1.48. **Characteristics**: white to gray, occasionally colorless, yellow to brown. Luster: vitreous, cleavage surfaces mother-of-pearl; transparent. Cleavage: perfect. Malleable; greasy to the touch; soluble in warm water. Taste: sour. Low melting point; flame test: green. Crystals (triclinic) pseudo-hexagonal, tabular, sometimes acicular. **Aggregates**: flaky, scaly, crusty, powdery; present at hot spring deposits and from sublimation associated with volcanic vents. **Found in**: Tuscany, Vesuvius/Italy; Kamchatka/Russia; Ladakh/India; California, Nevada/USA. **Similar to**: borax, kernite.

Sal Ammoniac Ammonium chloride ④ Paricutin/Mexico

NH$_4$Cl

Streak white. **Mohs' hardness** 1–2. **Specific gravity** 1.53. **Characteristics**: colorless, white, sometimes yellow to brown. Luster: opaque; transparent. Cleavage: imcomplete. Fracture: conchoidal, crumbly, moderate, malleable but tough; easily soluble in water. Taste: stinging, salty. Crystals: (cubic) cubic, octahedral; rare and small. **Aggregates**: rough, crusty, skeletal, stalactitic, botryoidal, fibrous and crumbly; present at volcanic vents, on burning coal fields, as layers of minable ore and coal, in guano. **Accompanied by**: phosphorite. **Found in**: Ruhr valley, Saarland, Saxony/Germany; Etna, Vesuvius/Italy; Hekla/Iceland; California, Hawaii/USA; Chile; Peru. **Similar to**: alunite.

Epsonite bitter salt

Mg[SO$_4$] · 7 H$_2$O

⑤ California/USA

Streak white. **Mohs' hardness** 2–2$\frac{1}{2}$. **Specific gravity** 1.68. **Characteristics**: white, sometimes greenish, reddish, yellowish. Luster: transparent to translucent. Cleavage: perfect. Fracture: conchoidal, brittle; easily soluble in water. Taste: bitter-salty. Crystals: (rhombic) prismatic, acicular, filamentary, fibrous; rare. **Aggregates**: fibrous with silky luster, radial, stalactitic, grainy, crumbly as cottony rosettes, crusty as deposits in salt springs and ore bodies; present as deposits in salt lakes and in arid steppe regions. **Accompanied by**: anhydrite, carnallite, gypsum, halite, calcite. **Found in**: Lower Saxony/Germany; Czech Republic; Serbia; Montenegro; Surry/England; Colorado/USA; Kazakhstan; Crimea/Ukraine. **Similar to**: Kieserite.

Sulfur p. 42, sepiolite p. 42, serpentine p. 48, chrysocolla p. 134

Ozokerite earth wax
Mixture of hydrocarbons

① Pribram/Czech Republic 1:3

Streak white, also brown. **Mohs' hardness** 1–2. **Specific gravity** 1.1–1.2. **Characteristics:** yellow to greenish, brown to black. Luster: greasy, opaque. Cleavage: none. Fracture: shallow conchoidal to hook-shaped. Malleable to brittle. Odor: waxy. Melting point between 50–100°C. Crystals: none, amorphous. **Aggregates:** rough, fibrous, tabular, botryoidal; present as impregnations or in the pore space of sandstone and slate. **Found in:** Galizia/Poland, Romania; Trinidad; Venezuela.

Mellite honey stone
$Al_2[C_{12}O_{12}] \cdot 18\,H_2O$

② Thuringia/Germany
1:2

Streak white. **Mohs' hardness** 2–2½. **Specific gravity** 1.6. **Characteristics:** honey to wax-yellow, brown to reddish, seldom white. Luster: vitreous; greasy; transluscent. Cleavage: incomplete. Fracture: conchoidal, somewhat brittle. Blue fluorescence under ultraviolet light; soluble in nitric acid and potassium hydroxide. Crystals: (tetragonal) dipyramidal, small, often convex, rough faces; isolated intergrowth and surficial crystals; rare. **Aggregates:** rough, small, fine-grained or nodular; present in crevices and cavities in lignite and anthracite, sometimes in sandstone. **Accompanied by:** ordinary coal. **Found in:** Saxony, Thuringia/Germany; Czech Republic; Seine/France, Tula/Russia. **Similar to:** amber.

Kernite
$Na_2[B_4O_6(OH)_2] \cdot 3\,H_2O$

③ Kern Co., California/USA

Streak white. **Mohs' hardness** 2½–3. **Specific gravity** 1.9. **Characteristics:** when fresh colorless and transparent, but usually white and opaque. Luster: vitreous, on cleavage surface silky to mother-of-pearl. Cleavage: perfect. Fracture: dendritic, splintery, brittle. Flame test: yellow. Crystals: (monoclinic) prismatic, pyramidal, wedge-shaped, tabular mass; rare. **Aggregates:** rough, coarsely spar-like with fibrous structure; present in tabular or irregular masses, in borate deposits. **Accompanied by:** borax, colemanite, ulexite. **Found in:** California/USA; Argentina; Turkey; Catalonia/Spain. **Similar to:** borax, sassoline.

Sylvite
KCl

④ with yellowish halite;
Kern Co., California/USA

Streak white. **Mohs' hardness** 1½–2. **Specific gravity** 1.9–2.0. **Characteristics:** colorless, gray, white, yellowish to reddish, seldom blue or violet. Luster: greasy-vitreous; transparent, also often cloudy. Cleavage: perfect. Fracture: uneven, brittle. Taste: bitter, pungent, salty. Flame test: violet. Easily water-soluble; when contaminated hygroscopic; good heat conductor. Crystals: (cubic) cubic, octahedral in geodes and crevices. **Aggregates:** granular, rough, dense, seldom dendritic; found in potassium hydroxide salt deposits, with halite to form rock (sylvinite), on crevices in halite and anhydrite rocks; rarely found associated with volcanic vents or as deposits in deserts and steppe regions. **Accompanied by:** halite, gypsum and anhydrite, carnallite, polyhalite, kieserite, kainite. **Found in:** Baden, eastern Harz mountains, Lower Saxony/Germany; Galicia/Poland; Urals/Russia; Alsace-Lorraine/France; Etna, Vesuvius/Italy; Saskatchewan/Canada; New Mexico, Texas/USA; Chile; Peru; India. **Similar to:** halite, anhydrite.

32

Streak

white and
colorless

Mohs' h. — 1 ◄

2 ◄

3 ◄

4 ◄

5 ◄

6 ◄

7 ◄

8 ◄

9 ◄

10 ◄

S. gravity — 1 ◄

2 ◄

3 ◄

4 ◄

5 ◄

6 ◄

7 ◄

Carnallite

$KMgCl_3 \cdot 6\,H_2O$

① Hattorf, Philippsthal, Hesse/Germany
② Röbling, Halle/Germany 1:½

Streak white. **Mohs' hardness** 1–2. **Specific gravity** 1.6. **Characteristics**: yellow to white, reddish, seldom white, colorless or blue. Luster: greasy-vitreous, usually with a metallic sheen, turning dull soon after exposure to air; translucent to transparent. Cleavage: none. Fracture: conchoidal, brittle; highly hygroscopic; dissolves easily in water (with a crackling sound). Generally highly fluorescent. Taste: biting, bitter. Crystals: (rhombic) pseudohexagonal, barrel-shaped, tabular mass, scattered, or in pore space; rare. **Aggregates**: rough, grainy, sometimes fibrous; present in rock-forming carnallite as important source of potassium in potash mines; as concretions and as recent deposits in salt lakes. **Accompanied by**: anhydrite, halite, kainite, kieserite, sylvite, boracite, polyhalite. **Found in**: Lower Saxony, Hesse, near the towns of Magedburg, Halle, Erfurt/Germany; Galicia and Catalonia/Spain; Urals/Russia; Iran; Libya; Saskatchewan/Canada; New Mexico, Texas, Utah/USA.

Aluminite

$Al_2[(OH)_4\,|\,SO_4] \cdot 7\,H_2O$

③ More, Halle/Germany 1:2

Streak white. **Mohs' hardness** 1–2. **Specific gravity** 1.6–1.8. **Characteristics**: white to yellow, gray. Luster: dull, transparent to opaque. Cleavage: incomplete. Fracture of aggregate crumbly, soft, easy to crush; soluble in acid. Crystals: (rhombic or monoclinic) indiscernible. **Aggregates**: botryoidal, reniform, tuberous, crumbly, minutely flaky, occasionally spherolitic; present in layered clay, sand, and gypsum deposits, and in coal ore. **Found in**: Saxony/Germany; Bohemia/Czech Republic; Sussex/England; vicinity of Paris/France; Punjab/Pakistan; Colorado, Missouri, Utah/USA. **Similar to**: alunite.

Natrite soda

$Na_2CO_3 \cdot 10\,H_2O$

④ Kazakhstan 1:½

Streak white. **Mohs' hardness** 1–1½. **Specific gravity** 1.42–1.47. **Characteristics**: colorless, gray-white, yellowish. Luster: vitreous, dull; transparent to translucent. Cleavage: complete. Fracture: conchoidal, crumbly. Flame test: yellow; melts at 32°C. Easily soluble in water. Crystals: (monoclinic) large crystals unknown in nature. **Aggregates**: granular, dendritic, acicular, as a crust and dusting; present in salt lake deposits, deposits covering the soil in arid regions, and volcanic vent deposits. **Found in**: region around Vesuvius, Etna/Italy; Hungary; Armenia; Kazakhstan; Egypt; Tanzania; Gobi desert/Mongolia; Tibet/China; California, Nevada/USA. **Similar to**: borax, colemanite.

Struvite

$(NH_4)Mg[PO_4] \cdot 6\,H_2O$

⑤ Hamburg/Germany

Streak white. **Mohs' hardness** 1½–2. **Specific gravity** 1.7. **Characteristics**: color: yellow or brownish, seldom colorless, white after dehydration. Luster: vitreous, after dehydration dull; transparent to translucent. Cleavage: complete. Fracture: uneven, moderate; piezo- and pyroelectric. Crystals: (rhombic) short prismatic, wedge-shaped, also in a tabular mass. **Aggregates**: present in recent sediments with a high proportion of organic matter, also in guano, cesspits, and ditches. **Found in**: Hamburg/Germany; Limfjord/Denmark; Victoria/Australia; Papland/South Africa; Réunion Island/Indian Ocean.

Streak

white and
colorless

Mohs' h. — 1 ◄

2 ◄

3 ◄

4 ◄

5 ◄

6 ◄

7 ◄

8 ◄

9 ◄

10 ◄

S. gravity — 1

2 ◄

3 ◄

4 ◄

5 ◄

6 ◄

7 ◄

Amber

① Palmnicken/Poland 1:2

Approximately $C_{10}H_{16}O$

Streak white. **Mohs' hardness** 2–2½. **Specific gravity** 1.05–1.30. **Characteristics**: light yellow to brown, also red to almost colorless, green, blue, and black, occasionally cloudy or streaky. Cleavage: none. Fracture: conchoidal, brittle; becomes electrically charged when rubbed, attracting small particles. Can be ignited by a match, giving off a resinous smell; floats on the surface of a saline solution. Crystals: none, amorphous; amber is the fossilized, hardened resin of the pine tree, *Pinus succinifera*, formed in the Eocene period about 50 million years ago. **Aggregates**: tuberous, stalactitic, layered; often containing inclusions of insects and parts of plants; present in the so-called blue earth amber-bearing clay and coastal deposits. **Found in**: Samland/Poland; Atlantic coast/USA; Dominican Republic. **Similar to**: resins, synthetics, yellow glass, ambroid, mellite.

Gaylussite

② Amboseli Sea/Kenya 1:2

$CaNa_2[CO_3]_2 \cdot 5\,H_2O$

Streak white. **Mohs' hardness** 2½–3. **Specific gravity** 1.99. **Characteristics**: white, colorless, gray, yellowish. Luster: dull-vitreous. transparent to translucent. Cleavage: complete. Fracture: conchoidal, brittle; easily soluble in water. Crystals: (monoclinic) flat, elongated wedge-shaped, octahedral, faces usually rough. **Aggregates**: rough, grainy, dispersed; present in salt lakes, desert sands, or in saline-rich soil (such as marshlands). **Found in**: California, Nevada, Wyoming/USA; Venezuela; Gobi desert/Mongolia; Madrid/Spain.

Halotrichite

③ Colorado/USA 1:4

$FeAl_2[SO_4]_4 \cdot 22\,H_2O$

Streak white. **Mohs' hardness** 1½. **Specific gravity** 1.73–1.79. **Characteristics**: white, colorless, grayish, yellowish. Luster: vitreous to silky; translucent. Cleavage: incomplete. Fracture: fibrous, brittle; easily water soluble. Taste: pungent. Crystal: (monoclinic) acicular and fibrous. **Aggregates**: rough, grainy, dispersed; present in brown coal, ore mines, and slate containing pyrite; by product in fumeroles. **Found in**: Rhineland/Germany; Czech Republic; Campania/Italy; Urals/Russia; Iran; Chile; California, New Mexico/USA.

Ulexite

④ Boron, California/USA
⑤ Ihn, Hemmersdorf, Saarland/Germany

$NaCa[B_5O_6(OH)_6] \cdot 5\,H_2O$

Streak white. **Mohs' hardness** 1–2½. **Specific gravity** 1.96. **Characteristics**: crystals colorless with vitreous luster, white fibrous aggregates with silky sheen, otherwise dull; transparent to translucent. Cleavage: perfect. Fracture: fibrous, soft; water soluble. Flame test: yellow. Crystals: (triclinic) acicular, scaly, short prismatic; very rare and very small. **Aggregates**: cottony fibrous; small aggregates with parallel fibrous structure have light conducting abilities, so-called television stone; present in terraced salt deposits, rarely as deposits associated with volcanic springs. **Accompanied by:** gypsum, anhydrite, glauberite, halite, borax, trona, colemanite, calcite. **Found in**: Tuscany/Italy; Kazakhstan; California, Nevada/USA; Atacama/Chile; Argentenia, Peru. **Similar to**: colemanite, datolite. See also ill. p. 19.

Gypsum selenite
CaSO$_4$ · 2 H$_2$O

① Tuscany/Italy
② Thüringia/ Germany
③ Sahara/Tunisia
④ Valencia/Spain 1:2

Streak white. **Mohs' hardness** 1½–2. **Specific gravity** 2.2–2.4. **Characteristics:** colorless, white, multicolored. Luster: vitreous, cleavage surfaces mother-of-pearl, fibrous aggregates display silky sheen; transparent to translucent. Cleavage: perfect. Fracture: conchoidal, fibrous, soft to brittle, malleable but not flexible; poor heat conductor; turns cloudy when heated; sometimes fluorescent and phosphorescent under ultraviolet light. Crystals: (monoclinic) prismatic, tabular, lenticular; occurring intergrown and as surficial growth; frequent twinning and pseudomorphs. **Aggregates:** rough, granular, parallel fibrous (fibrous gypsum), scaly, dense (alabaster); rosette-shaped (desert-, gypsum-, or sandrose), with strong snake-like layers, often contaminated with bitumen (stink gypsum), rock-forming, leaf-layered, transparent shapes are called "lady's ice" or "Mary's glass"; present in salt lakes, salt and iron ore mines, as concretions in clay-rich rock formations, deposits in deserts, and old iron ore mines. **Accompanied by:** anhydrite, halite, aragonite, dolomite, boracite. **Found in:** Harz mountains, Thüringia/Germany; Tyrol/Austria; Alsace, region around Paris/France; Tunisia; Morocco; Uzbekistan; Western Ural region/Russia; New Mexico, Utah/USA; Chile. **Similar to:** anhydrite, gypsum; calcite; marble; talc; muscovite; brucite, glauberite, celestite.

Artinite
Mg$_2$[(OH)$_2$ | CO$_3$] · 3 H$_2$O

⑤ San Bernito Co., California/USA

Streak white. **Mohs' hardness** 2½. **Specific gravity** 2.03. **Characteristics:** white, grayish, seldom colorless. Luster: crystals are vitreous, fibrous aggregates silky; transparent. Cleavage: perfect. Fracture: fibrous, brittle; soluble in cold hydrochloric acid (foaming). Crystals: (monoclinic) acicular to thin tabular; always surficial growth. **Aggregates:** small fibrous, radial tufts, also crusty, and in thin-fibrous masses; present on crevices in serpentinite and serpentinized peridotite. **Accompanied by:** hydromagnesite, actinolite, aragonite, brucite, dolomite, natrolite, serpentine. **Found in:** Steiermark/Austria; Lombardy/Italy; California, Nevada, Pennsylvania/USA; Urals/Russia. **Similar to:** hydromagnesite, actinolite, aragonite, natrolite.

Brucite
Mg(OH)$_2$

⑥ Pennsylvania/USA

Streak white. **Mohs' hardness** 2½. **Specific gravity** 2.4. **Characteristics:** white, gray, greenish, bluish, yellow to brown. Luster: vitreous, on cleavage surfaces mother-of-pearl; transparent to translucent. Cleavage: perfect. Fracture: flaky, soft, malleable; greasy to the touch; easily soluble in acid. Crystals: (trigonal) tabular, pointed prismatic; rare. **Aggregates:** rough, bladed, scaly, small fibrous, granular; present in zones of serpentinization, marble, chloritic and dolomitic slate. **Accompanied by:** hydromagnesite aragonite, calcite, chlorite, dolomite, magnesite, periclase, serpentine, talc. **Found in:** Steiermark/Austria; Trento/Italy; Sweden; Quebec/Canada; California, Nevada, Pennsylvania/USA; Urals/Russia. **Similar to:** alunite, chlorite, gibbsite, gypsum, pyrophylite, talc, muscovite.

pharmacolite p. 46, serpentine p. 48, gibbsite p. 62

Halite
NaCl

Streak white. **Mohs' hardness** 2. **Specific gravity** 2.1–2.2. **Characteristics:** colorless to white, reddish, yellow, blue, gray to black. Luster: vitreous to opaque. Cleavage: perfect. Fracture: conchoidal, somewhat brittle; good heat conductor. Flame test: yellow. Taste: salty; easily soluble in water, hygroscopic when contaminated. Crystals (cubic) cubes, rarely octahedral; usually surficial growth. **Aggregates:** rough, granular, fibrous, dense, crusty; present in drusy cavities, as surficial growth, by-product of volcanic sublimation; rock-forming (rock salt). **Accompanied by:** anhydrite, sylvanite, carnallite, kainite, kieserite, gypsum. **Found in:** Lower Saxony, Magdeburg/Germany; Salzkammergut/ Austria; Alsace/France; Caspian Sea/Turkey; Iran; Utah, California, southern states/USA. **Similar to:** sylvanite, carnallite, fluorite, boracite.

Trona
$Na_3H[CO_3]_2 \cdot 2\ H_2O$

Streak white. **Mohs' hardness** $2\frac{1}{2}$–3. **Specific gravity** 2.1–2.2. **Characteristics:** colorless, white, grayish, yellow, brownish. Luster: vitreous to silky, dull; transparent to translucent. Cleavage: perfect. Fracture: conchoidal to uneven, brittle; soluble in hydrochloric acid. Crystals: (monoclinic) tabular, prismatic. **Aggregates:** granular, dendritic crusts; developing in surfaces, also in layers; present in salt lakes, on desert surfaces, in lava pockets. **Accompanied by:** borax, soda, hanksite, thenardite, glauberite. **Found in:** Egypt; Libya; Kenya; Wyoming, California/USA; Venezuela; Iran; Tibet/China; Manchuria. **Similar to:** borax.

Kainite
$KMg[Cl\,|\,SO_4] \cdot 3\ H_2O$

Streak white. **Mohs' hardness** $2\frac{1}{2}$–3. **Specific gravity** 2.1–2.2. **Characteristics:** colorless to white, red, yellowish, gray, blue. Luster: translucent. Cleavage: perfect. Fracture: splintery, brittle; easily soluble in water. Flame test: orange-yellow. Taste: bitter-salty. Crystals: (monoclinic) thick tabular, pyramid-shaped; rare. **Aggregates:** rough, fine- or sugar-grained, dense, fibrous; rock-forming with halite (kainitite); present in slate quarries. **Accompanied by:** sylvanite, halite, carnallite, kieserite, polyhalite, anhydrite. **Found in:** Lower Saxony, Hesse, Magdeburg/Germany; Galicia/Poland; Ukraine; New Mexico, Texas/ USA. **Similar to:** carnallite, kieserite.

Palygorskite
$(Mg,Al)_2[OH\,|\,Si_4O_{10}] \cdot 4\ H_2O$

Streak white. **Mohs' hardness** 2–$2\frac{1}{2}$. **Specific gravity** 2.1–2.3. **Characteristics:** white, gray, yellowish, brownish. Luster: vitreous, silky, dull; translucent to opaque. Cleavage: complete. Fracture: indeterminable; malleable in thin layers, highly porous. Crystals: (monoclinic or rhombic) microscopically small. **Aggregates:** finely fibrous, fine-grained, felt-like (so-called mountain leather, mountain cork, and mountain wood is matted palygorskite, chrysotile, or actinolite); present in tailings of weathered serpentinite or granitic rocks. **Accompanied by:** calcite, barite, chalcedony, opal, chlorite, magnesite. **Found in:** Wallis/ Switzerland; Czech Republic; Shetland Island/Scotland; Ukraine; Morocco; Georgia/USA. **Similar to:** sepiolite, chrysotile.

chrysocolla p. 134, chalcanthite p. 210

Sulfur
S

① with calcite; Sicily/Italy

Streak white. **Mohs' hardness** 2. **Specific gravity** 2.0–2.1. **Characteristics:** white, yellow, brownish black. Luster: adamantine; resinous to greasy; translucent. Cleavage: incomplete. Fracture: conchoidal to uneven, very brittle. Extensive double-refraction; negatively charged when rubbed. Flame of a match: will melt sulfur when held into flame. Body temperature: (holding sulfur in the palm of the hand) will cause mineral to shatter; soluble in carbon disulfide. Crystals: (rhombic) dipyramidal, tabular; surficial growth. **Aggregates:** rough, grainy, fibrous, crumbly, powdery, dense, stalactitic, as surficial growth and impregnation; present in association with volcanic vents, thermal springs, salt mines, ore as well as coal mines. **Accompanied by:** calcite, gypsum, anhydrite, celestite, aragonite, halite. **Found in:** Liparian Islands/Italy; Japan; Indonesia; Don River region, middle Asia/Russia; Texas, Louisiana/USA; Mexico. **Similar to:** realgar; sphalerite, wulfenite, orpiment, uranophane.

Whewellite
Ca[C$_2$O$_4$] · H$_2$O

② Burgk, Dresden/Germany

Streak white. **Mohs' hardness** 2$\frac{1}{3}$–3. **Specific gravity** 2.2. **Characteristics:** colorless, white, yellowish. Luster: vitreous to mother-of-pearl; transparent to translucent. Cleavage: perfect. Fracture: conchoidal; easily soluble in acid. Crystals: (monoclinic) columnat, tabular, large well-developed faces; often with twinning. **Aggregates:** star-shaped; present in rock formations near coal and oil deposits, in ore mines. **Accompanied by:** barite, calcite, siderite, ankerite, pyrite, marcasite, magnetite. **Found in:** Saxony/Germany; Bohemia/Czech Republic; Alsace/France; Tuscany, Sardinia/Italy; Romania; Kuban and Transbaikal region/Russia; Utah, Ohio/USA. **Similar to:** barite.

Nitratite Chile salt peter
NaNO$_3$

③ Chile 1:10

Streak white. **Mohs' hardness** 1$\frac{1}{2}$–2. **Specific gravity** 2.2–2.3. **Characteristics:** colorless, white, also gray, yellow, brownish, reddish. Luster: vitreous to dull; transparent. Cleavage: perfect. Fracture: conchoidal, brittle. Taste: bitter-salty, cooling. Flame test: yellow. Easily soluble in water, somewhat hygroscopic. Crystal: (trigonal) rhombohedral; very rare; often twinning. **Aggregates:** rough, fine-grained; present in Chile, where mineral deposits are well-developed, otherwise occurs as crusts and other surficial deposits. **Accompanied by:** halite, galuberite, epsomite, gypsum, anhydrite. **Found in:** Chile; Bolivia; Peru; Egypt; India; trans-Caspian region/Russia; California/USA. **Similar to:** calcite.

Sepiolite meerschaum
Mg$_4$[(OH)$_2$ | Si$_6$O$_{15}$] · 6 H$_2$O

④ Eskishehir/Turkey

Streak white. **Mohs' hardness** 2–2$\frac{1}{2}$. **Specific gravity** 2.0–2.1. **Characteristics:** white, gray, yellowish, blue-green, reddish. Luster: dull, opaque. Cleavage: perfect. Fracture: conchoidal, moderate. When wet: soft; when dry: hard. Feels like soap; sticks to tongue. Floats on water; soluble in acid. Crystals: (rhombic) microscopically small. **Aggregates:** rough, tuberous, small-particled; present as concretions in serpentinite. **Accompanied by:** magnesite, chlorite, chalcedony, opal. **Found in:** Anatolia/Turkey; Samos Island/Greece; Madrid/Spain; Morocco; Tanzania; Kenya; Crimea/Ukraine; Texas, New Mexico/USA. **Similar to:** palygorskite.

Paragonite

① with blue kyanite 1:2

$NaAl_2[(OH,F)_2 \mid AlSi_3O_{10}]$

Streak white. **Mohs' hardness** 2–2½. **Specific gravity** 2.8–2.9. **Characteristics:** white, light green, also colorless. Luster: mother-of-pearl; transparent to translucent. Cleavage: perfect. Fracture: flaky, elastic. Crystals: (monoclinic) unknown. **Aggregates:** finely scaled to dense; small blades scattered throughout; present in schist, gneiss, common quartz deposits, fine-grained sediments; slates. **Accompanied by:** staurolite, kyanite, actinolite, muscovite, biotite, quartz, tremolite. **Found in:** Tessin/Switzerland; Tyrol/Austria; Piemonte/ Italy; Urals/Russia; Colorado, Virginia/USA. **Similar to:** sericite.

Zinnwaldite

② Zinnwald, Erzgebirge/Germany

$K(Li,Fe,Al)_3[(F,OH)_2 \mid AlSi_3O_{10}]$

Streak white. **Mohs' hardness** 2–3. **Specific gravity** 2.9–3.2. **Characteristics:** yellow to brown, gray, also violet, green, black. Luster: vitreous, on cleavage surface mother-of-pearl; transparent to opaque. Cleavage: perfect. Fracture: flaky, elastic; soluble in acid. Flame test: red. Crystals: (monoclinic) flat, hexagonal surfaces; rare. **Aggregates:** scaly, foliated; present in granite pegmatite, granite, greisen, zinc-ore deposits. **Accompanied by:** scheelite, wolframite, topaz, fluorite, quartz. **Found in:** Bavarian Forest, Saxony/Germany; Bohemia/ Czech Republic; Cornwall/England; Virginia/USA. **Similar to:** lepidolite.

Lepidolite

③ Minas Gerais/Brazil

$K(Li,Al)_3[(F,OH)_2 \mid (Si,Al)_4O_{10}]$

Streak white. **Mohs' hardness** 2–3. **Specific gravity** 2.8–2.9. **Characteristics:** pink to soft-violet, seldom white, gray, yellow, greenish. Luster: vitreous, on cleavage surface mother-of-pearl; transparent to translucent. Cleavage: perfect. Fracture: flaky, elastic. Flame test: carmine red. Crystals: (monoclinic) foliated tabular, hexagonal surfaces; rare. **Aggregates:** scaly, foliated, fine-grained, tabular; present in granite pegmatite, granite, geodes in disintegrated weathered granite, zinc ore deposits. **Accompanied by:** tourmaline, topaz, spodumene, amblygonite, feldspar, quartz, muscovite, beryl, cassiterite, fluorite. **Found in:** Saxony/Germany; Mahren/Czech Republic; Elba/Italy; Sweden; Urals/Russia; California, Maine/USA; Quebec/Canada; Madagascar; Nambia. **Similar to:** zinnwaldite, muscovite.

Phlogopite

④ Templeton, Ontario/Canada

$KMg_3[(F,OH)_2 \mid AlSi_3O_{10}]$

Streak white. **Mohs' hardness** 2–2½. **Specific gravity** 2.75–2.97. **Characteristic:** reddish brown to brownish red, yellowish, green, also gray, white, colorless. Luster: vitreous, on cleavage surfaces mother-of-pearl; transparent to translucent. Cleavage: perfect. Fracture: flaky, elastic; often asterismic; soluble in sulfuric acid. Crystals: (monoclinic) tabular, with six-sided surfaces, seldom prismatic. **Aggregates:** foliated, scaly, rough; present in ultrabasic magmatite, pegmatite, marble. **Accompanied by:** diopside, scapolite, apatite, feldspar, garnet, wollastonite, forsterite, spinel, graphite, calcite. **Found in:** Tessin/Switzerland; Sweden; Finland; Italy; Baikal region/Russia; Ontario/ Canada; California, Colorado/USA; Madagascar; South Africa. **Similar to:** biotite, diaspore, astrophyllite.

biotite p. 50, muscovite p. 50, kämmererite p. 68, vivianite p. 210

Glauberite

CaNa$_2$[SO$_4$]$_2$

① Boron, California/USA

Streak white. **Mohs' hardness** 2½–3. **Specific gravity** 2.7–2.8. **Characteristics**: gray, colorless, yellowish, red. Luster: vitreous to greasy, on cleavage surfaces mother-of-pearl; translucent to transparent. Cleavage: perfect. Fracture: conchoidal, brittle. Flame test: yellow. Exposed to air: powdery; soluble in water and hydrochloric acid. Taste: bitter-salty. Crystals: (monoclinic) tabular, prismatic, dipyramidal. **Aggregates**: granular, dense, crumbly, bladed, crusty, layered; present in and associated with salt beds, nitrate deposits, cavities associated with dormant volcanoes, fumeroles. **Accompanied by**: halite, gypsum, anhydrite, sylvanite, polyhalite, thenardite, sassolite, sodium nitrate. **Found in**: Lower Saxony, Magdeburg/Germany; Salzburg/Austria; Lothringen/France; Liparian Islands/Italy; India; Ukraine; Arizona, California/USA. **Similar to**: gypsum, thenardite.

Pharmacolite

CaH[AsO$_4$] · 2 H$_2$O

② Richelsdorf, Hesse/Germany

Streak white. **Mohs' hardness** 2–2½. **Specific gravity** 2.5–2.7. **Characteristics**: white, gray, colorless, greenish, reddish. Luster: silky; transparent to translucent. Cleavage: perfect. Fracture: uneven. Crystals: (monoclinic) acicular. **Aggregates**: radial; botryoidal, as surficial growth or dusting; present in arsenic ore deposits. **Accompanied by**: erythrite, skutterudite, nickeline, chloantite, annabergite. **Found in**: Black Forest, Harz mountains/Germany; Bohemia/Czech Republic; Alsace/France; California, Nevada/USA. **Similar to**: arsenolite.

Talc

Mg$_3$[(OH)$_2$ | Si$_4$O$_{10}$]

③ Futu Pass, Florence/Italy

Streak white. **Mohs' hardness** 1. **Specific gravity** 2.7–2.8. **Characteristics**: green, yellow, brownish, white, colorless. Luster: mother-of-pearl, greasy; translucent to transparent. Cleavage: perfect. Fracture: uneven, inelastic malleable, poor heat conductor; greasy to the touch. Crystals: (monoclinic) very small, pseudohexagonal or rhombic; pseudomorphic. **Aggregates**: scaly-foliated, conchoidal, dense (steatite); present in limestone or dolomite, metamorphic rocks. **Accompanied by**: magnesite, serpentine, dolomite, chlorite, apatite, magnetite, pyrite, quartz. **Found in**: Fichtel mountains, Saxony/Germany; Piemonte/Italy; Transvaal/South Africa; Madras/India; Arizona, California/USA. **Similar to**: pyrophyllite, brucite, muscovite, biotite, gypsum, chlorite, serpentine.

Cryolite

Na$_3$[AlF$_6$]

④ with galena;
Ivigtut/Greenland
⑤ Ivitgut/Greenland

Streak white. **Mohs' hardness** 2½–3. **Specific gravity** 2.95. **Characteristics**: white, colorless, brownish, reddish, gray to black. Luster: vitreous; transparent. Cleavage: none. Fracture; uneven. Flame test: reddish-yellow. Easily soluble in sulfuric acid. Crystals: (monoclinic) cubic, short-columned; usually with twinning. **Aggregates**: rough, with flat, parquet-like crystals, spar-like coarse-grained to dense; present in pegmatite, associated with granite. **Accompanied by**: siderite, quartz, fluorite, barite, galena, topaz, zircon, pyrite, sphalerite, chalcocite, kassiterite, wolframite, columbite. **Found in**: west Greenland; Colorado/USA; Urals/Russia; Nigeria. **Similar to**: fluorite, barite, topaz, anhydrite.

Serpentine

$Mg_6[(OH)_8 \mid Si_4O_{10}]$

① chrysotile; Quebec/Canada
② antigorite; Norway

Streak white. **Mohs' hardness** $2\frac{1}{2}$–4. **Specific gravity** 2.0–2.6. **Characteristics:** green, gray to black, white, brownish. Luster: greasy to silky, dull; transparent to opaque. Cleavage: perfect. Fracture: conchoidal, splintery, moderate, fibrous pieces inelastic, malleable; soluble in hydrochloric acid and sulfuric acid. Crystals: (monoclinic) unknown; fibrous serpentine (chrysotile); foliated serpentine (antigorite); dense and very finely fibrous (asbestos); pseudomorphic. **Aggregates:** fine-grained, dense, foliated, fibrous, crusty. So-called mountain leather (mountain wood, mountain cork) is often felted chrysotile; present in layers within slate limestone and marble; serpentinite. **Accompanied by:** chlorite, olivine, chromite, magnetite, dolomite, talc, quartz, opal. **Found in:** Fichtel Mountains, Thüringen, Saxony/Germany; Tyrol/Austria; Urals/Russia; Quebec/Canada; South Africa; Zimbabwe. **Similar to:** palygorskite, chlorite, talc, tremolite, actinolite, garnierite.

Annabergite

$Ni_3[AsO_4]_2 \cdot 8\,H_2O$

③ Laurio/Greece 1:10

Streak white. **Mohs' hardness** 2. **Specific gravity** 3.0–3.1. **Characteristics:** green, white, gray, Luster: dull, transparent to opaque. Cleavage: perfect. Fracture: bladed, moderate, small blade-shaped pieces are malleable; soluble in acid. Crystals: (monoclinic) prismatic, tabular, acicular foliated; rare. **Aggregates:** rough, dense, crumbly, crusty, present in nickel deposits. **Accompanied by:** chloanthite, nickeline, erythrite, pharmacolite, proustite, siderite, barite, calcite. **Found in:** Siegerland, Hesse, Harz mountains, Saxony/Germany; Dauphiné/France; Sardinia/Italy; Spain; Ontario/Canada; Nevada/USA. **Similar to:** malachite, chrysocolla.

Thenardite

Na_2SO_4

④ San Luis, California/USA

Streak white. **Mohs' hardness** $2\frac{1}{2}$–3. **Specific gravity** 2.7. **Characteristics:** colorless, gray, brownish, reddish. Luster: vitreous and resinous; transparent to translucent. Cleavage: perfect. Fracture: uneven, brittle; easily soluble in water. Flame test: yellow. Taste: salty. Crystals: (rhombic) dipyramidal, tabular, often with twinning. **Aggregates:** granular, crumbly, as crust and as bloom; present in salt lakes, deserts, terrestrial salt mines, associated with volcanic vents. **Accompanied by:** glauberite, gypsum, epsomite, halite, soda, sodium nitrate. **Found in:** Sicily/Italy; Kazakhstan; Arizona, California/USA; Chile; Peru. **Similar to:** glauberite.

Pyrophylite

$Al_2[(OH)_2 \mid Si_4O_{10}]$

⑤ Indian Gulch, California/USA

Streak white. **Mohs' hardness** 1–$1\frac{1}{2}$. **Specific gravity** 2.7–2.9. **Characteristics:** white, yellow, green. Luster: mother-of-pearl, dull; translucent to opaque. Cleavage: perfect. Fracture: uneven, gentle, malleable; greasy to the touch. Crystals: (monoclinic) tabular, foliated, never individually. **Aggregates:** radial, foliated, rough, dense, present in slate, quartz veins, veins of ore, cavities associated with dormant volcanoes. **Accompanied by:** quartz, kyanite, sillimanite, amblygonite, andalusite, kassiterite, mica, hematite, lazulite. **Found in:** Eifel Mountains, Saxony/Germany; Switzerland; Urals/Russia; California, Georgia/USA; Brazil; South Africa. **Similar to:** talc, brucite, margarite, jadeite.

1 ◄
2 ◄
3 ◄
4 ◄
5 ◄
6 ◄
7 ◄
8 ◄
9
10 ◄

1 ◄
2
3 ◄
4 ◄
5 ◄
6 ◄
7 ◄

Hydrozincite zinc bloom

① Yazd/Iran 1:2

$Zn_5[(OH)_3 \mid CO_3]_2$

Streak white. **Mohs' hardness** 2–2½. **Specific gravity** 3.2–3.8. **Characteristics**: white, gray, pink, colorless. Luster: vitreous to silky, dull; transparent to opaque. Cleavage: perfect. Fracture: crumbly, brittle; soluble in hydrochloric acid. Light blue fluorescence under ultraviolet light. Crystals: (monoclinic) tabular, very small. **Aggregates**: rough, crumbly, dense, botryoidal, crusty; stalactitic, as dusting on crusts, present in oxidized zones in zinc mines. **Accompanied by**: mica, smithsonite, hemimorphite, wulfenite. **Found in**: Black Forest, Westfalia/Germany; Kärnten/Austria; Santander/Spain; Nevada/USA; West Australia. **Similar to**: smithsonite.

Biotite

② Miask, Urals/Russia

$K(Mg,Fe^{2+},Mn^{2+})_3[(OH,F)_2 \mid (Al,Fe^{3+},Ti^{3+})Si_3O_{10}]$

Streak white. **Mohs' hardness** 2½–3. **Specific gravity** 2.7–3.3. **Characteristics**: black, dark brown, bronze-colored. Luster: vitreous, on cleavage side mother-of-pearl; translucent to opaque. Cleavage: perfect, with hexagonal contour. Fracture: foliated, elastic malleable. Strong pleochroism; easily soluble in sulfuric acid. Crystals: (monoclinic) tabular, foliated, and columnar; intergrown and surficial growth. **Aggregates**: bladed, foliated; present particularly in granitic rocks, pegmatite, gneiss, mica slate. **Accompanied by**: muscovite, amphibole (hornblende), quartz, feldspars. **Found in**: Alps/Austria; Vesuvius/Italy; Scandinavia; Scotland; Urals/Russia; California, Idaho/USA. **Similar to**: phlogopite, muscovite, chlorite, gold.

Arsenolite

③ St. Andreasberg, Harz mountains, Lower Saxony, Germany 1:10

As_2O_3

Streak white. **Mohs' hardness** 1½. **Specific gravity** 3.1. **Characteristics**: white, colorless, yellowish, bluish. Luster: vitreous; transparent to opaque. Cleavage: complete. Fracture: conchoidal; soluble in warm water and hydrochloric acid; very poisonous. Crystals (cubic) octahedral, very small. **Aggregates**: powdery, radial-fibrous, as crust; present in deposits of arsenic minerals, ore veins. **Accompanied by**: arsenopyrite, skutterudite. **Found in**: Black Forest, Saxony/Germany; Bohemia/Czech Republic; Alsace/France; California/Nevada/USA. **Similar to**: pharmacolite.

Muscovite

④ Urals/Russia 1:2

$KAl_2[(OH,F)_2 \mid AlSi_3O_{10}]$

Streak white. **Mohs' hardness** 2–3. **Specific gravity** 2.7–3.1. **Characteristics**: colorless, yellowish, greenish (fuchsite), silvery. Luster: vitreous, on cleavage surfaces mother-of-pearl; transparent to translucent. Cleavage: perfect. Fracture: foliated, elastic malleable. Crystals: (monoclinic) tabular with hexagonal contours, individual pyramidal; intergrown and surficial growth. **Aggregates**: foliated (sericite), dense; present in pegmatites, rock-forming particularly in granite, phyllite, mica slate, gneiss, sandstone. **Accompanied by**: biotite, lepidolite, feldspar, quartz, topaz, wolframite, cassiterite. **Found in**: Taunus Mountains/Germany; Tyrol/Austria; Tessin/Switzerland; South Tyrol/Italy; Urals, middle Siberia/Russia; Bihar/India; Transvaal/South Africa; Ontario/Canada; New Hampshire, South Dakota/USA. **Similar to**: biotite, phogopite, paragonite, lepidolite, margarite, chlorite, brucite, gypsum.

---

zinnwaldite p. 44, annabergite p. 48, kämmererite p. 68, autunite p. 192, aurichalcite p. 212

Stolzite
Pb[WO₄]

Streak white. **Mohs' hardness** 2½–3. **Specific gravity** 7.9–8.2. **Characteristics**: reddish, gray, yellow, brown, green. Luster: greasy to resinous; transparent. Cleavage: incomplete. Fracture: conchoidal, brittle. Crystals: (tetragonal) dipyramidal, massive tabular, short columnar; intergrown and surficial growth. **Aggregates**: rough, spherical, conical; present in oxidized zones of wolframite deposits. **Accompanied by**: scheelite, quartz, fluorite. **Found in**: Saxony/Germany; Bohemia/Czech Republic; Piemonte/Italy; England; Nigeria; Arizona, Utah/USA; New South Wales/Australia. **Similar to**: scheelite, wulfenite.

Leadhillite
Pb₄[(OH)₂ | SO₄ | (CO₃)₂]

Streak white. **Mohs' hardness** 2½. **Specific gravity** 6.45–6.55. **Characteristics**: colorless, white, gray, blue. Luster: adamantine, mother-of-pearl, greasy; transparent to translucent. Cleavage: complete. Fracture: conchoidal, brittle; soluble in diluted nitric acid. Crystals: (monoclinic) pseudohexagonal, tabular, also pseudorhombohedral. **Aggregates**: rough, granular, scaly, crusted; present in oxidized zones of lead-ore deposits. **Accompanied by**: cerussite, galena, anglesite, phosgenite. **Found in**: Kärten/Austria; Sardinia/Italy; Scotland; Tunisia; Namibia; Arizona, Nevada, Utah/USA. **Similar to**: cerussite, anglesite.

Silver
Ag

Streak white. **Mohs' hardness** 2½–3. **Specific gravity** 9.6–12.0. **Characteristics**: silver-white, yellowish, brown, gray or black tarnish. Luster: metallic, in thin layers blue transparent, otherwise opaque. Cleavage: none. Fracture: hook-shaped, very malleable, supple; soluble in nitric acid and in concentrated hydrochloric acid; good heat conductor. Crystals: (cubic) cubic, octahedral, dodecahedral, usually distorted; pseudomorphic. **Aggregates**: rough as clumps and grains; loose and wire-shaped as pure metal; moss-like, dendritic as inclusions; present in ore veins, occasionally in placers. **Accompanied by**: argentite (silver sulfide), proustite, pyrargyrite, stephanite, polybasite, siderite, chloanthite, copper, galena, cerrussite, pyrite, barite, fluorite, calcite. **Found in**: Saxony, Harz mountains/Germany; Bohemia/Czech Republic; Norway; Ontario/Canada; Colorado/USA; Mexico; Bolivia; Peru; Chile; Altai/Russia; Australia. **Similar to**: dyscrasite, argentite, pure antimony, platinum, pure arsenic.

Senarmontite
Sb₂O₃

Streak white. **Moh's hardness** 2–2½. **Specific gravity** 5.5. **Characteristics**: colorless, white to gray. Luster: adamantine, greasy; translucent to transparent. Cleavage: important. Fracture: conchoidal, brittle; often high degree of double refraction; soluble in hydrochloric acid. Crystals: (cubic) octahedral, often with curved surfaces; rare; dimorph with valentinite. **Aggregates**: rough, granular, dense, crusty; present in oxidized zones of antimony ore deposits. **Accompanied by**: valentinite, antimonite, kermesite, boulangerite. **Found in**: Saxony/Germany; Bohemia/Czech Republic; Isére/France; Sardinia/Italy; Algeria; Quebec/Canada; California, South Dakota/USA. **Similar to**: boracite.

bismutite p. 168, calomel p. 194, aurichalcite p. 212, caledonite p. 212

Valentinite

Sb$_2$O$_3$

① Pezinok, Czech Republic 1:10

Streak white. **Mohs' hardness** 2½–3. **Specific gravity** 5.6–5.8. **Characteristics**: colorless, white, gray, yellowish. Luster: adamantine, on cleavage surface mother-of-pearl; transparent. Cleavage: complete. Fracture: uneven, brittle, fragile; easily soluble in acid. Crystals: (rhombic) prismatic to acicular, tabular, multifaceted; sometimes pseudomorphic; dimorph with senarmontite. **Aggregates**: rough, granular, radial, fibrous, fan-shaped as deposits; present in oxidized zones, particularly in antimony-bearing ore. **Accompanied by**: senarmontite, antimonite. **Found in**: Harz mountains, Saxony/Germany; Bohemia/Czech Republic; Dauphiné/France; Sardinia/Italy; Algeria; Bolivia; Quebec/Canada; California, Oregon/USA. **Similar to**: cerussite.

Chlorargyrite

AgCl

② St. Andreadberg,
Harz mountains,
Lower Saxony/Germany 1:2

Streak white. **Mohs' hardness** 1½–2. **Specific gravity** 5.5–5.6. **Characteristics**: initially colorless, with adamantine luster and translucent, under light becoming gray, brownish to black with metallic, waxy luster or dull horn-like, opaque. Cleavage: none. Fracture: hook-shaped, supple, can be cut with a knife; soluble in ammonia. Crystals: (cubic) cube-like, very small and very rare. **Aggregates**: rough, crusty, reniform, stalactitic, dendritic, parallel-fibrous; present in oxidized zones of silver-bearing ore deposits, particularly as impregnations in sandstone. **Accompanied by**: silver, argentite, cerussite, barite, calcite. **Found in**: Saxony/Germany; Bohemia/Czech Republic; Idaho, Nevada/USA; Atacama/Chile; Bolivia; New South Wales/Australia; Altai/Russia. **Similar to**: calomel, pure silver.

Phosgenite

Pb$_2$[Cl$_2$ | CO$_3$]

③ Monte Poni, Sardinia/Italy 1:2

Streak white. **Mohs' hardness** 2–3. **Specific gravity** 6.0–6.3. **Characteristics**: white, gray, yellow, also colorless and greenish. Luster: greasy adamantine; translucent to transparent. Cleavage: complete. Fracture: conchoidal and gentle; soluble in diluted nitric acid. Sometimes yellow fluorescence under ultraviolet light. Crystals: (tetragonal) prismatic, pyramidal, tabular, often multifaceted; usually surficial deposits. **Aggregates**: rough, granular; present in oxidized zones of lead ore deposits. **Accompanied by**: cerussite, anglesite. **Found in**: Upper Silesia/Poland; Derbyshire/England; Sardinia/Italy; Greece; Namibia; California, Colorado/USA; Argentina. **Similar to**: cerussite, anglesite, barite.

Mercury

Hg

④ Almadén/Spain 1:4

Streak white. **Mohs' hardness** none. **Specific gravity** 13.6. **Characteristics**: zinc-white, often with a gray coating. Luster: strongly metallic; opaque. Fumes very poisonous. Crystals: none. Liquid solidifies at −38.9°C to form rhombohedral crystals in the tetragonal crystal system, **Aggregates**: impregnation or single droplets on the surface of the source stone, particularly cinnabar; present in oxidized zones of mercury ore deposits; occasionally in ore veins or associated with volcanics. **Accompanied by**: cinnabar. **Found in**: Rhine Palatinate/Germany; Cuidad/Spain; Croatia; Serbia; Tuscany/Italy; California, Texas/USA; Peru.

Laumonite

① Unterberg, Southern Tirol/Italy 1:2

$Ca[AlSi_2O_6]_2 \cdot 4\ H_2O$

Streak white. **Mohs' hardness** 3–3½. **Specific gravity** 2.25–2.35. **Characteristics**: colorless, white, yellow, reddish. Luster: vitreous, on cleavage surfaces mother-of-pearl. Will turn dull when exposed to air, crumbly, transparent to opaque. Cleavage: complete. Fracture: uneven, brittle; soluble in hydrochloric acid. Crystals: (monoclinic) narrow columnar, vertically striped. **Aggregates**: stalk-like, fibrous, rough; present in crevices and pore space of magmatites and metamorphic rocks, occasionally in veins of ore. **Accompanied by**: heulandite, stilbite, chabazite, analcite, prehnite, apophyllite, chlorite, albite, quartz, calcite. **Found in**: Rheinland-Pfalz, Saxony/Germany; Tessin/Switzerland; southern Tirol/Italy; California, New Jersey/USA. **Similar to**: feldspars.

Hydromagnesite

② San Benito Co., California/USA

$Mg_5[OH \mid (CO_3)_2]_2 \cdot 4\ H_2O$

Streak white. **Mohs' hardness** 3½. **Specific gravity** 2.2. **Characteristics**: white, colorless. Luster: vitreous; transparent to translucent. Cleavage: complete. Fracture: uneven, brittle. Soluble in diluted hydrochloric acid, effervescence. Greasy to the touch. Crystals: (monoclinic) pseudorhombic, acicular, tabular, usually very small. **Aggregates**: rough, radial filaments, wart-like, crusty, crumbly; present as a product of weathering in serpentinites and other magnesium-rich deposits in cavities in volcanic rocks. **Accompanied by**: brucite, artinite, opal, calcite and dolomite. **Found in**: Steiermark/Austria; Mähren/Czech Republic; Trentino/Italy; Iran; British Columbia/Canada; California, Nevada, New York/USA. **Similar to**: artinite.

Gyrolite

③ with acicular okenite; Poona/India

$NaCa_{16}(Si_{23}Al)O_{60}(OH)_8 \cdot 14\ H_2O$

Streak white. **Mohs' hardness** 3–4. **Specific gravity** 2.3–2.4. **Characteristics**: colorless, white. Luster: vitreous; transparent to translucent. Cleavage: complete. Fracture: uneven, brittle. Crystals: (trigonal or hexagonal) not known. **Aggregates**: rough, fibrous, radial, as concretion; present in cavities of weathered calc-silicate rocks. **Accompanied by**: apophyllite, prehnite. **Found in**: Bohemia/Czech Republic; Northern Ireland; Skye/Scotland; Nova Scotia/Canada; California/USA; India. **Similar to**: prehnite.

Variscite

④ Perth/Australia 1:2

$Al[PO_4] \cdot 2\ H_2O$

Streak white. **Mohs' hardness** 4–5. **Specific gravity** 2.5. **Characteristics**: green, white, bluish, colorless; transparent to opaque. Cleavage: incomplete. Fracture: conchoidal, brittle; greasy to the touch. Crystals: (rhombic) tabular, short prismatic, small, rare. **Aggregates**: rough, dense, tuberous, crusty; present in crevices and pore space in aluminum-rich deposits, particularly graywacke and slate. **Accompanied by**: wavellite, strengite, quartz. **Found in**: Vogtland/Germany; Steiermark/Austria; Arkansas, Utah/USA; Bolivia; Queensland/Australia. **Similar to**: wavellite, strengite, chalcedony, opal, chrysoprase, chrysocolla, turquoise, wardite.

kernite p. 32, gaylussite p. 36, serpentine p. 48, chrysocolla p. 134

Phillipsite

① Tuscany/Italy 1:2

KCa[Al$_3$Si$_5$O$_{16}$] · 6 H$_2$O

Streak white. **Mohs' hardness.** 4–4½. **Specific gravity** 2.2. **Characteristics:** colorless, white, gray, yellowish, reddish. Luster: vitreous; transparent to translucent. Cleavage: incomplete. Fracture: uneven, brittle; soluble in acid. Crystals: (monoclinic) tabular, columnar, small; usually twinning and quadrupling; almost always surficial covering. **Aggregates:** radial, spherical, rough, present in cavities of basaltic rock, in terrestrial salt lakes, in deep ocean floor sediments. **Accompanied by:** chabazite, harmotome, natrolite, analcite. **Found in:** Vogelsberg, Kaiserstuhl/Germany; Bohemia/Czech Republic; Ireland; Iceland; Vesuvius/Italy; California, Hawaii/USA; Chile; Pacific Ocean basin. **Similar to:** harmotome, heulandite, stilbite, chabazite.

Okenite

② Poona/India 1:2

Ca$_{10}$[Si$_6$O$_{16}$ | (Si$_6$O$_{15}$)$_2$] · 18 H$_2$0

Streak white. **Mohs' hardness** 4½–5. **Specific gravity** 2.3. **Characteristics:** white, yellow, bluish. Luster: mother-of-pearl; translucent to transparent. Cleavage: complete. Fracture: uneven, brittle. Flame test: orange. Crystals: (triclinic) flat-acicular. **Aggregates:** small fibrous, radial, rough; present in cavities of volcanic rocks. **Accompanied by:** prehnite, gyrolite. **Found in:** Iceland; Greenland; USA; Chile; Bombay/India; Faeroe Islands/Denmark. **Similar to:** natrolite.

Apophyllite

③ Poona/India 1:2

KCa$_4$[(F,OH) | (Si$_4$O$_{10}$)$_2$] · 8 H$_2$O

Streak white. **Mohs' hardness** 4½–5. **Specific gravity** 2.3–2.4. **Characteristics:** colorless, white, yellow to brown, reddish, greenish. Luster: mother-of-pearl, vitreous; transparent to translucent. Cleavage: perfect. Fracture: uneven, brittle; soluble in hydrochloric acid. Flame test: violet. Crystals: (tetragonal) dipyramidal, prismatic, cubic, tabular; often rough, uneven surfaces; almost always surficial growth. **Aggregates:** bladed, scaly, granular, dense; present in volcanic rock, ore veins and alpine crevices. **Accompanied by:** analcite, prehnite, heulandite, natrolite, scolecite, stilbite, calcite. **Found in:** Harz mountains, Siebenbirge/Germany; Bohemia/Czech Republic; Dolomite Alps/Italy; Norway; Bombay/Italy; New Jersey/USA; Mexico; Brazil. **Similar to:** chabazite, heulandite, fluorite, ludlamite, datolite.

Heulandite

④ Poona/India

Ca[Al$_2$Si$_7$O$_{18}$] · 6 H$_2$0

Streak white. **Mohs' hardness** 3½–4. **Specific gravity** 2.2. **Characteristics:** colorless, white, gray, yellowish, red. Luster: on cleavage surface mother-of-pearl; transparent to translucent. Cleavage: perfect. Fracture: uneven, brittle; easily soluble in hydrochloric acid. Crystals: (monoclinic) tabular, short columnar; surficial growth. **Aggregates:** bladed, scaly, radial, also rough, spar-like; present in cavities of volcanic rocks, in crevices of metamorphic rocks, less often in ore veins. **Accompanied by:** stilbite, chabazite, scolecite, pectolite, calcite, quartz. **Found in:** Rheinland-Pflaz, Harz mountains/Germany; Wallis/Switzerland; Dolomite Alps/Italy; Iceland; Norway; Ukraine; Bombay/India; New Jersey/USA. **Similar to:** phillipsite, apophyllite, stilbite, feldspar.

kainite p. 40, trona p. 40, serpentine p. 48, whewellite p. 42

Harmotome

Ba[Al$_2$Si$_6$O$_{16}$] · 6 H$_2$O

Streak white. **Mohs' hardness** 4^1/$_2$. **Specific gravity** 2.44–2.50. **Characteristics**: colorless, white, gray, yellowish, pink. Luster: vitreous, transparent to translucent; dull. Cleavage: incomplete. Fracture: uneven to conchoidal, brittle; easily soluble in hydrochloric acid. Crystals: (monoclinic) columnar, usually interpenetration twinning; surficial growth. **Aggregates**: radial; present in ore veins, in cavities in volcanic rock. **Accompanied by:** heulandite, stilbite, galena, barite, sphalerite, calcite. **Found in:** Harz mountains/Germany; Bohemia/Czech Republic; Norway; Scotland; Saskatchewan, Ontario/Canada; New York/USA. **Similar to:** phillipsite.

Gonnardite

Na$_2$Ca[Al$_2$,Si$_3$O$_{10}$]$_2$ · 7 H$_2$O

Streak white. **Mohs' hardness** 4^1/$_2$–5. **Specific gravity** 2.25. **Characteristics**: white, colorless. Luster: vitreous to silky; transparent. Cleavage: none. Fracture: fibrous, brittle. Crystals: (rhombic) fibrous, acicular, usually very small; rare. **Aggregates**: dense, fibrous, radial; present in cavities in volcanic rock. Accompanied by: phillipsite, thomsonite, wollastonite, pyrite, calcite. **Found in:** Vogelsberg, Eifel/Germany; Steiermark/Austria; Sicily/Italy; Auvergne/France; Norway; California/USA. **Similar to:** thomsonite, scolecite, natrolite.

Stilbite

NaCa$_2$[Al$_5$Si$_{13}$O$_{36}$] · 14 H$_2$O

Streak white. **Mohs' hardness** 3^1/$_2$–4. **Specific gravity** 2.1–2.2. **Characteristics**: colorless, white, gray, yellowish, reddish. Luster: on cleavage surface mother-of-pearl; translucent to transparent. Cleavage: complete. Fracture: uneven, brittle; soluble in hydrochloric acid. Crystals: (monoclinic) columnar, tabular; usually combined in sheaflike bundles of interpenetration twinnings. **Aggregates**: dendritic, radial; present in cavities of magmatites and metamorphic rocks, in ore veins. **Accompanied by:** chabazite, laumonite, scolecite, heulandite, calcite. **Found in:** Harz mountains/Germany; Tessin/Switzerland; Scotland; Faeroe Islands/Denmark; Iceland; Norway; Bombay/India; California, Oregon, Washington/USA. **Similar to:** heulandite, prehnite, phillipsite.

Chabazite

(Ca,Na$_2$)[Al$_2$Si$_4$O$_{12}$] · 6 H$_2$O

Streak white. **Mohs' hardness** 4–5. **Specific gravity** 2.1. **Characteristics**: colorless, white, reddish, brown. Luster: transparent to translucent. Cleavage: incomplete. Fracture: uneven, brittle; soluble in hydrochloric acid. Crystals: (trigonal) cubic, rhombohedral; always surficial growth; often twinning. **Aggregates**: rough, crusty; present in drusy cavities and in crevices of magmatites, particularly basalt and phonolite; also as deposits in hot springs. **Accompanied by:** natrolite, stilbite, heulandite, analcite, orthoclase, albite, quartz, fluorite, epidote, calcite, phillipsite. **Found in:** Vogelsberg, Westerwald, Rheinland-Pfalz/Germany; Bohemia/Czech Republic; Iceland; Faeroe Islands/Denmark; Vogesen/France; southern Tirol/Austria; Elba, Sardinia/Italy; New Jersey, Oregon/USA; New Zealand. **Similar to:** apophyllite, fluorite, calcite, dolomite.

chrysoberyl p. 134, serpierite p. 214

Wavellite

Al$_3$[(OH)$_3$ | (PO$_4$)$_2$] · 5 H$_2$0

① Arkansas/USA

Streak white. **Mohs' hardness** 3$\frac{1}{2}$–4. **Specific gravity** 2.3–2.4. **Characteristics**: green, yellowish, gray, colorless. Luster: vitreous to silky; transparent. Cleavage: incomplete. Fracture: uneven, brittle; soluble in hydrochloric acid. Crystals: (rhombic) prismatic, thin acicular; rare. **Aggregates**: radial, spheroidal, reniform, crusty; present in crevices and layers of siliceous schist, sandstone, zinc ore veins and phosphate deposits. **Accompanied by**: strengite, hematite, limonite, pyrolusite. **Found in**: Hesse, Thüringen, Sachsen/Germany; Cornwall, Devonshire/England; Arkansas, Pennsylvania/USA; Brazil; Bolivia. **Similar to**: variscite, natrolite, gibbsite, prehnite, calcite, aragonite.

Gmelinite

(Na$_2$Ca)[Al$_2$Si$_4$O$_{12}$] · 6 H$_2$O

② Glenarm, Antrim/Ireland 1:3

Streak white. **Mohs' hardness** 4$\frac{1}{2}$. **Specific gravity** 2.1. **Characteristics**: white, yellowish, reddish, also colorless. Luster: vitreous; transparent to translucent. Cleavage: incomplete. Fracture: uneven, brittle. Crystals: (hexagonal) dipyramidal, thick tabular; often twinning. **Aggregates**: isolated crystal groups; present in cavities in volcanic rock. **Accompanied by**: chabazite, analcite, phillipsite, thomsonite. **Found in**: Siegerland, Harz mountains/Germany; Antrim/Ireland; Skye/Scotland; Vincenza/Italy; Nova Scotia/Canada; New Jersey, Oregon/USA; Victoria/Australia.

Gibbsite hydrargillite

Al(OH)$_3$

③ Laurion/Greece

Streak white. **Mohs' hardness** 2$\frac{1}{2}$–3$\frac{1}{2}$. **Specific gravity** 2.3–2.4. **Characteristics**: colorless, white, gray, greenish, bluish. Luster: vitreous, on cleavage surface mother-of-pearl; transparent to translucent. Cleavage: perfect. Fracture: uneven, tough; malleable in thin layers. Crystals: (monoclinic) pseudohexagonal-tabular; often twinning; small and very rare. **Aggregates**: radial fibrous, scaly, botryoidal, wart-like, crusty; present in talc and serpentine deposits, also found mixed with bauxite and on the floor of tropical forests. **Accompanied by**: diaspore, boehmite, natrolite, limonite, calcite. **Found in**: Vogelsberg, Rhön/Germany; southern France; Hungary; Guinea; Jamaica; Arizona, Arkansas, California/USA; northern Australia. **Similar to**: wavellite, brucite, chalcedony.

Colemanite

Ca[B$_3$O$_4$(OH)$_3$] · H$_2$O

④ Ankara/Turkey

Streak white. **Mohs' hardness** 4–4$\frac{1}{2}$. **Specific gravity** 2.4. **Characteristics**: colorless, white, yellowish, gray. Luster: vitreous to adamantine; transparent to translucent. Cleavage: complete. Fracture: uneven, conchoidal, brittle; soluble in warm hydrochloric acid. Flame test: green. Crystals: (monoclinic) short to long columnar, tabular. **Aggregates**: rough, granular, dense, dendritic, bladed; present in dried salt beds. **Accompanied by**: ulexite, borax, boracite, kernite, realgar, celestite, halite, gypsum, calcite. **Found in**: Anatolia/Turkey; Kazakhstan; California, Nevada/USA; Chile; Argentina. **Similar to**: ulexite, datolite, borax, soda, danburite.

Calcite
Ca[CO$_3$]

① Namibia 1:2
② Berchtesgaden/
   Germany
③ Chihuahua/Mexico

Streak white. **Mohs' hardness** 3. **Specific gravity** 2.6–2.8. **Characteristics:** colorless, white, gray, yellow to brown, reddish, seldom green, bluish, black. Luster: vitreous; translucent to transparent. Cleavage: perfect; rhombohedral cleavage fragments. Fracture: conchoidal, brittle; high double refraction. Fluorescence under ultraviolet light: red, yellow, blue. Easily soluble in cold, diluted hydrochloric acid (effervescence). Crystals: (trigonal) occurring in several hundred crystallographic forms and several thousand combinations thereof; basic shapes are rhombohedral, prismatic; almost always surficial growth, particularly in drusy cavities and other hollow spaces; often twinning, pseudomorphic. **Aggregates:** rough, granular, dense, spar-like, dendritic, fibrous, crumbly, stalactitic, oolitic, as concretions and contributing to the fossilization process; rock-forming; principle constituent in limestone, calc-precipitates, marble, carbonatite; as cement in many other rocks. **Accompanied by:** quartz, mica, dolomite, sulfur, many ore minerals. **Found in:** northern and southern Calcite Alps; Jura Mountains/France; Switzerland; southern Germany; Harz mountains, Erzgebirge/Germany; Bohemia/Czech Republic; Champagne/France; Cumberland/England; Ireland; Ontario/Canada; Colorado, Missouri, South Dakota/USA; Mexico; Crimea/Ukraine; Siberia/Russia. **Similar to:** dolomite, aragonite, gypsum, anhydrite, quartz, barite, fluorite, chabazite.

Alunite
KAl$_3$[(OH)$_6$] | (SO$_4$)$_2$]

④ Taiwan

Streak white. **Mohs' hardness** 3$\frac{1}{2}$–4. **Specific gravity** 2.6–2.9. **Characteristics:** colorless, white, gray, yellowish, reddish. Luster: vitreous; on cleavage surface mother-of-pearl; translucent to transparent. Cleavage: complete. Fracture: conchoidal, brittle, splintery; soluble in potassium leach and hot sulfuric acid. Crystals: (trigonal) rhombohedral, tabular, small and rare. **Aggregates:** rough, dense, granular, crumbly, fibrous; present in cavities in volcanic rock, bauxite, and on floor of tropical forests. **Accompanied by:** quartz, opal, sulfur, ammonium chloride, gypsum. **Found in:** Latium, Tuscany/Italy; Hungary; Greece; Uzbekistan; Azerbaijan; Colorado, Nevada/USA; Australia. **Similar to:** aluminite, sal ammoniac, brucite.

Coral
Ca[CO$_3$]

⑤ Calabria/Italy
⑥ Sicily/Italy

Streak white. **Mohs' hardness** 3–4. **Specific gravity** 2.6–2.7. **Characteristics:** red, pink, white. Luster: usually dull, sometimes waxy; translucent. Cleavage: none. Fracture: uneven, splintery, brittle; soluble in acid (effervescence). Crystals: (trigonal) microcrystalline. **Aggregates:** rough, dense, dendritic; present in reefs, atolls, and coral banks; skeletal deposits. **Found in:** coast of the western Mediterranean countries; Gulf of Biscay; Canary Island; Malayan archipelago; Midway Islands; Japan; Hawaii/USA. **Similar to:** glass, horn, (Indian) rubber, bones, synthetic substances.

The very rare blue and black corals are organic substances and are found in the Malayan archipelago, along the coast of north Australia and the Red Sea.

lepidolite p. 44, zinnwaldite p. 44, glauberite p. 46, cryolite p. 46

Streak

white and
colorless

Mohs' h.

1 ◄
2 ◄
3 ◄
4 ◄
5 ◄
6 ◄
7 ◄
8 ◄
9 ◄
10 ◄

S. gravity
1 ◄
2 ◄
3 ◄
4 ◄
5 ◄
6 ◄
7 ◄

Aragonite
Ca[CO₃]

① Arizona/USA
② Morocco 1:2
④ Karlsbad/Czech Republic

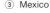

Streak white. **Mohs' hardness** 3½–4. **Specific gravity** 2.95. **Characteristics:** colorless, white, gray, yellow-green, bluish, reddish. Luster: on cleavage face greasy; translucent to transparent. Cleavage: incomplete. Fracture: conchoidal, brittle; easily soluble in hydrochloric acid (effervescence). Crystals: (rhombic) prismatic, tabular, acicular, intergrown, and surficial growth; often twinning and quadrupling, pseudomorphic. **Aggregates:** rough, crusty, dendritic, radial, stalactically branched; striped, oolitic, powdery; present in crevices and cavities in younger volcanic rocks, aragonitic muds, in ore veins, as deposits in hot springs, in supporting structures of mollusks, material of pearls. **Accompanied by:** natrolite, chabazite, harmotome, gypsum, sulfur, limonite, siderite. **Found in:** Kaisersthul/Kärnten/Austria; Bohemia/Czech Republic; Aragonia/Spain; Vesuvius, Sicily/Italy; southwest France; Arizona, New Mexico/USA; New Zealand. **Similar to:** calcite, strontianite, celestite, barite, natrolite.

Anhydrite
Ca[SO₄]

③ Mexico

Streak white. **Mohs' hardness** 3½. **Specific gravity** 2.9–3.0. **Characteristics:** colorless, white, gray, bluish, reddish. Luster: vitreous and mother-of-pearl; transparent. Cleavage: complete, square-shaped fragments. Fracture: conchoidal, splintery, brittle; volume increases and turns slowly into gypsum under humid conditions. Not easily soluble in acid; easily soluble as a powder in sulfuric acid. Flame test: dull red. Crystals: (rhombic) cubic, prismatic, tabular, intergrown, and surficial growth. **Aggregates:** rough, granular, spar-like, fibrous, dense, often contaminated; present in salt beds, ore deposits, in pegmatites, and alpine crevices; also as an exhalation product of volcanic activities, and rock-forming as alteration product. **Accompanied by:** halite, gypsum, sylvanite, carnallite, kainite, polyhalite, kieserite, boracite, dolomite. **Found in:** lower Saxony, eastern Harz mountains/Germany; Tessin/Switzerland; Kärnten/Austria; Urals/Russia; Louisiana, Texas/USA; Chile; western Australia. **Similar to:** gypsum, calcite, cryolite, barite.

Magnesite
Mg[CO₃]

⑤ Tuscany/Italy

Streak white. **Mohs' hardness** 4–4½. **Specific gravity** 2.9–3.1. **Characteristics:** colorless, white, yellow to brown, also gray to black. Luster: vitreous to dull; transparent to translucent. Cleavage: perfect. Fracture: conchoidal, brittle; in powder form soluble in warm hydrochloric acid; occasionally green or blue fluorescence under ultraviolet light. Crystals: (trigonal) rhombohedral, columnar, thick tabular; mostly intergrowth; rare. **Aggregates:** rough, granular, spar-like, dendritic, dense, crumbly; present in talc and chlorite slate; serpentinite, dolomite, in individual layers in veins, rarely in pegmatites. **Accompanied by:** calcite, aragonite, dolomite, serpentine, chlorite, talc, opal, chalcedony, gypsum. **Found in:** Tyrol, Kärnten, Steiermark/Austria; Mähren/Czech Republic; Euboea/Greece; Piemonte, Tuscany/Italy; Norway; Sweden; Urals/Russia; Manchuria/China; California, Nevada/USA. **Similar to:** calcite, dolomite, siderite, ankerite.

serpentine p. 48, thenardite p. 48, biotite p. 50, muscovite p. 50

Dolomite

$CaMg[CO_3]_2$

① with calcite;
Durham/England
② Arkansas/USA

Streak white. **Mohs' hardness** 3½–4. **Specific gravity** 2.85–2.95. **Characteristics:** white, gray, yellow to brown, reddish, also colorless to black. Luster: vitreous to mother-of-pearl; transparent to translucent. Cleavage: complete. Fracture: conchoidal and brittle; easily soluble in warm hydrochloric acid, in powder form also in cold hydrochloric acid. Crystals: (trigonal) rhombohedral, intergrown and surficial growth; parallel twinning, pseudomorphic. **Aggregates:** rough, granular, spar-like, dendritic, dense; present in ore and mineral veins, in chlorite and talc slate; rock-forming. **Accompanied by:** calcite, gypsum, quartz, pyrite, realgar, tremolite, wollastonite, ankerite. **Found in:** northern Bavaria, Eifel, Erzgebirge/Germany; Tyrol/Austria; Wallis, Switzerland; Dolomite Alps/Italy; Cornwall/England; Urals/Russia; Quebec/Canada; Iowa, Missouri/USA; Mexico. **Similar to:** calcite, magnesite, chabazite, siderite, gypsum, anhydrite, quartz.

Polyhalite

$K_2Ca_2Mg[SO_4]_4 \cdot 2\ H_2O$

③ Hallein/Austria 1:½

Streak white. **Mohs' hardness** 3–3½. **Specific gravity** 2.8. **Characteristics:** red, yellow, white, gray. Luster: greasy, vitreous, resinous; transparent. Cleavage: perfect. Fracture: fibrous, brittle. Taste: bitter. Flame test: violet. Soluble in water. Crystals: (triclinic) prismatic; mostly intergrowth; small and rare; often twinning. **Aggregates:** rough, fibrous, rarely dendritic, bladed, granular; present in salt mines. **Accompanied by:** halite, anhydrite, gypsum, kieserite, carnallite. **Found in:** Lower Saxony, upper Bavaria, Magdeburg/Germany; Salzkammergut/Austria; Lothringen/France; New Mexico, Texas/USA; Chile. **Similar to:** kieserite, gypsum.

Kämmererite

$(Mg,Cr)_6[(OH)_8(AlSi)_3O_{10}]$

④ Guleman/Turkey

Streak white. **Mohs' hardness** 2–3. **Specific gravity** 2.6–3.3. **Characteristics:** red, violet. Luster: vitreous, mother-of-pearl, dull; transparent to translucent. Cleavage: complete. Fracture: bladed, in thin layers nonelastic, malleable; soluble in hydrochloric and sulfuric acid. Crystals: (monoclinic) columnar, barrel-shaped, pyramidal. **Aggregates:** bladed, crumbly, as surficial deposits; present in chromite deposits. **Accompanied by:** chromite, uvarovite. **Found in:** Steiermark/Austria; Silesia/Poland; Piemonte/Italy; Turkey; Urals, Caucasus/Russia; California, Texas/USA.

Ankerite

$Ca(Fe^{2+},Mg,Mn)[CO_3]_2$

⑤ Sunk, Steiermark/Austria

Streak white, also light gray and light brown. **Mohs' hardness** 3½–4. **Specific gravity** 2.9–3.8. **Characteristics:** yellow to brown, white, gray. Luster: vitreous to mother-of-pearl; transparent to translucent. Cleavage: complete. Fracture: uneven, brittle. Soluble (effervescence) in warm hydrochloric acid; occasional yellow or red fluorescence under ultraviolet light. Crystals: (trigonal) rhombohedral. **Aggregates:** rough, spar-like, granular, dense; present in ore veins and alpine crevices. **Accompanied by:** calcite, siderite, quartz, dolomite, galena. **Found in:** Steiermark, Kärnten/Austria; Hungary; Lancashire/England; South Dakota/USA. **Similar to:** dolomite, magnesite, siderite.

margarite p. 72, wollastonite p. 94, serpierite p. 214

Kieserite

① Hanover/Germany

$Mg[SO_4] \cdot H_2O$

Streak white. **Mohs' hardness** $3\frac{1}{2}$. **Specific gravity** 2.57. **Characteristics:** colorless, white, yellowish, gray, reddish. Luster: vitreous, transparent, dull. Cleavage: complete. Difficult to dissolve in water. Crystals: (monoclinic) dipyramidal; rarely well-developed; usually dispersed. **Aggregates:** rough, fine-grained, rarely large-grained; present either layered or scattered in salt mines, particularly in potassium salt mines. **Accompanied by:** halite, polyhalite, sylvite, anhydrite, carnallite, kainite. **Found in:** Lower Saxony, Hessia, Magdeburg/Germany; Salzburg/Austria; Poland; Sicily/Italy; New Mexico, Texas, Utah/USA; Punjab/India. **Similar to:** epsomite, polyhalite, kainite.

Hanksite

② Boron, California/USA 1:2

$KNa_{22}[Cl \mid (CO_3)_2 \mid (SO_4)_9]$

Streak white. **Mohs' hardness** $3–3\frac{1}{2}$. **Specific gravity** 2.56. **Characteristics:** colorless, white, yellow, gray to black. Luster: vitreous; transparent to translucent. Cleavage: perfect. Fracture: uneven, brittle. Taste: salty. Sometimes yellow fluorescence under ultraviolet light. Crystals: (hexagonal) tabular to short prismatic, dipyramidal; often interpenetration twinning. **Aggregates:** in groups with interpenetrating crystals; present in salt mines, specifically in borax, and soda mines. **Accompanied by:** borax, soda, halite, trona. **Found in:** California/USA. **Similar to:** quartz.

Strengite

③ Svappavaara/Sweden

$Fe^{3+}[PO_4] \cdot 2\,H_2O$

Streak white. **Mohs' hardness** $3–4\frac{1}{2}$. **Specific gravity** 2.8–2.9. **Characteristics:** red, violet, white, yellow, greenish, and almost colorless. Luster: vitreous; transparent to translucent. Cleavage: perfect. Fracture: conchoidal to uneven, brittle; soluble in hydrochloric acid. Crystals: (rhombic) pseudohexagonal, tabular, short prismatic, often multifaceted; rare. **Aggregates:** radial, spherical, botryoidal, as crusts and surface covering; present in drusy cavities of phosphate-bearing pegmatites and ore deposits. **Accompanied by:** wavellite, vivianite, dufrenite, cacoxenite, limonite, quartz. **Found in:** Hesse, Oberpfalz, Thüringen/Germany; Portugal; Lappland/Sweden; Alabama, California/USA. **Similar to:** variscite, amethyst, scorodite.

Pectolite

④ Rauschermühle/Germany

$NaCa_2[Si_3O_8(OH)]$

Streak white. **Mohs' hardness** $4\frac{1}{2}–5$. **Specific gravity** 2.8–2.9. **Characteristics:** white, gray, sometimes greenish, yellowish, colorless. Luster: vitreous; transparent to translucent. Cleavage: perfect. Fracture: conchoidal to uneven, brittle; soluble in hydrochloric acid. Flame test: yellow. Crystals: (triclinic) occasionally columnar, commonly dentritic, fibrous, acicular; rare. **Aggregates:** rough, dense, radial, spheroidal; also parallel fibrous; present in crevices and drusy cavities in basic volcanic rocks, sometimes in metamorphic rocks. **Accompanied by:** natrolite, laumontite, heulandite, thomsonite, prehnite, diopside, calcite. **Found in:** Rheinland-Pfalz/Germany; Bohemia/Czech Republic; Skye/Scotland; Ontario, Quebec/Canada; New Jersey, New York/USA. **Similar to:** wollastonite, tremolite.

Ludlamite
$(Fe^{2+},Mg,Mn^{2+})_3[PO_4]_2 \cdot 4\,H_2O$

① Trepca/Serbia

Streak white. **Mohs' hardness** 3–4. **Specific gravity** 3.1–3.2. **Characteristics:** light to apple green, seldom colorless. Luster: vitreous; transparent to translucent. Cleavage: perfect. Fracture: uneven, brittle; soluble in acid. Flame test: green. Crystals: (monoclinic) tabular. **Aggregates:** rough, granular, spar-like; present in oxidation zones of ore veins, in granite pegmatites. **Accompanied by:** vivianite, triphylite. **Found in:** northern Bavaria/Germany; Cornwall/England; Serbia; Montenegro; Idaho, New Hampshire/USA. **Similar to:** apophyllite, chalcedony.

Astrophyllite
$(K,Na)_3(Fe^{2+},Mn^{2+})_7Ti_2[(O,OH)_7 \mid Si_8O_{24}]$

② Mt. St. Hilaire/Canada 1:2

Streak white, also brownish. **Mohs' hardness** 3–3½. **Specific gravity** 3.3–3.4. **Characteristics:** yellow to brown, olive. Luster: vitreous; cleavage face mother-of-pearl; transparent to translucent. Cleavage: complete. Fracture: bladed, brittle; obvious pleochroism; slowly soluble in acid. Crystals: (triclinic) tabular, bladed; rare. **Aggregates:** radial; present in basic plutonites. **Accompanied by:** quartz, feldspars, mica, aegerine, zircon, titanite. **Found in:** Norway; Quebec/Canada; Colorado/USA; Kola/Russia. **Similar to:** muscovite, biotite, phlogopite.

Margarite
$CaAl_2[(OH)_2 \mid Al_2Si_2O_{10}]$

③ Chester, Massachusetts/USA

Streak white. **Mohs' hardness** 4–4½. **Specific gravity** 3.0–3.1. **Characteristics:** gray, white, reddish, yellow, green. Luster: mother-of-pearl; translucent. Cleavage: perfect. Fracture: bladed, brittle; somewhat soluble in warm hydrochloric acid. Crystals: (monoclinic) tabular with hexagonal contours; very rare. **Aggregates:** bladed, scaly, granular; present in schists, emery deposits. **Accompanied by:** corundum, staurolite, tourmaline, emerald, magnetite, rutile. **Found in:** Tyrol/Austria; St. Gotthard/Switzerland; southern Tirol/Italy; Naxos/Greece; Turkey; Urals/Russia; Pennsylvania/USA. **Similar to:** pyrophyllite, muscovite.

Fluorite
CaF_2

④ with barite;
Oberpfalz/Germany
⑤ Pöla, Erzgebirge/
Germany

Streak white. **Mohs' hardness** 4. **Specific gravity** 3.1–3.2. **Characteristics:** violet, blue, black, yellow to brown, green, pink, often zoned colors, seldom colorless. Luster: vitreous; transparent to translucent. Cleavage: complete. Fracture: conchoidal, splintery, brittle. Flame test: dull red. Often violet, blue, or green fluorescence under ultraviolet light. Sometimes radioactive. Crystals: (cubic) octahedral, rhombododecahedral; usually surface growth. **Aggregates:** rough, spar-like, macrocrystalline to dense, rarely dendritic or crumbly; present in veins, pegmatites, and alpine crevices, as by-products of many rocks. **Accompanied by:** barite, apatite, calcite, tourmaline, topaz, quartz, siderite, galena, sphalerite, kieserite. **Found in:** Harz mountains, eastern Bavaria, Thüringen/Germany/ Tauern/Austria; St. Gotthard/Switzerland; Derbyshire/England; Spain; Urals/Russia; Kazakhstan; Illinois/USA; Namibia. **Similar to:** apatite, barite, chalcedony, calcite, halite, apophyllite.

zinnwaldite p. 44, biotite p. 50, muscovite p. 50, magnesite p. 66

Streak

white and colorless

Mohs' h.

S. gravity

Betafite

$(Ca,Na,U)_2(Ti,Nb,Ta)_2O_6(OH)$

① Antsirabe/Madagascar 1:3

Streak white, sometimes gray and yellowish. **Mohs' hardness** 3–5½. **Specific gravity** 3.7–5.2. **Characteristics:** greenish brown to black, yellowish. Luster: resinous, on cleavage face greasy; transparent to opaque. Cleavage: none. Fracture: conchoidal, uneven, brittle; soluble in acid; strongly radioactive. Crystals: (cubic) octahedral and dodecahedral, tabular. **Aggregates:** crusty, granular, dense; present in granite pegmatites. **Accompanied by:** fergusonite, euxenite, allanite. **Found in:** Norway; Baikal Lake/ Russia; Madagascar; Ontario/Canada; Colorado/USA; Brazil. **Similar to:** pyrochlore, magnesite, scheelite, euxenite, uraninite.

Triphylite

$Li(Fe^{2+},Mn^{2+})[PO_4]$

② Hagendorf, Bavaria/Germany

Streak gray-white. **Mohs' hardness** 4–5. **Specific gravity** 3.4–3.6. **Characteristics:** greenish, blue, brownish. Luster: vitreous, greasy; transparent to translucent. Cleavage: complete. Fracture: splintery, uneven, brittle. Flame test: red. Easily soluble in hydrochloric acid. Crystals: (rhombic) prismatic; always intergrown; rare. **Aggregates:** dense, rough-granular, spar-like; present in granite pegmatites, tin ore veins. **Accompanied by:** cassiterite, spodumene, amblygonite, apatite, beryl. **Found in:** northern Bavaria/Germany; Portugal; Sweden; Namibia; Manitoba/Canada; Connecticut, South Dakota/ USA; Tasmania/Australia.

Kyanite disthene

$Al_2[O \mid SiO_4]$

③ Alpe Spondar, Tessin/Switzerland 1:2

Streak white. **Mohs' hardness** 4–4½ vertically, 6–7 horizontally. **Specific gravity** 3.5–3.7. **Characteristics:** blue, yellowish, green, white, pink, seldom colorless. Luster: vitreous, mother-of-pearl; transparent to translucent. Cleavage: complete. Fracture: fibrous, uneven, brittle. Crystals: (triclinic) linearly columnar, mostly intergrown. **Aggregates:** irregularly radial, bladed, seldom dense; present in metamorphic rocks, pegmatites, sand and gravel deposits. **Accompanied by:** staurolite, andalusite, corundum, mica, garnet, tourmaline, quartz. **Found in:** Tyrol/Austria; Tessin/Switzerland; southern Tirol/Italy; Assam/ India; western Australia; Virginia/USA; Brazil. **Similar to:** sillimanite, dumortierite, actinolite, glaucophane.

Celestite

$Sr[SO_4]$

④ Madagascar

Streak white. **Mohs' hardness** 3–3½. **Specific gravity** 3.9–4.0. **Characteristics:** light blue, white, yellowish, gray, colorless, seldom reddish and greenish. Luster: vitreous to mother-of-pearl; transparent to translucent. Cleavage: complete. Fracture: conchoidal, uneven, brittle. Flame test: carmine red. Soluble as powder in concentrated hydrochloric acid. Crystals: (rhombic) prismatic, tabular, mostly surficial growth. **Aggregates:** granular, spar-like, dense, dendritic, small, tuberous; present in limestone and gypsum stone, in cavities in volcanic rocks, in veins. **Accompanied by:** calcite, aragonite, gypsum, anhydrite, sulfur, galena, sphalerite. **Found in:** Kaiserstuhl, Thüringen/Germany; Sicily, Vicenza/Italy; Granada/Spain; southwest England; Madagascar; Tennessee/ USA; Turkestan. **Similar to:** barite, gypsum, calcite, aragonite, strontianite, cerussite.

ankerite p. 68, kämmererite p. 68, scorodite p. 140, sphalerite p. 198

Boehmite

AlO(OH)

① Le Duc, Provence/France

Streak white. **Mohs' hardness** 3. **Specific gravity** 3.07. **Characteristics:** colorless, white, yellowish to brown. Luster: vitreous, mother-of-pearl, dull; transparent. Cleavage: perfect. Fracture: uneven, brittle. Crystals: (rhombic) microscopically small and tabular. **Aggregates:** rough and crumbly; present with bauxite. **Accompanied by:** diaspore, gypsite, limonite. **Found in:** southern France; Serbia; Montenegro; Hungary; Urals/Russia; California, Georgia/USA; Jamaica; Surinam/Indonesia. **Similar to:** diaspore.

Siderite

Fe[CO$_3$]

② iron ore; Steiermark/Austria

Streak white. **Mohs' hardness** 4–4$\frac{1}{2}$. **Specific gravity** 3.7–3.9. **Characteristics:** yellowish to brown, black, seldom white; occasionally tarnished in different colors. Luster: vitreous, mother-of-pearl; transparent to translucent. Cleavage: complete. Fracture: conchoidal, spar-like, brittle; easily soluble in warm hydrochloric acid; occasional lemon-yellow fluorescence under ultraviolet light. Crystals: (trigonal) rhombohedral, scalenohedral. **Aggregates:** rough, spar-like, granular, dense, radial, botryoidal, oolitic; as concretion (clay ironstones) present in peat bogs. **Accompanied by:** quartz, barite, calcite, galena, sphalerite, ankerite. **Found in:** Siegerland, northern Bavaria, Saxony/Germany; Kärnten, Steiermark, Austria; Czech Republic; Cornwall/England; Lorraine/France; Spain; Connecticut/USA. **Similar to:** calcite, dolomite, smithsonite, sphalerite, ankerite.

Rhodochrosite

Mn[CO$_3$]

③ St. Luis/Argentina
④ Saxony/Germany

Streak white. **Mohs' hardness** 3$\frac{1}{2}$–4. **Specific gravity** 3.3–3.6. **Characteristics:** pink, gray, brown to black, seldom colorless. Luster: vitreous; transparent to opaque. Cleavage: complete. Fracture: uneven, brittle; easily soluble in warm hydrochloric acid. Crystals: (trigonal) rhombohedral, scalenohedral; surface growth. **Aggregates:** rough, granular, spar-like, dense, radial, botryoidal, stalactitic, crusty; occasionally with ragged rings; present in oxidized zones of ore veins, as stalagmites in abandoned mines. **Accompanied by:** rhodonite, manganite, quartz, fluorite, barite, limonite. **Found in:** Saxony, Siegerland/Germany; Romania; Huelva/Spain; Pyrenees/France; South Africa; Colorado, Montana/USA; Mexico; Argentina; Urals/Russia. **Similar to:** rhodonite, calcite, dolomite, siderite, ankerite.

Strontianite

Sr[CO$_3$]

⑤ on barite; Koentiz, Thüringen/Germany

Streak white. **Mohs' hardness** 3$\frac{1}{2}$. **Specific gravity** 3.7–3.8. **Characteristics:** colorless, gray, white, yellow, green, reddish. Luster: vitreous, on cleavage face greasy; transparent to translucent. Cleavage: incomplete. Fracture: conchoidal, brittle. Flame test: red. Easily soluble in warm hydrochloric acid (effervescence). Occasional blue fluorescence under ultraviolet light. Crystals: (rhombic) acicular, prismatic, tabular. **Aggregates:** rough, radial, crusty, reniform, as concretions; present in ore veins, limestone, and marl. **Accompanied by:** calcite, barite, galena, pyrite, celestite. **Found in:** Harz mountains, Münsterland, Saxony/Germany; Steiermark/Austria; Scotland; Arizona, California/USA. **Similar to:** aragonite, calcite, natrolite, barite, celestite.

Mimetite

Pb₅[Cl | (AsO₄)₃]

① Tsumeb/Namibia 1:2
② Mexico

Streak white. **Mohs' hardness** 3½–4. **Specific gravity** 7.1. **Characteristics:** yellow, greenish, sometimes colorless, gray, white, brown, reddish. Luster: adamantine, greasy, transparent to translucent. Cleavage: none. Fracture: conchoidal to uneven, brittle; soluble in nitric acid and potassium leach. **Crystals:** (hexagonal) prismatic, tabular, acicular, surface growth. **Aggregates:** botryoidal, crusty, reniform, crumbly; present in oxidized zones of lead ore veins. **Accompanied by:** galena, cerussite, anglesite, pyromorphite, wulfenite, limonite. **Found in:** Erzgebirge/Germany; Czech Republic; Cornall, Cumberland/ England; Sweden; Sardinia/Italy; Turkestan; Namibia; Nevada/USA; Mexico. **Similar to:** pyromorphite, vanadinite, apatite, wulfenite, crocoite.

Cerussite

Pb[CO₃]

③ Tsumeb/Namibia 1:2

Streak white. **Mohs' hardness** 3–3½. **Specific gravity** 6.4–6.6. **Characteristics:** colorless, white, gray, yellow, brown, black. Luster: adamantine, greasy, vitreous; transparent to opaque. Cleavage: incomplete. Fracture: conchoidal, very brittle; soluble in nitric acid (effervescence); blue-green fluorescence under ultraviolet light. Crystals: (rhombic) tabular, prismatic, dipyramidal, acicular; twinning and pseudomorphic. **Aggregates:** dense, rough, crusty, reniform, dendritic, crumbly; present in oxidized zones of lead ore veins. **Accompanied by:** galena, anglesite, pyromorphite, hemimorphite, smithsonite. **Found in:** Siegerland/ Germany; Czech Republic; Sardinia/Italy; Zambia; Namibia; Colorado/USA; Altai Mountains/Russia; Australia. **Similar to:** anglesite, celestite, barite, phosgenite, scheelite.

Adamite

Zn₂[OH | AsO₄]

④ Mapimi/Mexico

Streak white. **Mohs' hardness** 3½. **Specific gravity** 4.3–4.5. **Characteristics:** colorless, white, yellow, green, pink to violet. Luster: vitreous; transparent to translucent. Cleavage: complete. Fracture: conchoidal, uneven, brittle; distinct pleochroism; easily soluble in hydrochloric acid; sometimes lemon-yellow fluorescence under ultraviolet light. Crystals: (rhombic) prismatic to acicular, tabular, surface growth. **Aggregates:** fine-grained, radial, crusty, crumbly; present in oxidized zones of zinc veins. **Accompanied by:** smithsonite, hemimorphite, azurite. **Found in:** Attica/Greece; Var/France; Namibia; Utah/USA; Mexico; Chile. **Similar to:** olivine, libethenite.

Witherite

Ba[CO₃]

⑤ Alston Moor/England

Streak white. **Mohs' hardness** 3–3½. **Specific gravity** 4.3. **Characteristics:** colorless, white, gray, yellowish. Luster: vitreous or dull, on cleavage face greasy; transparent to translucent. Cleavage: incomplete. Fracture: uneven, brittle. Flame test: yellowish green. Soluble in diluted hydrochloric acid (effervescence). **Witherite is poisonous in powder form.** Crystals: (rhombic) prismatic, dipyramidal; penetration twinning. **Aggregates:** rough, botryoidal, radial, bladed, crusty; present in veins. **Accompanied by:** barite, galena, sphalerite, calcite. **Found in:** Steiermark/Austria; England; Turkmenistan; California, Illinois/USA. **Similar to:** strontianite, cerussite, quartz.

silver p. 52, stolzite p. 52, valentinite p. 54, phosgenite p. 54,
betafite p. 74, scheelite p. 114, bismutite p. 168, platinum p. 168

Anglesite

① Tsumeb/Namibia

Pb[SO₄]

Streak white. **Mohs' hardness** 3–3½. **Specific gravity** 6.3–6.4. **Characteristics:** colorless, gray to blackish, brownish. Luster: adamantine, greasy; transparent to translucent. Cleavage: incomplete. Fracture: conchoidal, brittle; soluble in potassium leach and warm sulfuric acid. Crystals: (rhombic) prismatic and tabular; surface growth. **Aggregates:** rough, granular, crusty, reniform, crumbly; present in oxidized zones of galena deposits, as a volcanic sublimation product. **Accompanied by:** galena, cerussite, phosgenite, sphalerite, smithsonite, limonite. **Found in:** Siegerland/Germany; Kärnten/Austria; Sardinia/Italy; Wales; Scotland; Spain; Urals/Russia; Namibia; Missouri/USA. **Similar to:** cerussite, scheelite, barite, phosgenite.

Barite baryte

Ba[SO₄]

② with chalcosite; Alston Moor/England

④ barite rose; Rockenberg, Hesse/Germany

Streak white. **Mohs' hardness** 3–3½. **Specific gravity** 4.48. **Characteristics:** colorless, white, yellow to brown, reddish, blue, green, gray to black. Luster: on cleavage face mother-of-pearl; translucent to transparent. Cleavage: complete. Fracture: conchoidal, uneven, brittle. Flame test: yellow-green. Slowly soluble in concentrated sulfuric acid. Sometimes radioactive. Crystals: (rhombic) tabular, prismatic; surface growth. **Aggregates:** rough, bladed, spar-like, reniform, rosette-like (barite rose), granular, dense, as concretions; present in ore veins, sandstone, magmatites. **Accompanied by:** galena, siderite, sphalerite, quartz, fluorite. **Found in:** Westphalia, Harz mountains/Germany; Czech Republic; England; Urals/Russia; Colorado/USA; western Australia. **Similar to:** aragonite, feldspars, anglesite.

Pyromorphite

③ Freihung/Germany

Pb₅[Cl | (PO₄)₃]

Streak white. **Mohs' hardness** 3½–4. **Specific gravity** 6.7–7.1. **Characteristics:** green (green alteration of galena), brown (brown alteration of galena), yellow, reddish, white and colorless, also zoned colors. Luster: adamantine, greasy; transparent to translucent. Cleavage: none. Fracture: conchoidal to uneven, brittle; soluble in nitric acid and potassium leach. Crystals: (hexagonal) prismatic, tabular, acicular, dipyramidal, often barrel-shaped; pseudomorphic. **Aggregates:** botryoidal, radial, rough, present in oxidized zones of lead deposits. **Accompanied by:** mimetite, cerussite, galena, wulfenite. **Found in:** Harz mountains, Siegerland, Saxony/Germany; Czech Republic; England; Colorado/USA; Mexico. **Similar to:** mimetite, apatite, vanadinite.

Wulfenite yellow lead ore

⑤ Mezica/Slovenia

Pb[MoO₄]

Streak white. **Mohs' hardness** 3. **Specific gravity** 6.7–6.9. **Characteristics:** yellow, orange, colorless, gray. Luster: adamantine, resinous; transparent to translucent. Cleavage: incomplete. Fracture: conchoidal to uneven, brittle; slowly soluble in hydrochloric acid. Crystals: (tetragonal) tabular, pyramidal, acicular; usually surficial growth. **Aggregates:** rough, dense, crusty; present in oxidized zones of lead ore deposits. **Accompanied by:** galena, cerussite, pyromorphite, hydrozincite, smithsonite, calcite. **Found in:** Kärnten/Austria; Czech Republic; Slovenia; Morocco; DR Congo; Namibia; Arizona, Utah/USA, Mexico; Australia. **Similar to:** stolzite, sulfur, mimetite.

vanadinite p. 198, sphalerite p. 198, powellite p. 200, caledonite p. 212

Opal
$SiO_2 \cdot nH_2O$

① fire opal; Mexico
② prasopal; Mexico
③ precious opal; Andamooka/Australia 1:2
④ petrified wood opal; Oregon/USA
⑤ liver opal; Hungary

Streak white. **Mohs' hardness** $5\frac{1}{2}$–$6\frac{1}{2}$. **Specific gravity** 1.9–2.5. **Characteristics**: colorless, white, yellow to brown, red to orange (fire opal), green (prasopal), gray to black, occasionally rainbow-colored (precious opal). Luster: vitreous, waxy, mother-of-pearl; transparent (hyalite) to opaque (common opal), often cloudy (milky opal). Cleavage: none. Fracture: conchoidal, splintery, brittle; easily soluble in potassium leach. Noncrystalline: amorphous; only a very small occurrence of fine-crystalline cristobalite and tridymite, rarely represented in the quartz group. **Aggregates**: reniform, tuberous, botryoidal, crusty, layered, crumbly (siliceous earth), as concretions (chert or flint); present as filling in volcanic rock, often in sandstone or limestone, as deposits in hot springs (geyserite), as fossilization product (among other petrified wood). **Accompanied by**: zeolite, chalcedony, limonite. **Found in**: Hungary; Iceland; Turkey; Libya; Egypt; Tanzania; Kazakhstan; Montana, Nevada, Wyoming/USA; Hidalgo, Queretaro/Mexico; New South Wales, southern Australia, Queensland/Australia; New Zealand; New Caledonia. **Similar to**: chalcedony, variscite, smithsonite, hemimorphite, porcelain, glass, synthetic materials.

Scapolite

⑥ Baikal Lake/Russia

Mineral group series between marialite and meionite
marialite $Na_4[Cl \mid Al_3Si_9O_{24}]$
meionite $Ca_4[CO_3 \mid Al_6Si_6O_{24}]$

Streak white. **Mohs' hardness** 5–$6\frac{1}{2}$. **Specific gravity** 2.5–2.8. **Characteristics**: colorless, white, gray, yellow, green, blue, red to violet. Luster: vitreous, greasy; transparent to opaque. Cleavage: complete. Fracture: conchoidal, brittle; sometimes orange-yellow fluorescence under ultraviolet light. Crystals: (tetragonal) prismatic-pyramidal; surficial and intergrowth. **Aggregates**: rough, granular, dendritic, acicular, dense; present in magmatites, pegmatites, by-product of volcanic eruptions; in metamorphic rocks. **Accompanied by**: garnet, apatite, idocrase, epidote, augite, wollastonite. **Found in**: Eifel, eastern Bavaria/Germany; Tessin/Switzerland; Kärnten/Austria; Scandanavia; Kenya; Tanzania; Madagascar; Karelia, Baikal Lake/Russia; Myanmar; Ontario/Canada; California, New York/USA. **Similar to**: feldspars, idocrase, amblygonite, petalite, apatite, chrysoberyl.

Charoite

⑦ Jakutia/Russia

$K(Ca,Na)_2[(OH,F) \mid Si_4O_{10}] \cdot H_2O$

Streak white. **Mohs' hardness** 5–6. **Specific gravity** 2.5. **Characteristics**: violet. Luster: vitreous, silky; transparent to opaque. Cleavage: incomplete. Fracture: fibrous, tough. Crystals: (monoclinic) unknown. **Aggregates**: fibrous, dense; present in quartzite, as riverspar (fluorite). **Accompanied by**: aegirine, orthoclase. **Found in**: only eastern Siberia/Russia. **Similar to**: sodalite, azurite, lapis lazuli, lazulite.

variscite p. 56, apophyllite p. 58, okenite p. 58, chabazite p. 60

Thomsonite

NaCa$_2$[Al$_5$Si$_5$O$_{20}$] · 6 H$_2$O

① Giant's Causeway, Northern Ireland 1:3

Streak white. **Mohs' hardness** 5–5$\frac{1}{2}$. **Specific gravity** 2.3–2.4. **Characteristics:** white, gray, yellow, reddish, sometimes colorless, green. Luster: vitreous, on cleavage face mother-of-pearl; transparent to translucent. Cleavage: complete. Fracture: uneven to conchoidal, brittle; soluble in hydrochloric acid. Crystals: (rhombic) prismatic, columnar, tabular, vertical striped; rare and small, sometimes cross-shaped twinnings. **Aggregates:** rough, radial, dendritic, reniform, spheroidal; present in young, basic volcanics, rarely in sedimentary deposits. **Accompanied by:** natrolite, chabazite, phillipsite, calcite, analcite. **Found in:** Eifel, Erzgebirge/Germany; Czech Republic; Vesuvius/Italy; Skye/Scotland; Faeroe Islands/Denmark; Iceland; Nova Scotia/Canada; California, Colorado, Oregon/USA; India. **Similar to:** natrolite, phillipsite, gonnardite.

Cancrinite

in series with vishnevite

Na$_2$Ca$_2$[(CO$_3$)$_2$ | (AlSiO$_4$)$_6$] · 2 H$_2$O

② Blue Mountain, Ontario/Canada

Streak white. **Mohs' hardness** 5–6. **Specific gravity** 2.4–2.5. **Characteristics:** colorless, yellowish, pink, white. Luster: on cleavage face mother-of-pearl, vitreous; transparent to translucent. Cleavage: complete. Fracture: uneven, brittle; soluble in hydrochloric acid (effervescence). Crystals: (hexagonal) prismatic, short columnar, acicular; mostly intergrowth. **Aggregates:** rough, granular, dendritic; present as by-product in residual crystallization and of volcanic eruptions. **Accompanied by:** zeolite, nepheline, sanidine, sodalite, calcite. **Found in:** Eifel/Germany; Siebenbürgen/Romania; Norway; Sweden; Kola, Urals/Russia; Ontario/Canada; Colorado, Maine/USA. **Similar to:** nepheline, chondrodite, humite.

Mesolite

Na$_2$Ca$_2$[Al$_2$Si$_3$O$_{10}$]$_3$ · 8 H$_2$O

③ with hydrous scolecite; India

Streak white. **Mohs' hardness** 5–5$\frac{1}{2}$. **Specific gravity** 2.2–2.4. **Characteristics:** colorless, white. Luster: vitreous, silky, dull; transparent to translucent. Cleavage: complete. Fracture: conchoidal, brittle. Crystals: (monoclinic) long prismatic to acicular. **Aggregates:** delicately fibrous, also crumbly; present in volcanic cavities. **Accompanied by:** other zeolites, apophyllite. **Found in:** Thüringen/Germany; Northern Ireland; Faeroe Islands/Denmark; Skye/Scotland; Iceland; Greenland; Nova Scotia/Canada; California, Oregon/USA; Australia. **Similar to:** natrolite, scolecite.

Sodalite

Na$_8$[Cl$_2$ | (AlSiO$_4$)$_6$]

④ with white calcite; Canada 1:2

Streak white. **Mohs' hardness** 5–6. **Specific gravity** 2.1–2.3. **Characteristics:** blue, gray, white, colorless. Luster: vitreous, on cleavage face greasy; translucent to opaque. Cleavage: complete. Fracture: uneven, conchoidal, brittle; soluble in hydrochloric and nitric acid. Flame test: yellow. Crystals: (cubic) rhombododecahedral. Surface growth; occasional twinning. **Aggregates:** rough, granular, dense; present in metasomatized rocks, by foyaite (syenite), product of volcanic eruptions. **Accompanied by:** nepheline, leucite, cancrinite, augite, sanidine, zircon, titanite, hematite, barite. **Found in:** Eifel/Germany; Alban Mountains, Vesuvius/Italy; Siebenbürgen/Romania; Portugal; Ukraine; Kola/Russia; Arkansas, Maine/USA; Bolivia; Brazil. **Similar to:** analcite, leucite, lapis lazuli, lazulite, haüynite, charoite.

gonnardite p. 60, milarite p. 96, orthoclase p. 98, chalcedony p. 122

Haüynite

$Na_{5-6}Ca_2[(SO_4,Cl)_2 \mid Al_6Si_6O_{24}]$

① Italy 1:2
② Mendig, Eifel/Germany

Streak white. **Mohs' hardness** $5\frac{1}{2}$–6. **Specific gravity** 2.4–2.5. **Characteristics:** blue, occasionally gray, white, yellowish, reddish, seldom colorless, green. Luster: vitreous, on cleavage face greasy; transparent to translucent. Cleavage: complete. Fracture: conchoidal, uneven, brittle; easily soluble in hydrochloric acid. Crystals: (cubic) rhombododecahedral; sometimes octahedral; intergrowth and surface growth; every rare, small. **Aggregates:** rough, granular, in basic volcanics, and ejected blocks from volcanic eruptions. **Accompanied by:** nepheline, leucite, nosean, mellite, sanidine, augite, hornblende, idocrase. **Found in:** Eifel, Erzegebirge/Germany; Alban Mountains, Vesuvius/Italy; Auvergne/France; Baikal Lake/Russia; Morocco; Quebec/Canada; Montana, South Dakota/USA. **Similar to:** sodalite, lapis lazuli, nosean.

Leucite

$K[AlSi_2O_6]$

③ Resina/Italy

Streak white. **Mohs' hardness** $5\frac{1}{2}$–6. **Specific gravity** 2.5. **Characteristics:** white-gray, seldom colorless, usually dull. Luster: on cleavage face vitreous and greasy; translucent to opaque. Cleavage: none. Fracture: conchoidal to uneven, brittle; soluble in hydrochloric acid. Crystals: (tetragonal) icositetrahedral; mostly intergrowth, pseudomorphic. **Aggregates:** rough, granular, rare; present in young basic magmatites, particularly in foyaite (syenite). **Accompanied by:** nepheline, apatite, augite, biotite, sanidine. **Found in:** Eifel, Kaiserstuhl/Germany; Czech Republic; Alban Mountains, Vesuvius/Italy; Turkestan; western Siberia/Russia; British Columbia/Canada; Arkansas, Wyoming/USA; Sao Paulo/Brazil. **Similar to:** analcite, sodalite, garnet.

Nosean

$Na_8[SO_4 \mid (AlSiO_4)_6] \cdot H_2O$

④ Laarcher Lake, Eifel/Germany 1:3

Streak white. **Mohs' hardness** $5\frac{1}{2}$. **Specific gravity** 2.3–2.4. **Characteristics:** gray, yellow to brown, blue, black, seldom white. Luster: vitreous and greasy; transparent to opaque. Cleavage: complete. Fracture: conchoidal, brittle; soluble in acid. Crystals: (cubic) rhombododecahedral, mostly intergrown; small and rare. **Aggregates:** rough, granular; present in young basic volcanics. **Accompanied by:** nepheline, leucite, haüynite, sanidine, biotite, zircon, augite. **Found in:** Eifel, Baden/Germany; Alban Mountains, Vesuvius/Italy; Cornwall/England; Colorado, South Dakota/USA; northern Chine. **Similar to:** sodalite, haüynite, zircon.

Petalite castor

$Li[AlSi_4O_{10}]$

⑤ reddish aggregate;
Meldon,
Devon/England 1:2

Streak white. **Mohs' hardness** 6–$6\frac{1}{2}$. **Specific gravity** 2.4. **Characteristics:** colorless, white, gray, reddish, green. Luster: vitreous, on cleavage face mother-of-pearl; transparent to translucent. Cleavage: complete. Fracture: conchoidal and brittle. Flame test: carmine red. Crystals: (monoclinic) columnar, tabular; mostly scattered; very rare and small. **Aggregates:** rough, spar-like, granular, bladed, dense; present in granite pegmatites. **Accompanied by:** lepidolite, spodumene, tourmaline, quartz, arsenopyrite, pollucite. **Found in:** Elba/Italy; Sweden; Finland; Zimbabwe; South Africa; Namibia; Manitoba/Canada; Maine, Massachussets/USA; western Australia. **Similar to:** spodumene, amblygonite, scapolite, feldspars, glass.

Analcite analcime

(1) Farmsen/Germany

$Na[AlSi_2O_6] \cdot H_2O$

Streak white. **Mohs' hardness** $5–5\frac{1}{2}$. **Specific gravity** 2.2–2.3. **Characteristics**: colorless, white, gray, yellow, reddish, green. Luster: vitreous; transparent to translucent. Cleavage: none. Fracture: uneven, conchoidal, brittle. Flame test: yellow. Crystals: (cubic) icositetrahedral, also hexahedral; usually surface growth; psuedomorphic. **Aggregates**: rough, granular, dense, crumbly, crusty; present in basalt, ore veins. **Accompanied by**: leucite, natrolite, nepheline, thomsonite, chabazite, stilbite, apophyllite, prehnite, chlorite, calcite. **Found in**: Harz mountains/Germany; Czech Republic; Sicily, Trient/Italy; Faeroe Islands/Denmark; Norway; Caucasus, Urals/Russia; Colorado, New Jersey/USA. **Similar to**: leucite, sodalite, garnet.

Tridymite

(2) Colli Euganei/Italy 1:4

SiO_2

Streak white. **Mohs' hardness** $6\frac{1}{2}–7$. **Specific gravity** 2.27. **Characteristics**: colorless, white, gray. Luster: vitreous; transparent to translucent. Cleavage: none. Fracture: conchoidal, brittle; soluble in hot soda solution. Crystals: (rhombic or triclinic) tabular with hexagonal contours; surface growth, often twinning and tripling. **Aggregates**: scaly, fan-like, spheroidal, rough; present in cavities of acidic volcanics, by-product after volcanic eruptions, in sandstone. **Accompanied by**: quartz, sanidine, hematite, augite, hornblende. **Found in**: Siebengebirge, Eifel/Germany; Hungary; Auvergne/France; Scotland; Colorado, Oregon/USA; Mexico. **Similar to**: sanidine.

Scolecite

(3) with pink stilbite and green apophyllite; Poona/India

$Ca[Al_2Si_3O_{10}] \cdot 3 H_2O$

Streak white. **Mohs' hardness** $5–5\frac{1}{2}$. **Specific gravity** 2.3–2.4. **Characteristics**: colorless, white. Luster: vitreous and silky; transparent. Cleavage: perfect. Fracture: conchoidal, brittle; soluble in hydrochloric acid. Crystals: (monoclinic) prismatic to acicular. **Aggregates**: radial, fibrous; present in drusy cavities in granite and syenite, in alpine and young volcanic crevices. **Accompanied by**: laumontite, heulandite, stilbite, apophyllite. **Found in**: Iceland; Faeroe Islands/Demark; Scotland; Trient, Vesuvius/Italy; Caucasus, Urals/Russia; Bombay/India; California, Colorado/USA; Rio Grande do Sul/Brazil. **Similar to**: natrolite, mesolite, gonnardite.

Natrolite

(4) Westerwald/Germany

$Na_2[Al_2Si_3O_{10}] \cdot 2 H_2O$

Streak white. **Mohs' hardness** $5–5\frac{1}{2}$. **Specific gravity** 2.2–2.3. **Characteristics**: white, yellowish to brown, reddish, colorless. Luster: vitreous, silky; mother-of-pearl; transparent to translucent. Cleavage: complete. Fracture: conchoidal, brittle; will melt in the flame of a candle. Flame test: yellow. Soluble in hydrochloric acid. Occasional orange fluorescence under ultraviolet light. Crystals: (rhombic) prismatic to acicular, filamentary; usually surface growth. **Aggregates**: radial, spheroidal, rough, powdery; present in cavities in volcanics, in ore veins. **Accompanied by**: zeolite, benitoite, neptunite, andesine, apophyllite, calcite. **Found in**: Baden, Hesse, Harz mountains, Erzgebirge/Germany; Czech Republic; Auvergne/France; southern Tirol/Italy; Iceland; Faeroe Islands/Denmark; Kola, Urals/Russia; California, New Jersey/USA. **Similar to**: mesolite, scolecite, thomsonite, wavellite, aragonite, gonnardite.

Tremolite

① Campolungo,
Tessin/Switzerland 1:2

$Ca_2Mg_5[OH\,|\,Si_4O_{11}]_2$

Streak white. **Mohs' hardness** $5\frac{1}{2}$–6. **Specific gravity** 2.9–3.1. **Characteristics:** white, gray, greenish. Luster: vitreous, silky; transparent to opaque. Cleavage: complete. Fracture: fibrous, brittle. Crystals: (monoclinic) long prismatic, acicular. **Aggregates:** dendritic, radial, feltlike (asbestos); present in marble, talc slate, serpentine. **Accompanied by:** calcite, dolomite, talc, serpentine, diaspore. **Found in:** eastern Bavaria/Germany; Tessin/Switzerland; Tyrol/Austria; Novara/Italy; Finland; Baikal Lake, Urals/Russia; Namibia; Quebec/Canada; Arizona, New York/USA. **Similar to:** wollastonite, pectolite, zoisite, clinozoisite, diaspore, serpentine.

Amblygonite

② Viitaniemi/Finland 1:½

$(Li,Na)Al[(F,OH)\,|\,PO_4]$

Streak white. **Mohs' hardness** 6. **Specific gravity** 3.0–3.1. **Characteristics:** white, gray, yellow to brown, greenish, bluish. Luster: vitreous, on cleavage face mother-of-pearl; transparent to translucent. Cleavage: complete. Fracture: uneven to conchoidal, brittle. Flame test: carmine red. Soluble in sulfuric acid. Crystals: (triclinic) dipyramidal-distorted; rare; sometimes twinning. **Aggregates:** rough, spar-like, granular; present in pegmatites, granite. **Accompanied by:** cassiterite, apatite, feldspars, quartz, spodumene, lepidolite. **Found in:** Creuse/France; Estremadura/Spain; Finland; Sweden; Kazakhstan; Namibia; South Dakota, Maine/USA; Brazil. **Similar to:** feldspars, petalite, spodumene, calcite, brazilianite.

Pollucite

③ Bernic Lake, Manitoba/Canada

$(Cs,Na)_2[Al_2Si_4O_{12}]\cdot\frac{1}{2}$–$1\,H_2O$

Streak white. **Mohs' hardness** $6\frac{1}{2}$. **Specific gravity** 2.9. **Characteristics:** colorless, white, gray. Luster: vitreous; transparent to dull-translucent. Cleavage: none. Fracture: conchoidal to uneven, brittle; difficult to dissolve in hydrochloric acid. Crystals: (cubic) cubes; rare. **Aggregates:** rough, coarse- to fine-grained; present in crevices of granite and pegmatites. **Accompanied by:** petalite, lepidolite, amblygonite, spodumene, quartz, microcline. **Found in:** Elba/Italy; Sweden; Kazakhstan; Namibia; Manitoba, Quebec/Canada; Maine, South Dakota/USA. **Similar to:** quartz, hyalite.

Bertrandite

④ Aschamalm/Austria 1:8

$Be_4[(OH)_2\,|\,Si_2O_7]$

Streak white. **Mohs' hardness** $6\frac{1}{2}$–7. **Specific gravity** 2.6. **Characteristics:** colorless, white, light yellow. Luster: vitreous, mother-of-pearl; transparent to translucent. Cleavage: complete. Fracture: bladed, brittle. Crystals: (rhombic) tabular, prismatic; usually small; heart-shaped twinning; sometimes pseudomorphic. **Aggregates:** only groups of crystals; present in acidic volcanics, pegmatites, rarely in lead-ore veins. **Accompanied by:** beryl, phenakite, aegirine, riebeckite, barite, fluorite, tourmaline, apatite, adularia, opal, calcite. **Found in:** eastern Bavaria/Germany; Salzburg/Austria; Czech Republic; western France; Murcia/Spain; Norway; Namibia; eastern Siberia/Russia; Queensland/Australia; Colorado, Maine/USA; Chihuahua/Mexico. **Similar to:** barite, albite, muscovite, quartz.

pectolite p. 70, scapolite p. 82, fassaite p. 102, lazulite p. 106

Eudialyte
① Kola/Russia 1:2

$Na_{16},Ca_6(Fe^{2+},Mn^{2+})_3Zr_3[(OH,Cl)]_2 | Si_3O_9 | Si_9O_{27}]_2$

Streak white. **Mohs' hardness** 5–5½. **Specific gravity** 2.8–3.1. **Characteristics**: reddish brown, red, pink, yellow. Luster: transparent. Cleavage: incomplete. Fracture: uneven, brittle; will corrode in acid. Crystals: (trigonal) thick tabular, sometimes prismatic; usually intergrowth; seldom well-developed. **Aggregates**: rough, granular to dense; present in foyaites (syenites) and pegmatites. **Accompanied by**: zircon, nepheline, sodalite, molybdenite, aegirine, microcline. **Found in**: Norway; Kola/Russia; Greenland; Quebec/Canada; Arkansas, Montana/USA; Minas Gerais, Sao Paulo/Brazil; Transvaal/South Africa; Madagascar. **Similar to**: zircon, garnet.

Datolite
② with danburite;
Charcas/Mexcico

$Ca_2B_2[OH | SiO_4]_2$

Streak white. **Mohs' hardness** 5–5½. **Specific gravity** 2.9–3.0. **Characteristics**: colorless, white, yellow, greenish, seldom gray, reddish. Luster: vitreous, on cleavage face greasy; transparent to translucent. Cleavage: none. Fracture: uneven to conchoidal, brittle. Flame test: green. Lightly corrosive in hydrochloric acid. Crystals: (monoclinic) short prismatic, thick tabular, multifaceted; usually surficial growth. **Aggregates**: rough, granular to dense, fibrous, radial, reniform, crusty; present in cavities of base magmatites and metamorphic rocks; less often granite rocks, ore deposits, alpine crevices. **Accompanied by**: prehnite, apophyllite, wollastonite, diopside, magnetite, pure copper, quartz, calcite, chabazite, stilbite, heulandite. **Found in**: Black Forest, Harz mountains/Germany; southern Tirol/ Italy; Czech Republic; Norway; Transbaikal region; Urals/Russia; Tazmania/Australia; Michigan, New Jersey/USA. **Similar to**: ulexite, colemanite, prehnite, danburite, apophyllite.

Beryllonite
③ Newry, Maine/USA

$NaBe[PO_4]$

Streak white. **Mohs' hardness** 5½. **Specific gravity** 2.8. **Characteristics**: colorless, white, yellowish. Luster: vitreous, mother-of-pearl; translucent to transparent. Cleavage: complete. Fracture: conchoidal, brittle. Crystals: (monoclinic) short prismatic, tabular, multifaceted; occasional twinning. **Aggregates**: only in groups of crystals; present in granite pegmatites. **Accompanied by**: tourmaline, albite, muscovite, smoky quartz. **Found in**: Finland; Zimbabwe; Maine/USA. **Similar to**: many of the colorless minerals, apatite, glass.

Wardite
④ Yukon region/Canada 1:2

$NaAl_3[(OH)_4 | (PO_4)_2] \cdot 2 H_2O$

Streak white. **Mohs' hardness** 5. **Specific gravity** 2.8. **Characteristics**: blue-green, white, colorless. Luster: vitreous, greasy, dull; transparent to translucent. Cleavage: complete. Fracture: uneven, conchoidal, brittle. Crystals: (tetragonal) pyramidal, occasionally horizontally striped. **Aggregates**: rough, granular, fibrous, crusty, radial-tuberous; present in drusy cavities and crevices of pegmatites and phosphate-rich sedimentary rocks. **Accompanied by**: variscite, vivianite, amblygonite, lazulite, apatite. **Found in**: Creuse/France; California, New Hampshire, South Dakota, Utah/USA; Paraiba/Brazil. **Similar to**: turquoise, variscite.

anthophyllite p. 108, chalcedony p. 122, actinolite p. 144

Wollastonite

$Ca_3[Si_3O_9]$

① Auerbach, Bergstrasse,
Hesse/Germany

Streak white. **Mohs' hardness** 4½–5. **Specific gravity** 2.8–2.9. **Characteristics:** colorless, white, gray, yellowish, greenish, reddish. Luster: vitreous, on cleavage face mother-of-pearl, aggregates silky; translucent to transparent. Cleavage: complete. Fracture: fibrous and brittle; soluble in acid. Crystals: (monoclinic or triclinic) broad dendritic; fibrous, acicular, less often thick tabular; mostly surface growth; often twinning. **Aggregates**; spar-like, granular, radial, bladed, finely fibrous, rough; present in calc-silicate rocks, by-product of volcanic eruptions. **Accompanied by:** garnet, idocrase, diopside, epidote, graphite. **Found in:** Black Forest, Erzgebirge/Germany; Banat/Romania; Finland; Veltlin, Vesuvius/Italy; Bretagne/France; eastern Siberia, Urals/Russia; Namibia; California, New York/USA; Mexico. **Similar to:** pectolite, tremolite, scolecite, zoisite.

Nepheline

$KNa_3[AlSiO_4]_4$

② Vesuvius/Italy

Streak white. **Mohs' hardness** 5–6. **Specific gravity** 2.6–2.7. **Characteristics:** colorless, white, gray, yellowish to brownish, reddish and greenish. Luster: vitreous, on cleavage face greasy, transparent or opaque-dull (eläolite). Cleavage: incomplete. Fracture: conchoidal to brittle. Flame test: yellow. Soluble in hydrochloric acid. Crystals: (hexagonal) prismatic, short columnar, less often thick tabular; intergrowth and surface growth. **Aggregates:** rough, granular to dense, present in basic magmatites and pegmatites; by-products of volcanic eruptions; seldom in metamorphic rocks. **Accompanied by:** feldspars, leucite, sodalite, melilite, cancrinite, augite, aegirine, hornblende, apatite. **Found in:** Kaiserstuhl, Odenwald, Saxony/Germany; Siebenbürgen/Romania; Portugal; Kola, Urals/Russia; Transvaal/South Africa; Ontario/Canada; Montana/USA. **Similar to:** cancrinite, melilite, cordierite, apatite, quartz.

Carpholite

$Mn^{2+}Al_2[(OH)_4 \,|\, Si_2O_6]$

③ Schlaggenwald/
Czech Republic 1:2

Streak white. **Mohs' hardness** 5–5½. **Specific gravity** 2.9–3.0. **Characteristics:** straw yellow, yellow-green, yellow-brown. Luster: silky; translucent. Cleavage: complete. Fracture: fibrous, brittle; easily soluble in acid. Crystals: (rhombic) filamentary. **Aggregates:** finely fibrous, radial, bundle-like, matted; seldom rough; present in schist, lead-ore deposits. **Accompanied by:** fluorite, quartz, cassiterite. **Found in:** Harz mountains/Germany; Czech Republic; Macedonia; Ardennes/Belgium.

Melilite

$(Ca,Na)_2(Al,Mg,Fe^{2+})[(Al,Si)SiO_7]$

④ with nepheline; Üdersdorf, Eifel/Germany 1:4
⑤ Capo di Bove/Italy

Streak white to gray. **Mohs' hardness** 5–6. **Specific gravity** 2.9–3.0. **Characteristics:** yellow, brown, gray, sometimes colorless. Luster: vitreous, on fresh cleavage faces greasy; transparent to translucent. Cleavage: incomplete. Fracture: conchoidal, brittle; easily soluble in acid. Crystals: (tetragonal) thick tabular, short columnar, usually small, intergrowth and surface growth; sometimes crosslike twinning. **Aggregates:** rough, granular, present in basic volcanics. **Accompanied by:** perovskite, olivine, hornblende, augite, nepheline, leucite, apatite, calcite. **Found in:** Eifel, Kaiserstuhl/Germany; Czech Republic; Vesuvius/Italy; Kola/Russia; Madagascar; Quebec/Canada; Colorado, Hawaii/USA; Rurengo/Mexico. **Similar to:** nepheline.

arfvedsonite p. 216, odontolite p. 216

Streak

white and
colorless

Mohs' h.
1 ◀
−
2 ◀
−
3 ◀
−
4 ◀
−
5 ◀
6 ◀
7 −
8 ◀
9 ◀
10 ◀

S. gravity
1 ◀
−
2 ◀
−
3 ◀
−
4 ◀
−
5 ◀
−
6 ◀
7 ◀

Turquoise

① Arizona/USA 1:2

$Cu(Al,Fe^{3+})_6[(OH)_2 | PO_4]_4 \cdot 4 H_2O$

Streak white. **Mohs' hardness** 5–6. **Specific gravity** 2.6–2.9. **Characteristics:** azure blue to apple green. Luster: vitreous, waxy, also dull; opaque. Cleavage: none. Fracture: conchoidal, brittle; distinct pleochroism; soluble in acid. Crystals: (triclinic) short prismatic; very small and very rare. **Aggregates:** rough, finely granular to dense, finely fibrous, botryoidal, crusty, accumulating in crevices, especially in tachytes, slate, sandstone. **Accompanied by:** limonite, chalcedony. **Found in:** Thüringen, Vogtland/Germany; Silesia/Poland; Iran; Turkestan; Manchuria/China; Sinai/Egypt; Arizona, Nevada, New Mexico/ USA. **Similar to:** chrysocolla, variscite, vivianite, garnierite, odontolite, wardite.

Brazillianite

② Minas Gerais/Brazil

$NaAl_3[(OH)_2 | PO_4]_2$

Streak white. **Mohs' hardness** 5½. **Specific gravity** 2.98. **Characteristics:** yellow to greenish yellow. Luster: vitreous; transparent to translucent. Cleavage: complete. Fracture: conchoidal, brittle. Flame test: yellow. Soluble in acid. Crystals: (monoclinic) short prismatic, multifaceted. **Aggregates:** spheroidal, radial fibrous, rough; present in pegmatites. **Accompanied by:** apatite, amblygonite, tourmaline, wardite, lazulite, muscovite, albite. **Found in:** Minas Gerais, Parabia/Brazil; New Hampshire/USA. **Similar to:** amblygonite, beryl, chrysoberyl, topaz, albite,

Milarite

③ Habachtal/Austria

$KCa_2AlBe_2[Si_{12}O_{30}] \cdot H_2O$

Streak white. **Mohs' hardness** 5½–6. **Specific gravity** 2.5–2.6. **Characteristics:** colorless, light green, yellow-green. Luster: vitreous, greasy; transparent to translucent. Cleavage: none. Fracture: conchoidal to uneven, brittle. Crystals: (hexagonal) prismatic, acicular, seldom thick tabular; usually surface growth. **Aggregates:** crystalline groups; present in alpine crevices; pegmatites. **Accompanied by:** anatase, brookite, chlorite, bertrandite, albite, adularia, quartz. **Found in:** Bavarian Forest, Thüringen/Germany; Graubünden/ Switzerland; Czech Republic; Salzburg, eastern Tyrol/Austria; Kola/Russia; Namibia; Mexico; Brazil. **Similar to:** beryl, apatite, phenakite.

Prehnite

④ Radatual,
Harz mountains/Germany

$Ca_2Al_2[(OH)_2 | Si_3O_{10}]$

Streak white. **Mohs' hardness** 6–6½. **Specific gravity** 2.8–3.0. **Characteristics:** colorless, white, gray, greenish, yellowish, reddish. Luster: vitreous, mother-of-pearl; transparent to translucent. Cleavage: incomplete. Fracture: uneven, brittle; only slowly soluble in hydrochloric acid. Crystals: (rhombic) tabular, short columnar; often distorted; single crystals rare; occasionally pseudomorphic. **Aggregates:** rough, fan-shaped, radial, spheroidal, reniform; present in basic magmatites, slate, alpine crevices. **Accompanied by:** stilbite, heulandite, pectolite, epidote, calcite, laumontite. **Found in:** Black Forest, Rhein-Pfalz, Thüringer Forest/Germany; Tyrol/Austria; Graubünden/Switzerland; southern Tirol/Italy; Dauphiné/France; Bombay/India; Caucasus, Urals/Russia; Michigan, New Jersey/USA. **Similar to:** stilbite, wavellite, datolite.

Streak

white and
colorless

Mohs' h.
1 ◀
―
2 ◀
―
3 ◀
―
4 ◀
―
5 ◀
―
6 ◀
―
7 ◀
―
8 ◀
―
9 ◀
―
10 ◀

S. gravity
1 ◀
―
―
2 ◀
―
―
3 ◀
―
―
4 ◀
―
―
5 ◀
―
―
6 ◀
―
7 ◀

Orthoclase Feldspars

K[AlSi$_3$O$_8$]

Streak white. **Mohs' hardness** 6. **Specific gravity** 2.53–2.56. **Characteristics:** colorless, white, yellow to brown, meat red to reddish brown, green. Luster: vitreous, mother-of-pearl; transparent to translucent to opaque. Cleavage: complete, cleavage angle 90°. Fracture: conchoidal, uneven, splintery, brittle. Crystals: (monoclinic) orthoclase; (triclinic) microcline; prismatic, tabular, rhombohedral, often multifaceted; intergrowth and surface growth; often twinning and pseudomorphic. **Aggregates:** rough, spar-like, granular; intergrowth with quartz (graphic granite); combined with magmatites, metamorphic rocks; less often in sedimentary rocks; well-developed crystals in pegmatites, in crevices and veins. **Accompanied by:** quartz, plagioclase, mica, tourmaline, topaz, garnet.

Orthoclase

② Saxony/Germany
③ Arendal/Norway

Milky white, reddish white, light pink to meat red; usually cloudy, opaque, seldom clear yellow; often interpenetration twinning (among others: Carlsbad twinning); sometimes faint reddish-orange fluorescence under ultraviolet light. **Found in:** eastern Bavaria/Germany; Tauern/Austria; Tessin/Switzerland; Sweden; Norway; Canada; California/USA; Madagascar; Myanmar. **Similar to:** feldspars, barite, calcite.

Adularia

⑥ Wallis/Switzerland

Variety of orthoclase; transparent, faintly cloudy to milky white; almost always surface growth in drusy cavities and alpine crevices; often sprinkled or intergrown with chlorite. **Found in:** Graubünden, Tessin/Switzerland; Tauern/Austria; Sri Lanka; South Africa.

Sanidine

④ Vetralla, Latium/Italy

Colorless, transparent to opaque gray, gray brownish; large tabular and scattered crystals in young volcanic rocks. **Found in:** Siebengebirge/Germany; Vesuvius/Italy; Caucasus/Russia. **Similar to:** cancrinite, tridymite.

Moonstone

Variety of adularia or sanidine. Colorless, yellowish, milky, cloudy with bluish-white tint, and wavelight light reflections, particularly distinct when curved; weak bluish or orange fluorescence under ultraviolet light. **Found in:** Sri Lanka; India; Myanmar; western Australia; Tanzania; Madagascar; Virginia/USA; Brazil. **Similar to:** chalcedony, glass imitations.

Microline

① Setesdalen/Norway

Usually white, gray, yellowish, reddish; cloudy to opaque. **Found in:** eastern Bavaria/Germany; Scandanavia; Karelia, Urals/Russia; New Hampshire/USA; India. **Similar to:** feldspars, barite, dolomite.

Amazonite

⑤ Pikes Peak, Colorado/USA

Variety of microline. Green, bluish green, usually striped or spotted; opaque to translucent. **Found in:** Colorado/USA; Brazil; India; Madagascar; Urals/Russia. **Similar to:** jadeite, nephrite, turquoise.

Plagioclase Feldspars

solid solution

Albite Na[AlSi$_3$O$_8$]   Anorthite Ca[Al$_2$Si$_2$O$_8$]

Streak white. **Mohs' hardness** 6–6½. **Specific gravity** 2.61–2.77. **Characteristics:** colorless, white, gray, green, reddish; occasionally colored labradorization. **Luster:** vitreous, dull, mother-of-pearl in cleavage faces; transparent to opaque. **Cleavage:** complete, cleavage angle approximately 86°. **Fracture:** conchoidal to uneven, brittle; partially soluble in acid. **Crystals:** (triclinic) tabular, prismatic; intergrowth, and surficial growth; twinning sometimes, always striped. **Aggregates:** rough, granular, crusty; present as by-product in magmatites, metamorphic rocks, less often in sedimentary rocks. **Accompanied by:** quartz, orthoclase, mica, chlorite, calcite, zeolite, augite, hornblende.

Albite

② Habachtal, Tyrol/Austria

Colorless, grayish white, seldom greenish, bluish, reddish; usually cloudy, transparent to opaque. Not easily soluble in acid. **Found in:** Tyrol/Austria; Switzerland; Elba, Trient/Italy; Czech Republic; Pyrenees; Maine/USA. **Similar to:** other plagioclase, orthoclase, barite.

Pericline

③ with chlorite covering; Tauern/Austria

Variety of albite; white or greenish due to chlorite dusting; milky to cloudy. particularly frequent in chlorite slate in alpine crevices.

Oglioclase

Colorless, white, gray, greenish, yellowish, reddish; transparent, cloudy. Not easily soluble in acid; crystals mostly intergrown. **Similar to:** other feldspars.

Aventurine Feldspar sunstone

① polished; Norway

Variety of oglioclase; orange, reddish brown; opaque. Metallic sparkling due to intergrown hematite or goethite. **Found in:** USA; Canada; India; Norway; Russia. **Similar to:** aventurine quartz.

Andesine

White, gray, yellowish, greenish; transparent to opaque. Not easily soluble in acid. **Found in:** eastern Bavaria/Germany; Czech Republic; Hungary; Caucasus/Russia; South America. **Similar to:** other feldspars.

Labradorite

④ spectrolite; Finland
⑤ Antsirabé/Madagascar

White, gray, brown, bluish; transparent to opaque; sometimes blue, green, reddish labradorization. Crystals are rare. Soluble in acid. **Found in:** Labrador/Canada; Mexico; Madagascar; Ukraine. The finished variety from Finland is called spectrolite.

Bytownite

White, gray, brownish, bluish; transparent to opaque. Occasionally colored iridescence; soluble in acid. **Found in:** Harz mountains/Germany; Sicily/Italy; Albania; Slovenia; Serbia; Corsica/France; Canada. **Similar to:** labradorite.

Anorthite

Colorless, white, gray, reddish; transparent, cloudy, opaque. Soluble in acid. **Found in:** Italy, India, Japan. **Similar to:** other feldspars.

Apatite

$Ca_5[(F,Cl,OH)|(PO_4)_3]$

① with quartz rock crystal; Mexico 1:2
② Kragerö/Norway

Streak white. **Mohs' hardness** 5. **Specific gravity** 3.16–3.22. **Characteristics:** colorless, white, also many other colors. Luster: vitreous, on cleavage face greasy; transparent to opaque. Cleavage: incomplete. Fracture: conchoidal to uneven, brittle; sometimes bluish fluorescence under ultraviolet light. Easily soluble in acid. Occasionally radioactive. Crystals: (hexagonal) short and long columnar, thick tabular, dipyramidal, acicular, often multifaceted; intergrown and surface growth. **Aggregates:** rough, granular to dense; fibrous, radial, reniform; present in alpine crevices, magmatites and metamorphic rocks; on magnetite and cassiterite deposits, individual layers of sediments and concretions. **Accompanied by:** magnetite, cassiterite, sphene, rutile, wolframite, zircon, topaz. **Found in:** Eifel, Erzgebirge/Germany; Tyrol/Austria; Switzerland; Dauphené/ France; Sweden; Norway; Kola, Urals/Russia; Mexico; Montana/USA. **Similar to:** pyromorphite, mimetite, nepheline, milarite, beryl, quartz.

Fassaite

$Ca(Mg,Fe,Al)[(Si,Al)_2O_6]$

③ with calcite; Fassatal, southern Tirol/Italy

Streak greenish white. **Mohs' hardness** 6. **Specific gravity** 2.9–3.3. **Characteristics:** light to dark green, black. Luster: vitreous, transparent to opaque. Cleavage: incomplete. Fracture: uneven to conchoidal, brittle. Crystals: (monoclinic) short prisms, multifaceted; intergrowth and surficial growth. **Aggregates:** rough, granular to dense; present in marble, as by-product of volcanic eruptions. **Accompanied by:** grossular, idocrase, spinel, calcite, dolomite. **Found in:** southern Tirol, Vesuvius/Italy; Scotland; Sweden; Montana/USA; Sri Lanka. **Similar to:** diopside, grossular, idocrase.

Chondrodite

$(Mg,Fe^{2+})_5[(OH,F)_2|(SiO_4)_2]$

④ New York/USA 1:2

Streak white. **Mohs' hardness** 6–6½. **Specific gravity** 3.1–3.2. **Characteristics:** yellow, brown, red, rarely green. Luster: transparent to translucent. Cleavage: incomplete. Fracture: conchoidal to uneven, brittle. Crystals: (monoclinic) short columnar, usually small, multifaceted; often twinning. **Aggregates:** rough, granular, as impregnation; present in limestone and dolomite marble, ore veins, as by-product of volcanic eruptions. **Accompanied by:** magnetite, sphalerite, galena, idocrase, spinel. **Found in:** Fichtelgebirge, Erzgebirge/Germany; Vogesen/ France; Sweden; Finland; Ontario/Canada; New York/USA. **Similar to:** cancrinite, olivine.

Diaspore

$AlO(OH)$

⑤ Mineral Co., Nevada/USA

Streak white. **Mohs' hardness** 6½–7. **Specific gravity** 3.3–3.5. **Characteristics:** colorless, white, gray, yellow to brownish, green to blue. Luster: vitreous, mother-of-pearl on cleavage faces; transparent to translucent. Cleavage: complete. Fracture: uneven, brittle; sometimes distinct pleochroism. Crystals: (rhombic) tabular, small, rare, often twinning. **Aggregates:** rough, bladed, radial; present in metamorphic rocks, rock-forming in lime-bauxites. **Accompanied by:** corundum, hematite, kyanite, spinel, dolomite, calcite. **Found in:** Switzerland; Tyrol/Austria; Greece; Norway; Urals/Russia; South Africa; Colorado/USA. **Similar to:** phlogopite, boehmite, tremolite.

kyanite p. 74, triphylite p. 74, amblygonite p. 90, tremolite p. 90, eudialyte p. 92, bronzite p. 110, rhodonite p. 110, sphene p. 110

Streak

white and
colorless

Mohs' h.
1 ◄

2 ◄

3 ◄

4 ◄

5 ◄

6 ◄

7 ◄

8 ◄

9 ◄

10 ◄

S. gravity
1 ◄

2 ◄

3 ◄

4 ◄

5 ◄

6 ◄

7 ◄

Enstatite

① Kragerö/Norway

$Mg_2[Si_2O_6]$

Streak white. **Mohs' hardness** 5–6. **Specific gravity** 3.1–3.3. **Characteristics:** grayish white, yellowish to brown, greenish, seldom colorless or white. **Luster:** vitreous; transparent to opaque. **Cleavage:** incomplete, cleavage angle 85°. **Fracture:** conchoidal to uneven, brittle. **Crystals:** (rhombic) short prismatic, thick tabular; rare. **Aggregates:** rough, spar-like, granular; present in silicic acid-poor magmatites, metamorphic rocks, sometimes rock-forming. **Accompanied by:** apatite, olivine, phlogopite, diopside, augite, hornblende. **Found in:** Harz mountains/Germany; Scotland; Ireland; Norway; Caucasus, Urals/Russia; Greenland; California/USA; South Africa. **Similar to:** hypersthene, diopside, andalusite.

Idocrase vesuvianite

② California/USA

$Ca_{19}(Mg,Fe^{2+},Ti)_4Al_9[(OH,F)_{10} \,|\, (SiO_4)_{10} \,|\, (Si_2O_7)_4]$

Streak white. **Mohs' hardness** 6½. **Specific gravity** 3.27–3.45. **Characteristics:** gray, yellow, brown, green, black, seldom blue. **Luster:** vitreous, on cleavage faces greasy; transparent to opaque. **Cleavage:** incomplete. **Fracture:** uneven to conchoidal, also splintery, brittle; partially soluble in acid. **Crystals:** (tetragonal) short and long columnar; dipyramidal, acicular, mostly vertically striped; intergrowth and surface growth. **Aggregates:** rough, granular to dense, radial; present in metamorphic rocks, as by-product of volcanic eruptions, rarely in magmatites. **Accompanied by:** garnet, diopside, wollastonite, epidote. **Found in:** Erzgebirge/Germany; Switzerland; Tyrol/Austria; Piemonte, Vesuvius/Italy; Czech Republic; eastern Siberia/Russia; California/USA; Mexico. **Similar to:** scapolite, epidote, grossular, zircon.

Humite

③ Vesuvius/Italy 1:4

$(Mg, Fe^{2+})_7[(OH,F)_2 \,|\, (SiO_4)_3]$

Streak white. **Mohs' hardness** 6–6½. **Specific gravity** 3.1–3.2. **Characteristics:** yellowish to brown, orange to red. **Luster:** vitreous and resinous; transparent to translucent. **Cleavage:** incomplete. **Fracture:** uneven to conchoidal, brittle. **Crystals:** (rhombic) short columnar, multifaceted; very rare and usually small. **Aggregates:** rough, granular, as impregnation; present in metamorphosed limestones and dolomites, as by-product of volcanic eruptions, occasionally also in ore veins. **Accompanied by:** calcite, dolomite, spinel, magnetite, sphalerite, galena. **Found in:** Fichtelgebirge/Germany; Vesuvius/Italy; Andalusia/Spain; Sweden; New York/USA. **Similar to:** cancrinite.

Zoisite

④ Baja California/Mexico
⑤ zoisite-amphibolite with ruby; Tanzania
⑥ thulite; Lexviken/Norway 1:2
⑦ tanzanite; Tanzania

$Ca_2Al_3[O \,|\, OH \,|\, SiO_4 \,|\, Si_2O_7]$

Streak white. **Mohs' hardness** 6–6½. **Specific gravity** 3.15–3.36. **Characteristics:** gray, brownish, green, red (thulite), blue (tanzanite). **Luster:** vitreous, mother-of-pearl; transparent to opaque. **Cleavage:** complete. **Fracture:** uneven, brittle. **Crystals:** (rhombic) prismatic, acicular, vertically striped; mostly intergrowth. **Aggregates:** rough, spar-like, dendritic, fibrous; present in metamorphic rocks. **Accompanied by:** epidote, idocrase, quartz, feldspars, kyanite. **Found in:** Erzgebirge/Germany; Kärnten/Austria; Wallis/Switzerland; southern Tirol/Italy; Altai, Urals/Russia; Tanzania; Namibia; Wyoming/USA. **Similar to:** tremolite, sillimanite, clinozoisite.

andalusite p. 126, jadeite p. 126, axinite p. 128, olivine p. 132

Diopside

$CaMg[Si_2O_6]$

① Outokumpu/Finland
② diallage; Bad Harzburg/Germany

Streak white. **Mohs' hardness** 5–6½. **Specific gravity** 3.3–3.4. **Characteristics:** light to dark green, emerald green (chromediopside), gray, yellow, bronze-like (diallage), blue to violet (violane), rarely colorless, white. Luster: vitreous; transparent to translucent. Cleavage: incomplete, cleavage angle approximately 90°. Fracture: uneven, brittle. Crystals: (monoclinic) short columnar, also tabular; intergrowth and surface growth; frequent twinning. Star diopside Abb. S. 19. **Aggregates:** rough, dendritic, radial, granular to dense; present in magmatites and metamorphic rocks, alpine crevices. **Accompanied by:** grossular, wollastonite, chlorite, calcite, magnetite, vesuvianite. **Found in:** Erzgebirge, Odenwald/Germany; Tyrol/Austria; Wallis/Switzerland; Sweden; Baikal Lake region, Urals/Russia; Madagascar; California, Montana/ USA. **Similar to:** fassaite, hypersthene, bronzite, augite.

Clinozoisite

$Ca_2(Al,Fe^{3+})Al_2[O \,|\, OH \,|\, SiO_4 \,|\, Si_2O_7]$

③ on scolecite;
Tessin/Switzerland 1:3

Streak white to gray. **Mohs' hardness** 6–7. **Specific gravity** 3.2–3.5. **Characteristics:** gray, yellow, greenish, pink, less often blue and colorless. Luster: vitreous; translucent to transparent. Cleavage: complete. Fracture: uneven, brittle. Crystals: (monoclinic) long and short prismatic, thick tabular, mostly vertically striped; often twinning. **Aggregates:** rough, dendritic, fibrous, granular; present in metamorphic rocks. **Accompanied by:** axinite, albite, actinolite, glaucophane, epidote, zoisite. **Found in:** Fichtelgebirge/Germany; Tyrol/Austria; Switzerland; Turin/Italy; Madagascar; Ontario/Canada; California, Nevada/ USA; Sonora/Mexico; Brazil. **Similar to:** zoisite, epidote, tremolite.

Lazulite

$(Mg,Fe^{2+})Al_2[OH \,|\, PO_4]_2$

④ Yukon/Canada

Streak white. **Mohs' hardness** 5–6. **Specific gravity** 3.0–3.4. **Characteristics:** light to dark blue, white. Luster: vitreous, greasy; opaque, transparent at the edges. Cleavage: incomplete. Fracture: uneven, brittle. Crystals: (monoclinic) long and short prismatic, thick tabular, mostly vertically striped; intergrowth and surface growth; rare, sometimes twinning. **Aggregates:** rough, granular to dense, as impregnation; present in quartzite, quartz deposits. **Accompanied by:** corundum, rutile, garnet, kyanite, quartz. **Found in:** Thüringer Forest/ Germany; Salzburg, Steiermark/Austria; Wallis/Switzerland; Sweden; Georgia, North Carolina/USA; Minas Gerais/Brazil. **Similar to:** sodalite, lapis lazuli, azurite, vivianite, charoite.

Sillimanite

$Al_2[O \,|\, SiO_4]$

⑤ New York/USA
⑥ Pennsylvania/USA 1:3

Streak white. **Mohs' hardness** 6–7. **Specific gravity** 3.2–3.3. **Characteristics:** gray, yellow to brown, greenish, less often bluish, white, colorless. Luster: vitreous, greasy, aggregates silky; transparent to translucent. Cleavage: complete. Fracture: uneven, brittle. Crystals: (rhombic) prismatic, acicular; intergrowth; very rare. **Aggregates:** dendritic, fibrous, radial, matted; present in metamorphic rocks. **Accompanied by:** quartz, feldspars, cordierite, andalusite, garnet, corundum, chrysoberyl, spinel. **Found in:** Bavarian Forest, Erzgebirge/Germany; Tyrol/ Austria; Trentot/Italy; South Africa; Idaho, New York/USA; Brazil; Assam/India; Sri Lanka; Myanmar. **Similar to:** kyanite, zoisite, andalusite, asbestos.

actinolite p. 144, augite p. 146, hedenbergite p. 146, hypersthene p. 170.

Hemimorphite

$Zn_4[(OH)_2 | Si_2O_7] \cdot H_2O$

① Chihuahua/Mexico

Streak white. **Mohs' hardness** 5. **Specific gravity** 3.3–3.5. **Characteristics:** colorless, white to gray, light green, bluish, yellowish to brown. Luster: vitreous, silky; transparent to translucent. Cleavage: complete. Fracture: conchoidal to uneven, brittle; soluble in hydrochloric acid. Crystals: (rhombic) tabular, prismatic to acicular; usually small, surface growth; widely distributed twinning, pseudomorphic. **Aggregates:** radial, reniform, stalactitic, seldom granular, dense or crusty; present in oxidized zones of lead-zinc deposits. **Accompanied by:** smithsonite, sphalerite, hydrozincite, aurichalcite, galena, cerussite. **Found in:** Rheinland/Germany; Kärnten/Austria; Sardinia/Italy; England; Transbaikal region/Russia; Algeria; Arizona, Colorado/USA; Mexico. **Similar to:** smithsonite, opal, topaz, chalcedony.

Kornerupine

$Mg_4Al_6[(O,OH)_2 | BO_4 | (SiO_4)_4]$

② Waldheim, Saxony/Germany 1:2

Streak white. **Mohs' hardness** 6–7. **Specific gravity** 3.3. **Characteristics:** white, yellow, green, pink, sometimes colorless and red. Luster: vitreous; transparent to translucent. Cleavage: incomplete. Fracture: conchoidal, brittle; strong pleochroism. Crystals: (rhombic) long prismatic, intergrowth. **Aggregates:** rough, thin dendritic, radial; present in gneissic rocks. **Accompanied by:** cordierite, tourmaline, zircon, spinel, kyanite, quartz, feldspars, biotite. **Found in:** Saxony/Germany; Finland; Ukraine; Kazakhstan; Madagascar; South Africa; Kenya; Tanzania; Sri Lanka; India; Myanmar; Greenland; Quebec/Canada. **Similar to:** enstatite, tourmaline.

Anthophyllite

$(Mg,Fe^{2+})_7[OH | Si_4O_{11}]_2$

③ Paaka/Finland 1:½

Streak white. **Mohs' hardness** 5½. **Specific gravity** 2.8–3.2. **Characteristics:** brown, yellowish gray. Luster: vitreous, seldom mother-of-pearl and silky; bronze-like glimmer; translucent. Cleavage: complete, cleavage angle approximately 125°. Fracture: uneven, fibrous, brittle; malleable in thin layers; lively pleochroism. Crystals: (rhombic) prismatic, rare. **Aggregates:** dendritic, fibrous (asbestiform), acicular, radial, dense, tough (nephrite); present in metamorphic rocks, sometimes rock-forming. **Accompanied by:** cordierite, biotite, feldspars, quartz. **Found in:** Bavarian Forest/Germany; Czech Republic; southern Tirol/Italy; Norway; Finland; Urals/Russia; South Africa; California/USA. **Similar to:** bronzite, hypersthene, tremolite, actinolite, jadeite.

Spodumene

$LiAl[Si_2O_6]$

④ hiddenite; Minas Gerais/Brazil 1:2
⑤ kunzite; Minas Gerais/Brazil

Streak white. **Mohs' hardness** 6½–7. **Specific gravity** 3.1–3.2. **Characteristics:** colorless, white, gray, yellow to green (hiddenite), pink to violet (kunzite). Luster: vitreous; on cleavage face mother-of-pearl; transparent to translucent. Cleavage: complete. Fracture: uneven, brittle. Flame test: intensively red. Sometimes distinct pleochroism. Crystals: (monoclinic) tabular, prismatic, horizontally striped; intergrowth and surface growth; twinning. **Aggregates:** rough, spar-like, wide dendritic; present in granite pegmatites, drusy cavities. **Accompanied by:** quartz, feldspars, beryl, tourmaline, amblygonite, triphyline, cassiterite. **Found in:** Sweden; Scotland; Zimbabwe; Namibia; Madagascar; South Dakota/USA; Brazil. **Similar to:** petalite, scapolite, amblygonite, feldspars.

arfvedsonite p. 216, odontolite p. 216

Mohs' h.	
1	◄
2	◄
3	◄
4	◄
5	◄
6	◄
7	◄
8	◄
9	◄
10	◄

S. gravity	
1	◄
2	◄
3	◄
4	◄
5	◄
6	◄
7	◄

Streak

white and
colorless

Mohs' h. ──── 1 ◄

2 ◄

3 ◄

4 ◄

──── 5 ◄

6 ◄

7 ◄

8 ◄

9 ◄

10 ◄

S. gravity ──── 1 ◄

2 ◄

3 ◄

4 ◄

5 ◄

6 ◄

7 ◄

Rhodonite

(Ca,Mg)(Mn^{2+},Fe^{2+})$_4$[Si$_5$O$_{15}$]

① New Jersey/USA

Streak white. **Mohs' hardness** 5½–6½. **Specific gravity** 3.4–3.7. **Characteristics**: light red, rose red, brownish red; often with black spots and veins. Luster: vitreous, on cleavage faces mother-of-pearl; transparent to opaque. Cleavage: complete. Fracture: conchoidal to uneven, brittle; slowly soluble in hydrochloric acid. Crystals: (triclinic) tabular, columnar, often with rounded edges, rare. **Aggregates**: rough, spar-like, granular, dense; present in manganese- and iron-ore veins; in tungstenite. **Accompanied by**: magnetite, braunite, hausmannite, rhodochrosite, quartz, garnet. **Found in**: Harz mountains/Germany; Piemonte/Italy; Romania; Sweden; Urals/Russia; New Jersey/USA; Brazil; India; Japan; New South Wales/Australia. **Similar to**: rhodochrosite.

Sphene titanite

CaTi[O | SiO$_4$]

② dusted with chlorite;
Zillertal/Australia

Streak white. **Mohs' hardness** 5–6. **Specific gravity** 3.3–3.6. **Characteristics**: yellow, green, brown, red, black. Luster: adamantine, vitreous, greasy; transparent to opaque. Cleavage: incomplete. Fracture: conchoidal, brittle; high double-refraction; soluble in sulfuric acid. Crystals: (monoclinic) envelope-shaped, tabular, prismatic; intergrowth and surface growth. **Aggregates**: rough, granular, scaly, present as by-product in magmatites and metamorphic rocks, in alpine crevices, sometimes on soapstone. **Accompanied by**: chlorite, hornblende, rutile, apatite, nepheline, feldspars, quartz, calcite. **Found in**: Bavarian Forest, Eifel, Saxony/Germany; Salzburg, Tyrol/Austria; Piemonte/Italy; St. Gotthard/Switzerland; Kola, Urals/Russia; Ontario/Canada; Maine, Massachussets/USA; Mexico; Minas Gerais/Brazil. **Similar to**: axinite, cassiterite, monazite, zircon, anatase.

Periclase

MgO

③ Vesuvius/Italy 1:8

Streak white. **Mohs' hardness** 5½–6. **Specific gravity** 3.6–3.9. **Characteristics**: colorless, gray-green, yellowish. Luster: transparent to translucent. Cleavage: complete. Fracture: conchoidal; soluble in acid as crystal is difficult, in powder form easy. Crystals: (cubic) cubes, octahedral; intergrowth and surface growth; usually small and rare; twinning. **Aggregates**: rough, granular; present in metamorphosed limestones and dolomites, by-product in volcanic eruptions. **Accompanied by**: calcite, hausmannite, magnesite, brucite. **Found in**: Sardinia, Vesuvius/Italy; Sweden; California/USA. **Similar to**: spinel.

Bronzite

(Mg,Fe)$_2$[Si$_2$O$_6$]

④ Kraubath, Steiermark/Austria

Streak white. **Mohs' hardness** 5–6. **Specific gravity** 3.2–3.6. **Characteristics**: brown, green, bronze-colored. Luster: metallic, silky; translucent to opaque. Cleavage: incomplete. Fracture: uneven, bladed, fibrous, brittle; weak pleochroism. Crystals: (rhombic) short columnar, seldom well-developed. **Aggregates**: rough, spar-like, granular; present in basic to intermediate magmatites and metamorphic rocks, rock-forming in bronzitite. **Accompanied by**: diopside, olivine, serpentine, ilmenite, magnetite, chromite. **Found in**: Harz mountains, Saxony/Germany; Steiermark/Austria; Norway; Urals/Russia; Transvaal/South Africa; Greenland; Colorado/USA. **Similar to**: hypersthene, anthophyllite, diopside, enstatite. Recently bronzite has been considered to be an iron-rich variety of enstatite.

Willemite

$Zn_2[SiO_4]$

① Congo

Streak white. **Mohs' hardness** $5\frac{1}{2}$. **Specific gravity** 4.0. **Characteristics:** colorless, white, yellow to green, less often pink, gray brown. Luster: vitreous, greasy; translucent to transparent. Cleavage: incomplete. Fracture: conchoidal, splintery, brittle. Sometimes greenish-yellow fluorescence under ultra-violet light; in powder form soluble in hydrochloric acid. Crystals: (trigonal) short and long columnar, usually small; sometimes pseudomorphic. **Aggregates:** rough, granular, crumbly; present in oxidized zones of lead, zinc, and zinc-manganese deposits. **Accompanied by:** franklinite, zincite, smithsonite, hydrozincite, hemimorphite, rhodonite, calcite. **Found in:** Rheinland/Germany; Zambia; Namibia; Kirghizstan; New Jersey, New Mexico/USA; southern Australia. **Similar to:** epidote, olivine.

Anatase

TiO_2

② red crystals; Val Vavona, Tessin/Switzerland 1:2

Streak white. **Mohs' hardness** $5\frac{1}{2}$–6. **Specific gravity** 3.8–3.9. **Characteristics:** blue-black, yellow to brown, reddish, rarely colorless. Luster: adamantine, metallic, greasy; translucent to transparent. Cleavage: complete. Fracture: conchoidal, uneven, brittle. Crystals: (tetragonal) pointed to flat pyramidal, tabular, small; often horizontally striped; usually surface growth. **Aggregates:** loose rounded grains, otherwise crystals; present in alpine crevices, magmatites, sedimentary rocks. **Accompanied by:** rutile, sphene, brookite, ilmenite, quartz rock crystal, adularia, albite, calcite, chlorite. **Found in:** eastern Bavaria, Thüringer Forest/Germany; Wallis/Switzerland; Salzburg, Tyrol/Austria; Norway; Urals/Russia; Colorado/USA; Minas Gerais/Brazil. **Similar to:** brookite, sphene.

Perovskite

$CaTiO_3$

③ Brennkogel, Hohe Tauern/Austria 1:3

Streak white to gray. **Mohs' hardness** $5\frac{1}{2}$. **Specific gravity** 4.0–4.8. **Characteristics:** black, reddish-brown, yellow. Luster: adamantine, metallic, greasy; opaque to transparent. Cleavage: incomplete to complete. Fracture: conchoidal to uneven, brittle; soluble in boiling sulfuric acid. Occasionally radioactive. Crystals: (rhombic) cubes, often striped; intergrowth and surface growth, sometimes twinning. **Aggregates:** rough, granular, microcrystalline, reniform, rarely crystal skeletons; present in metamorphic rocks, basalt, magnetite and chromite deposits. **Accompanied by:** nepheline, leucite, melilite, magnetite, sphene, chlorite, talc, calcite. **Found in:** Eifel/Germany; Wallis/Switzerland; Tyrol/Austria; Finland; Sweden; southern Tirol/Italy; Kola, Urals/Russia; Quebec/Canada; Colorado/USA; Sao Paulo/Brazil. **Similar to:** magnetite, melanite.

Benitoite

$BaTi[Si_3O_9]$

④ California/USA

Streak white. **Mohs' hardness** $6\frac{1}{2}$. **Specific gravity** 3.7. **Characteristics:** light to deep blue, rarely pink or colorless. Luster: vitreous; transparent to translucent, sometimes cloudy to speckled. Cleavage: none. Fracture: conchoidal, brittle; distinct pleochroism; lively blue fluorescence under ultraviolet light. Crystals: (trigonal) always dipyramidal; intergrowth; very rare. **Aggregates:** none; present in veins in glaucophane schist. **Accompanied by:** natrolite, neptunite, anatase, glaucophane. **Found in:** only Mt. Diablo, San Benito County, California/USA. **Similar to:** sapphire.

olivine p. 132, augite p. 146, hedenbergite p. 146, hypersthene p. 170

Brookite

① Uri/Switzerland 1:10

TiO₂

Streak white, yellowish to brownish. **Mohs' hardness** 5½–6. **Specific gravity** 4.1–4.2. **Characteristics:** yellowish to brown; almost black (arkansite), seldom colorless. **Luster:** adamantine, metallic; translucent to opaque. **Cleavage:** incomplete. **Fracture:** conchoidal, uneven, brittle. **Crystals:** (rhombic) thin tabular, prismatic, dipyramidal, often vertically striped, mostly small; individually occurring; pseudomorphic. **Aggregates:** scattered; present in alpine crevices, sandstones. **Accompanied by:** anatase, rutile, sphene, feldspars, quartz, hematite. **Found in:** Graubünden/Switzerland; Tyrol/Austria; Wales; Urals/Russia; USA; Brazil. **Similar to:** anatase.

Scheelite

② on quartz; Erzgebirge/Germany

Ca[WO₄]

Streak white. **Mohs' hardness** 4½–5. **Specific gravity** 5.9–6.1. **Characteristics:** gray to white, yellow to brownish, rarely colorless. **Luster:** greasy, adamantine; transparent. **Cleavage:** incomplete. **Fracture:** conchoidal, uneven, brittle; bluish to white fluorescence under ultraviolet light. **Crystals:** (tetragonal) dipyramidal, less often tabular, often striped along the edges; surface growth and intergrowth. **Aggregates:** rough, granular, crusty, as impregnation; present in pegmatites, alpine crevices, alluvial deposits. **Accompanied by:** cassiterite, wolframite, fluorite, quartz. **Found in:** Erzgebirge/Germany; Cornwall/ England; Caucasus/Russia; Namibia; California/USA; Brazil; Tasmania/Australia. **Similar to:** stolzite, anglesite, betafite, powellite.

Monazite

 ③ Namibia

(Ce,La,Nd,Th)[PO₄]

Streak white. **Mohs' hardness** 5–5½. **Specific gravity** 4.6–5.7. **Characteristics:** light yellow to dark brown, less often colorless, red, green. **Luster:** vitreous, resinous, greasy; translucent to opaque. **Cleavage:** complete. **Fracture:** conchoidal, brittle; green fluorescence under ultraviolet light, often radioactive; easily soluble in sulfuric acid, in hydrochloric acid difficult. **Crystals:** (monoclinic) thick tabular, prismatic; intergrowth and surface growth, often twinning. **Aggregates:** rough, granular; present in basic magmatites and pegmatites, in gneiss, alpine crevices, sand, gravel. **Accompanied by:** ilminite, zircon, rutile, anatase, magnetite, garnet, quartz, feldspars. **Found in:** France; Norway; Madagascar; India; Sri Lanka; USA; Brazil. **Similar to:** euxenite, fergusonite, thortvietite, titanite.

Smithsonite

④ New Mexico/USA
⑤ Tsumed/Namibia

ZnCO₃

Streak white. **Mohs' hardness** 5. **Specific gravity** 4.3–4.5. **Characteristics:** yellowish, brown, gray, green, bluish, reddish, less often colorless, white. **Luster:** vitreous, mother-of-pearl, greasy; transparent. **Cleavage:** complete. **Fracture:** uneven, conchoidal, brittle; easily soluble in warm acid. **Crystals:** (trigonal) rhombic, often pseudomorphic. **Aggregates:** rough, granular, dense, reniform, stalactitic, striped; present in oxidized zones of sulfur-rich lead-zinc deposits. **Accompanied by:** calcite, dolomite, sphalerite, hydrozincite, hemimorphite, malachite, galena, cerussite. **Found in:** Rheinland/Germany; Sardinia/ Italy; Greece; Australia; Namibia; Oklahoma/USA. **Similar to:** hydrozincite, siderite, hemimorphite, chalcedony.

betafite p. 74, perovskite p. 112, andradite p. 130, olivine p. 132

Beryl

Al$_2$Be$_3$[Si$_6$O$_{18}$]

① morganite; Kenya
② Utah/USA
③ emerald; Chivor/Columbia
④ in quartz; Brazil

Streak white. **Mohs' hardness** 7$\frac{1}{2}$–8. **Specific gravity** 2.63–2.91. **Characteristics**: colorless, or in many different shades. Transparent beryl crystals that come in beautiful colors are used for jewelry and have their own names: goshenite (colorless), emerald (green), aquamarine (blue), gold-beryl (golden yellow), heliodor (yellow-green), morganite (pink to violet). Luster: vitreous, dull; transparent to opaque. Cleavage: incomplete. Fracture: conchoidal to uneven, brittle. Crystals: (hexagonal) short or long prismatic; usually hexagonal, pyramidal, vertically striped, seldom tabular; intergrowth and surface growth; only occasional twinning. **Aggregates**: rough, dendritic; present in pegmatites, granites, mica schists, veins in limestone. **Accompanied by**: quartz, feldspars, calcite, chrysoberyl, topaz, apatite, phenakite, fluorite, wolframite, cassiterite. **Found in**: eastern Bavaria/Germany; Tyrol/Austria; Elba/Italy; Urals/Russia; Tanzania; Kenya; Zambia; Madagascar; Transvaal/South Africa; Namibia; California, Utah/USA; Columbia; Bahia/Brazil; India; Sri Lanka; Myanmar; South Korea; western Australia. **Similar to**: chrysoberyl, apatite, spinel, brazilianite, tourmaline.

Boracite

Mg$_3$[Cl|BO$_3$|B$_6$O$_{10}$]

⑤ Lüneburg/Germany

Streak white. **Mohs' hardness** 7–7$\frac{1}{2}$. **Specific gravity** 2.9–3.0. **Characteristics**: colorless, white, gray, yellow to brown, light blue, greenish. Luster: vitreous, adamantine; transparent to translucent. Cleavage: none. Fracture: conchoidal, brittle. Flame test: green. Slowly soluble in hydrochloric acid. Crystals: (cubic) cubes, tetrahedral, octahedral, dodecahedral, finely fibrous; always intergrowth; often twinning. **Aggregates**: rough, fibrous, tuberous, granular to dense; present in salt veins. **Accompanied by**: gypsum, anhydrite, halite, carnallite, sylvite, kieserite. **Found in**: Magdeburg, Niedersachsen/Germany; Yorkshire/England; Lorraine/France; California, Louisiana/USA; Namibia. **Similar to**: halite, fluorite, senarmontite.

Cordierite dichroite, iolite

Mg$_2$Al$_3$[AlSi$_5$O$_{18}$]

⑥ Kisco/Finland

Streak white. **Mohs' hardness** 7–7$\frac{1}{2}$. **Specific gravity** 2.5–2.8. **Characteristics**: gray, blue to violet, yellow to brown, greenish, also colorless. Luster: vitreous, on cleavage face greasy; transparent to translucent. Cleavage: incomplete. Fracture: conchoidal to uneven, brittle; very strong pleochroism, detectable with the naked eye. Crystals: (rhombic) short columnar with six or twelve sides and rounded edges; intergrowth and surface growth; rare; often twinning. **Aggregates**: rough, granular, dispersed; present in metamorphic rocks (rock-forming in cordierite gneiss), in magmatites, by-product of volcanic eruptions, as river gravel. **Accompanied by**: garnet, tourmaline, spinel, sillimanite, andalusite, quartz, feldspars, pyrrhotite, chalcopyrite. **Found in**: Bavarian Forest, Eifel, Saxony/Germany; Finland; Sweden; Norway; Urals/ Russia; Madagascar; Sri Lanka; Madras/India; Myanmar; Connecticut/USA; northwest Canada; Minas Gerais/Brazil. **Similar to**: quartz, nepheline, sapphire.

tridymite p. 88

Hambergite

① Gilgit/Pakistan 1:3

Be$_2$[(OH,F)|BO$_3$]

Streak white. **Mohs' hardness** 7½. **Specific gravity** 2.36. **Characteristics:** colorless, white, gray. Luster: vitreous; transparent to translucent. Cleavage: complete. Fracture: conchoidal, brittle; high double refraction; soluble in hydrochloric acid. Crystals: (rhombic) prismatic, tabular, vertically striped, multifaceted; also twinning. **Aggregates:** none; only individual crystals; present in pegmatites; veins in sedimentary deposits. **Accompanied by:** feldspars. **Found in:** Norway; Madagascar; Kashmir/India; California/USA; Brazil. **Similar to:** quartz rock crystal and many other colorless minerals, glass.

Danburite

② San Luis Potossi/Mexico

Ca[Be$_2$Si$_2$O$_8$]

Streak white. **Mohs' hardness** 7–7½. **Specific gravity** 2.9–3.0. **Characteristics:** colorless, yellowish to dark brown, pink. Luster: greasy; transparent to translucent. Cleavage: incomplete. Fracture: uneven to conchoidal, brittle. Flame test: green. Crystals: (rhombic) prismatic, pyramidal, sometimes vertically striped; usually surface growth. **Aggregates:** rough, granular; present in metamorphic rocks, marine salt deposits, alpine crevices, by-product of volcanic eruptions. **Accompanied by:** calcite, dolomite, quartz, datolite, prehnite, apophyllite, pyrite. **Found in:** Harz mountains/Germany; Graubünden/Switzerland; Madagascar; eastern Siberia/Russia; Myanmar; Kyushu/Japan; Connecticut, New York/USA; Mexico; Bolivia. **Similar to:** datolite, topaz, citrine, colemanite.

Phenakite

③ Sao Miguel de Kiraciala/Brazil

Be$_2$[SiO$_4$]

Streak white. **Mohs' hardness** 7½–8. **Specific gravity** 2.96–3.0. **Characteristics:** colorless, yellowish, pink. Luster: vitreous; transparent. Cleavage: incomplete. Fracture: conchoidal, brittle. Crystals: (trigonal) short columnar, tabular lens-shaped, often multifaceted, vertically striped; intergrowth and surface growth; often twinning. **Aggregates:** none; present in granite, pegmatites, mica schist, alpine crevices. **Accompanied by:** beryl, chrysoberyl, topaz, tourmaline, quartz, apatite, fluorite. **Found in:** Fichtelgebirge/Germany; Salzburg/Austria; Wallis/Switzerland; Norway; Vogesen/France; Transbaikal region, Urals/Russia; Namibia; California, Colorado/USA; Minas Gerais/Brazil. **Similar to:** quartz, topaz, milarite.

Euclase

④ Brazil
⑤ Brazil

AlBe[OH|SiO$_4$]

Streak white. **Mohs' hardness** 7½. **Specific gravity** 3.0–3.1. **Characteristics:** colorless, light green, light blue. Luster: vitreous; transparent to translucent. Cleavage: perfect. Fracture: conchoidal, brittle; weak pleochroism. Crystals: (monoclinic) long and short prisms, vertically striped, multifaceted; surface growth; rare. **Aggregates:** none; present in pegmatites, crevices and geodes, alluvial deposits. **Accompanied by:** beryl, topaz, tourmaline, quartz, feldspars, muscovite. **Found in:** Fichtelgebirge/Germany; Tauern/Austria; Ireland; Norway; Urals/Russia; DR Congo; Tanzania; India; Minas Gerais/Brazil; Colorado/USA. **Similar to:** quartz, aquamarine, hiddenite, albite.

bertrandite p. 90, tourmaline p. 124

Quartz macrocrystalline
SiO_2

Streak white. **Mohs' hardness** 7. **Specific gravity** 2.5–2.7. **Characteristics:** colorless, milky white, gray, and many other colors. Luster: vitreous, on cleavage face greasy; transparent to opaque. Cleavage: none. Fracture: conchoidal, splintery, brittle; soluble in hydrofluoric acid; poor heat conductor. Crystals: (trigonal) hexagonal prisms, pyramidal with dipyramidal ends; on prism faces almost always horizontally striped; intergrowth and surficial growth; anomalies in development sometimes lead to peculiarities in crystal structure such as inclusions of liquid, gas, or small crystals. Twinning fairly common, pseudomorphs frequent. **Aggregates:** rough, granular, dense, dendritic, radial (star quartz), as crystal groups; present in basic magmatites, pegmatites, sand, gravel, particularly in drusy cavities, occasionally rock-forming. **Accompanied by:** feldspars, mica, calcite, tourmaline, garnet, wolframite, galena, sphalerite, pyrite, molybdenite.

Rock Crystal
⑥ with pyrite; Trebca/Serbia

Colorless, transparent like water; crystal faces are well-developed on all sides. **Found in:** Brazil; Madagascar; central Switzerland; Tyrol/Austria; Tuscany/Italy; New York/USA. **Similar to:** many of the colorless minerals, glass.

Smoky Quartz
③ Graubünden/Switzerland

Smoky gray, brown to black (morion); transparent; often inclusion of rutile-like needles. **Found in:** Brazil; Madagascar; central Switzerland. **Similar to:** andalusite, axinite, sanidine, vesuvianite.

Amethyst
⑤ Rio Grande do Sul/Brazil

Violet, often whitish, striped, spotted; transparent; prominently developed crystal points. **Found in:** Brazil, Uruguay; Madagascar. **Similar to:** beryl, fluorite, kunzite, spinel, topaz, tourmaline, strengite, glass.

Citrine
④ heat-treated; Brazil

Light yellow to golden brown; transparent; many citrine crystals are yellowish through burning of smoky quartz or amethyst. **Found in:** Brazil; Madagascar; Colorado/USA. **Similar to:** beryl, orthoclase, topaz, tourmaline, danburite.

Rose Quartz
① Minas Gerais/Brazil

Pink, usually cloudy because of small fissures; very rare crystal; usually rough. **Found in:** Madagascar; Brazil. **Similar to:** tourmaline.

Aventurine Green, golden brown due to inclusion of fuchsite crystals, or metallic luster due to hematite particles; transparent to opaque. **Found in:** India; Brazil; Russia. **Similar to:** oligoclase (sunstone).

Prase Emerald quartz. Leek green due to inclusion of actinolite; transparent; rough. **Found in:** Scotland; North Caroline/USA; western Australia. **Similar to:** nephrite, jadeite.

Blue quartz Siderite, sapphire quartz. Blue; translucent to opaque; rough. **Found in:** Brazil; South Africa; USA. **Similar to:** lapis lazuli, dumortierite.

Tiger's Eye
② Oranje/South Africa

Golden yellow; opaque; formed through pseudomorphism of crocidolite in quartz while maintaining its fibrous structure. **Found in:** South Africa; western Australia; Myanmar; India; USA.

Quartz microcrystalline, chalcedony
SiO_2

Streak white. **Mohs' hardness** 6½–7. **Specific gravity** 2.57–2.64. **Characteristics**: milky white, gray, also all other shades; often spotted. Luster: waxy or dull; translucent to opaque. Cleavage: none. Fracture: uneven and brittle, splintery; soluble in a potassium solution. Crystals: (trigonal) none, only microcrystalline aggregate with fine fibres or grains. **Aggregates**: dense, botryoidal, reniform; glass bead-shaped, stalactitic; present in nodules, veins, sedimentary rocks as concretions and gravel. **Accompanied by**: macrocrystalline quartz, opal, calcite, chlorite, serpentine.

Chalcedony ② striped jasper; Brazil
White to gray, bluish; translucent. Natural chalcedony is never banded; blue-layered varities are artificially colored agate. **Found in**: Brazil; Uruguay; Madagascar; India. **Similar to**: opal, smithsonite.

Cornelian Flesh-red to brownish red; dull, translucent. **Found in**: India; Brazil; Uruguay; Australia; Romania. **Similar to**: opal.

Sard Reddish brown to dark brown; translucent. No clear distinction between sard and cornelian.

Chrysoprase ⑥ California/USA
Yellow-green to apple green; translucent to opaque; often cracked with irregular color distribution. **Found in**: Australia; Brazil; USA; Madagascar; South Africa; India. **Similar to**: jadeite, smithsonite, variscite.

Heliotrope bloodstone. Dark green with red sopts; opaque. **Found in**: India; China; Australia; Brazil; USA.

Dendritic Agate ④ Rio Grande do Sul/Brazil
Whitish gray, with dark or reddish brown deposits (dendrites) of iron and manganese compounds; translucent. **Found in**: Brazil; India; USA.

Moss Agate ⑤ Kathivar/India
Colorless or milky white, with moss-like green, brown or red deposits of stem-like hornblende, or of iron and manganese oxides; translucent. **Found in**: India; China; USA; Russia.

Agate ① Idar-Oberstein, Rheinlandpfalz/Germany
Every conceivable color possible, band-like stripes; translucent to opaque; in the midde of the agate nodule often drusy development of quartz rock crystal, amethyst, smoky quartz, calcite, hematite, siderite, zeolite. **Found in**: Brazil; Uruguay; China; India; Madagascar; Mexico; USA.

Onyx Single-colored chalcedony, black, brown, red; double-layered agate with the base black and the top white is also called onyx.

Jasper ③ Idar-Oberstein, Rheinlandpfalz/Germany
All shades; striped, spotted or flamed; opaque, finely grained, dense; always in combination with foreign materials. **Found in**: India, Russia, USA.

Petrified Wood ⑦ Arizona/USA 1:½
Mostly brown, gray, red; opaque; petrification of wood by jasper in combination with chalcedony and, less frequently, opal; pseudomorphism after wood. **Found in**: Arizona/USA; Egypt; Argentina.

Corundum

Al_2O_3

① ruby in quartz; Norway
② sapphite; Sri Lanka 1:3

Streak white. **Mohs' hardness** 9. **Specific gravity** 3.9–4.1. **Characteristics:** colorless (leuco sapphire), blue (sapphire), red (ruby), gray, yellow to brown, greenish; often spotted and zoned shadings. Luster: vitreous, dull; transparent to opaque. Cleavage: none. Fracture: conchoidal to splintery, brittle; occasional pleochroism more or less distinct; occasional asterism. Crystals: (trigonal) prismatic, dipyramidal, rhombohedral, tabular; often barrel-shaped and horizontally striped; usually intergrowth; frequent twinning. **Aggregates:** rough, spar-like, coarse and fine grained; a grainy mixture known as emery is a mixture of corundum and magnetite, quartz, hematite and ilmenite; present in plutonic rocks and pegmatites, metamorphic rocks, alluvial deposits. **Accompanied by:** spinel, garnet, zircon, rutile, tourmaline, topaz, calcite. **Found in:** Tessin/Switzerland; Norway; Turkey; Urals/Russia; Kenya; Tanzania; South Africa; Sri Lanka; Myanmar; Thailand; Australia; Ontario/Canada; Montana/USA. **Similar to:** chrysoberyl, spinel, benitoite, almandite, pyrope.

Chrysoberyl

Al_2BeO_4

③ Madagascar 1:3

Streak white. **Mohs' hardness** 8½. **Specific gravity** 3.7. **Characteristics:** yellow, yellow-green, brownish, light to emerald green. Luster: vitreous, cleavage face greasy; transparent to translucent. Cleavage: incomplete. Fracture: conchoidal to brittle; sometimes strong pleochroism. Varieties: alexandrite is green in daylight and red in artifical light; cymophane occasionally has "wavelike" light rays (chrysoberyl cat's eye). Crystals: (rhombic) thick tabular, short columnar, often striped; usually intergrowth; frequent twinning, intergrowth triplings. **Aggregates:** collection of loose grains; present in granite pegmatites, gneiss, mica schist, alluvial deposits. **Accompanied by:** beryl, garnet, tourmaline, spinel, phenakite. **Found in:** Sweden; Urals/Russia; Zimbabwe; Sri Lanka; Myanmar; USA; Brazil; Tasmania/Australia. **Similar to:** brazilianite, beryl, corundum, olivine, spinel.

Tourmaline

$(Na,Li,Ca)(Fe,Mg,Mn,Al)_3$
$Al_6[(OH)_4 | (BO_3)_3 | Si_6O_{18}]$

④ schorl in quartz;
Minas Gerais/Brazil
⑤ California/USA 1:½

Streak white. **Mohs' hardness** 7–7½. **Specific gravity** 3.0–3.3. **Characteristics:** colorless (achroite), black (schorl), brown (dravite), green (verdelite), blue (indicolite), red (rubellite), violet (siberite); often in different zoned shades. Luster: vitreous; transparent to opaque. Cleavage: none. Fracture: conchoidal to uneven, splintery, brittle; high double refraction; distinct to strong pleochroism. Crystals: (trigonal) prismatic, mostly elongated to acicular, with triangular cross sections and rounded sides, vertically striped; intergrowth and surface growth. **Aggregates:** dendritic, radial, seldom rough or dense; present in basic magmatites and pegmatites, metamorphic rocks, in alpine crevices, alluvial deposits. **Accompanied by:** quartz, beryl, topaz, apatite, fluorite, feldspars, mica. **Found in:** Harz mountains/Germany; Tyrol/Austria; Czech Republic; Elba/Italy; Cornwall/England; Russia; Tanzania; Madagascar; Mozambique; Namibia; Sri Lanka; New Hampshire/USA; Brazil; Tasmania/Australia. **Similar to:** epidote, neptunite, rutile, actinolite, emerald.

kyanite p. 74, diaspore p. 102, clinozoisite p. 106, sillimanite p. 106

Andalusite

$Al_2[O \,|\, SiO_4]$

① chiastolite; Chile
② in quartz; Czech Republic

Streak white. **Mohs' hardness** $7\frac{1}{2}$ (chiastolite $5\frac{1}{2}$). **Specific gravity** 3.1–3.2. Characteristics: gray, yellow, brown, red, green, seldom colorless. Luster: vitreous, dull; transparent to opaque. Cleavage: incomplete. Fracture: uneven, splintery, brittle; strong pleochrism. Crystals: (rhombic) thick columnar with almost square cross sections, seldom acicular; sometimes with carbonaceous inclusions that form in cross sections (chiastolite, hohlspat or cross stone). **Aggregates:** rough, dendritic, radial; present in metamorphic rocks, as gravel in alluvial deposits, seldom in granitic rocks. **Accompanied by:** sillimanite, cordierite, tourmaline, garnet, quartz. **Found in:** Fichtelgebirge/Germany; Austria; Pyrenees/France; Elba/Italy; Sweden; California/USA; Brazil. **Similar to:** enstatite, tourmaline, augite, hornblende.

Dumortierite

$Al_7[(O,OH)_3 \,|\, BO_3 \,|\, (SiO_4)_3]$

③ in quartz; California/USA

Streak white. **Mohs' hardness** 7–8. **Specific gravity** 3.3–3.4. **Characteristics:** blue to violet, gray, brownish red. Luster: vitreous, silky; translucent to opaque. Cleavage: incomplete. Fracture: uneven, conchoidal, brittle; strong pleochrism. Crystals: (rhombic) thin columnar, acicular; rare. **Aggregates:** thinly fibrous, radial; present in pegmatites and metamorphic rocks. **Accompanied by:** tourmaline, cordierite, kyanite. **Found in:** Poland; Lyon/France; Urals/Russia; Uzbekistan; Madagascar; Namibia; Nevada/USA; Brazil. **Similar to:** kyanite, lapis lazuli; azurite, sodalite.

Jadeite

$Na(Al,Fe^{3+})[Si_2O_6]$

④ partially cut; China

Streak white. **Mohs' hardness** 6–7. **Specific gravity** 3.2–3.4. **Characteristics:** green, white, yellowish, reddish, violet, green with black (chloromelanite); often spotted. Luster: vitreous, dull; translucent to opaque. Cleavage: incomplete. Fracture: uneven, conchoidal, splintery and brittle. Flame test: yellow; sometimes whitish fluorescence under ultraviolet light. Crystals: (monoclinic) short prismatic; rare. **Aggregates:** dense, finely fibrous to granular, matted; very tough; in combination with nephrite known as jade; present in serpentinites, as river gravel. **Accompanied by:** quartz, feldspars, diopside. **Found in:** Myanmar; China; Guinea; Japan; California/USA; Mexico. **Similar to:** nephrite, serpentine, chalcedony.

Staurolite

$(Fe^{2+},Mg,Zn)_2Al_9[O_6 \,|\, (OH,O)_2 \,|\, (SiO_4)_4]$

⑤ Bretagne/France
⑥ with kyanite;
   Tessin/Switzerland

Streak white. **Mohs' hardness** 7–$7\frac{1}{2}$. **Specific gravity** 3.7–3.8. **Characteristics:** reddish, brown, black-brown, black. Luster: vitreous, dull; on cleavage face greasy; translucent to opaque. Cleavage: incomplete. Fracture: conchoidal, uneven, splintery, brittle. Crystals: (monoclinic) short and long columnar; always intergrowth; interpenetration twinning at right angles or at 60°. **Aggregates:** often distinct intergrowth with kyanite; collections of individual crystals; present in metamorphic rocks, in sand. **Accompanied by:** kyanite, garnet, andalusite, quartz. **Found in:** Tessin/Switzerland; Steiermark/Austria; Czech Republic; Bretagne/France; Scotland; Namibia; Tennessee/USA. **Similar to:** tourmaline, garnet.

kornerupine p. 108, spodumene p. 108, euclase p. 118.

Diamond

C

① Namibia 1:3
② on kimberlite; South Africa

Streak white. **Mohs' hardness** 10. **Specific gravity** 3.47–3.55. **Characteristics**: yellowish, brown to black, less often colorless; occasionally green, blue, reddish. Luster: adamantine, dull; transparent to opaque. Cleavage: complete. Fracture: conchoidal, splintery, brittle. Crystals: (cubic) octahedral, dodecahedral, cubes; always intergrowth. **Aggregates**: radial, spheroidal (bort, carbonado); present in ancient volcanic pipes with kimberlite as "mother stone," alluvial deposits. **Accompanied by**: chromite, pyrope, spinel, zircon, olivine. **Found in**: South Africa; Namibia; Botswana; Angola; Ghana; DR Congo; Russia; India; Brazil; Venezuela; Canada; western Australia. **Similar to**: quartz, sapphire, topaz, zircon.

Topaz

$Al_2[(F,OH)_2 | SiO_4]$

③ Minas Gerais/Brazil 1:2

Streak white. **Mohs' hardness** 8. **Specific gravity** 3.5–3.6. **Characteristics**: colorless, yellow to brown, green, blue, violet, pink, red. Luster: vitreous; transparent to translucent. Cleavage: complete. Fracture: conchoidal to uneven, brittle. Crystals: (rhombic) short or long columnar, pyramidal; often multifaceted and striped; usually surface growth. **Aggregates**: rough, radial, dendritic, as impregnation; present in basic magmatites and pegmatites, alluvial deposits. **Accompanied by**: tourmaline, beryl, fluorite, cassiterite, wolframite, quartz. **Found in**: Saxony/Germany; Transbaikal region, Urals/Russia; Namibia; Sri Lanka; Pakistan; Myanmar; Colorado, Utah/USA; Mexico; Minas Gerais/Brazil. **Similar to**: quartz, chrysoberyl, cryolite, brazilianite, hemimorphite.

Axinite

$Ca_2Fe^{2+},Al_2[BO_3(OH) | Si_{14}O_{12}]$

④ dusted with chlorite;
Dauphiné/France

Streak white. **Mohs' hardness** 6½–7. **Specific gravity** 3.26–3.36. **Characteristics**: brown, gray, blue, violet; greenish, less often yellow, red; more often dusted with green chlorite. Luster: vitreous; transparent to translucent. Cleavage: incomplete. Fracture: conchoidal, brittle; strong pleochroism under ultraviolet light. Crystals: (triclinic) tabular, wedge-shaped, multifaceted, often striped; intergrowth and surface growth. **Aggregates**: rough, spar-like, dendritic, bladed, granular, present in drusy cavities in grantitic rocks, calc-cilicate rock, alpine crevices. **Accompanied by**: quartz, feldspars, calcite, chlorite, epidote, prehnite, tourmaline. **Found in**: Erzgebirge, Fichtelgebirge, Harz mountains/Germany; Switzerland; England; Russia; Nevada/USA; Australia. **Similar to**: titanite.

Spinel

$MgAl_2O_4$

⑤ pleonaste in calcite; Madagascar
⑥ Hunza-Tal/Pakistan 1:2

Streak white. **Mohs' hardness** 8. **Specific gravity** 3.6. **Characteristics**: yellow to brownish, blue to violet, red (ruby spinel), black (pleonaste, ceylonite), seldom colorless. Luster: vitreous; transparent to opaque. Cleavage: incomplete. Fracture: conchoidal, brittle. Crystals: (cubic) octahedral, dodecahedral; frequent twinning. **Aggregates**: intergrown crystals, rounded grains, present in metamorphic rocks, magmatites, by-products of volcanic eruptions, in alluvial deposits. **Accompanied by**: zircon, garnet, corundum, magnetite, calcite. **Found in**: Odenwald/Germany; Vesuvius/Italy; Sweden; Urals/Russia; Sri Lanka; India; Thailand; Myanmar; New York/USA; Brazil; Australia. **Similar to**: corundum, garnet, zircon, beryl.

olivine p. 132, zircon p. 132

Garnet

A group of differently colored minerals with similar crystal structures. **Streak** white. **Mohs' hardness** 6½–7½. **Specific gravity** 3.40–4.32. **Characteristics:** all colors except blue. **Luster:** vitreous, greasy, resinous; translucent to opaque. **Cleavage:** incomplete. **Fracture:** conchoidal to splintery, brittle. **Crystals:** (cubic) rhombododecahedral, icositerahedron; intergrowth, and surficial growth; seldom twinning. **Aggregates:** rough, grainy to dense; present in metamorphic rocks, also as gravel and sand in alluvial deposits. **Accompanied by:** quartz, feldspars, mica, calcite, chlorite, idocrase, magnetite, chromite, wollastonite.

Pyrope
② Rodhaugen Sunnmore/Norway 1:½

$Mg_3Al_2[SiO_4]_3$

Mohs' hardness 7–7½. **Specific gravity** 3.58–3.91. **Color:** bloodred with a brownish tint, reddish black, seldom light to dark red, rose red (rhodolite); always intergrowth. **Found in:** Czech Republic; India; Sri Lanka; Tanzania; South Africa; Australia. **Similar to:** almandine, ruby, spinel.

Almandine
⑧ zillertal; Tyrol/Austria

$Fe_3Al_2[SiO_4]_3$

Mohs' hardness 7–7½. **Specific gravity** 3.95–4.32. Colored dark red with violet tint, reddish brown, brownish black; always intergrowth. **Found in:** Oberpfalz/Germany; Tyrol/Austria; Sweden; Norway; Karelia, Urals/Russia; Sri Lanka; India; Afghanistan; Alaska/USA; Brazil. **Similar to:** pyrope, spessartite, ruby, spinel, glass imitations.

Spessartite
③ Madagascar

$Mn_3Al_2[SiO_4]_3$

Mohs' hardness 7–7½. **Specific gravity** 4.12–4.20. **Color:** orange to reddish brown, also pink. **Found in:** Spessart/Germany; Sweden; Madagascar; Sri Lanka; California/USA; Minas Gerais/Brazil. **Similar to:** almandine, hessonite.

Grossular
① hessonite; Italy

$Ca_3Al_2[SiO_4]_3$

Mohs' hardness 7–7½. **Specific gravity** 3.59–3.68. Colorless (leucogarnet), yellowish, green, emerald green (tsavorite), opaque green (hydrogrossular), brownish orange (hessonite); soluble in hot sulfuric acid. **Found in:** Elba, Piemonte/Italy; Tanzania; Kenya; South Africa; Sri Lanka; Pakistan; eastern Siberia/Russia; Canada; USA; Mexico. **Similar to:** demantoid, emerald, jadeite, idocrase, spessartite.

Andradite
④ Stanley Butte, Arizona/USA   ⑤ demantoid; Bernia/Italy
⑥ topazolite; California/USA

$Ca_3Fe_2[SiO_4]_3$

Mohs' hardness 6½–7½. **Specific gravity** 3.7–4.1. **Color:** usually brown, reddish brown to black (melanite), also colorless, green to emerald green (demantoid), yellow, yellow-green (topazolite); soluble in hot sulfuric acid. **Found in:** Fichtelgebirge/Germany; Austria; Switzerland; Piemonte/Italy; Urals/Russia; Namibia; British Columbia/Canada; Arkansas/USA. **Similar to:** grossular, olivine, emerald, idocrase, topaz.

Uvarovite
⑦ Urals/Russia 1:5

$Ca_3Cr_2[SiO_4]_3$

Mohs' hardness 7–7½. **Specific gravity** 3.40-3.77. **Color:** emerald green; soluble in hot sulfuric acid. **Found in:** Finland; Poland; Urals/Russia; Transvaal/South Africa; India; Tazmania/Australia; Quebec/Canada; Oregon/USA. **Similar to:** grossular, emerald, olivine.

YAG yttrium aluminum garnet ① polished 1:6
$Y_3Al_5O_{12}$

Streak white. **Mohs' hardness** $8-8\frac{1}{2}$. **Specific gravity** 4.6. **Characteristics:** colorless, yellow, green, brown, red, violet. Luster: transparent. Cleavage: none. Fracture: conchoidal, brittle. Crystals: (cubic) none; a synthetic product. **Similar to:** diamond, zircon, rock crystal, and synthetically produced "precious" stones.

Olivine peridot, chrysolite ② Dreiser Wether,
$(Mg,Fe)_2[SiO_4]$ Eifel/Germany

Streak white. **Mohs' hardness** $6\frac{1}{2}-7$. **Specific gravity** 3.27–4.20. **Characteristics:** green, yellowish, brown to red-brown; seldom colorless. Luster: on fractured surface greasy; transparent to translucent. Cleavage: incomplete. Fracture: conchoidal, brittle; in powder form soluble in sulfuric acid. Crystals: (rhombic) prismatic, thick tabular, usually intergrowth; twinning; pseudomorphic; olivine is in the mineral series forsterite ($Mg_2[SiO_4]$) to fayalite ($Fe_2[SiO_4]$). **Aggregates:** rough, granular, tubular; present in basic magmatites, in metamorphic rocks. **Accompanied by:** augite, hornblende, feldspars, garnet, diopside, spinel. **Found in:** Eifel/Germany; Steiermark/Austria; Egypt; South Africa; Caucasus, Urals/Russia; Myanmar; Arizona/USA. **Similar to:** chrysoberyl, chondrodite, willemite.

Cassiterite pewter stone ③ Ehrenfriedersdorf,
SnO_2 Saxony/Germany

Streak white to yellowish. **Mohs' hardness** 7. **Specific gravity** 6.8–7.1. **Characteristics:** brown to black, seldom yellow, gray, reddish, colorless. Luster: on fractured surface greasy; translucent, seldom transparent. Cleavage: incomplete. Fracture: conchoidal, brittle; occasionally distinct pleochroism. Crystals: (tetragonal) short columnar to acicular, sometimes with distinctly colored stripes; surface growth and intergrowth; twinning, pseudomorphic. **Aggregates:** rough, granular, radial glass bead-like (wood-tin), long acicular (needletin); present in pegmatites, veins, as impregnation (mountain-tin), alluvial deposits (placer-tin). **Accompanied by:** quartz, topaz, fluorite, wolframite, sphalerite, arsenopyrite, pyrrhotite, pyrite. **Found in:** Czech Republic; England; Nigeria; Malaysia; Indonesia; Mexico; Bolivia; Alaska/USA. **Similar to:** rutile, sphalerite, wolframite, sphene.

Zircon
$Zr[SiO_4]$ ④ southern Tirol/Italy 1:6

Streak white, **Mohs' hardness** $7-7\frac{1}{2}$. **Specific gravity** 3.9–4.8. **Characteristics:** brown, yellowish red to reddish brown (hyacinth), straw yellow, red, green, blue (starlite), also colorless. Luster: adamantine, fractured surface greasy; transparent to translucent. Cleavage: incomplete. Fracture: conchoidal, brittle; strong multiple refraction; sometimes weak pleochroism; occasionally yellowish fluorescence under ultraviolet light. Sometimes radioactive. Crystals: (tetragonal) short prismatic, dipyramidal; mostly intergrowth, seldom twinning. **Aggregates:** intergrown or loose grains; present in acidic magmatites and metamorphic rocks, sandstone, alluvial deposits. **Accompanied by:** spinel, corundum, garnet, feldspars, mica. **Found in:** Eifel/Germany; Austria; Florida/USA; Ontario/Canada; Brazil. **Similar to:** idocrase, rutile, cassiterite, spinel.

corundum p. 124, almandine p. 130, andradite p. 130, spessartine p. 130

Garnierite
$(Ni,Mg)_6[(OH)_8 \,|\, Si_4O_{10}]$

① Riddle, Oregon/USA

Streak light green. **Mohs' hardness** 2–4. **Specific gravity** 2.2–2.8. **Characteristics**: apple green, blue-green. Luster: greasy, waxy, dull; opaque. Cleavage: none. Fracture: conchoidal, brittle; soluble in warm hydrochloric acid. Crystals: (monoclinic) not known, amorphous. **Aggregates**: rough, stalactitic, botryoidal, bladed, granular, crumbly, dense; present as a product of weathering of ultrabasic magmatites and serpentinites. **Accompanied by**: serpentine, chlorite, magnesite, chalcedony, opal, limonite. **Found in**: Saxony/Germany; Urals/Russia; New Caledonia; Philippines; New Zealand; Borneo; Sulawesi/Indonesia; Oregon/USA; Cuba; Brazil. **Similar to**: serpentine, turquoise.

Chalcophyllite
$Cu_{18}Al_2[(OH)_9 \,|\, SO_4 \,|\, AsO_4]_3 \cdot 36\,H_2O$

② Redruth, Cornwall/England 1:3

Streak light green. **Mohs' hardness** 2. **Specific gravity** 2.4–2.6. **Characteristics**: bluish, light to emerald green. Luster: vitreous, on cleavage surfaces mother-of-pearl or adamantine; transparent to translucent. Cleavage: complete. Fracture: bladed, thin blades malleable; high double-refraction; easily soluble in acid and ammonia. Crystals: (trigonal) thin tabular; usually with hexagonal contours; small. **Aggregates**: bladed; rosette-shaped, crusty, present in drusy cavities of oxidized zones of copper deposits. **Accompanied by**: cuprite, malachite, azurite, tyrolite, devilline. **Found in**: Erzgebirge/Germany; Tyrol/Austria; Cap Garonne/France; Romania; England; Nevada, Utah/USA; Urals/Russia; Chile. **Similar to**: autunite, devilline.

Chrysocolla
$(Cu,Al)_2H_2[(OH)_4 \,|\, Si_2O_5] \cdot nH_2O$

③ Zacatecas/Mexico

Streak greenish white. **Mohs' hardness** 2–4. **Specific gravity** 1.9–2.3. **Characteristics**: greenish, bluish. Luster: vitreous, waxy, dull; transparent to opaque. Cleavage: none. Fracture: conchoidal, brittle; soluble in hydrochloric acid. Flame test: green. Crystals: (rhombic) seldom microcrystalline, usually amorphous. **Aggregates**: rough botryoidal, stalactitic, crusty, crumbly; dense, as surface covering; present in oxidized zones of copper deposits. **Accompanied by**: malachite, azurite, cuprite, dioptase. **Found in**: Baden, Erzgebirge/Germany; Cornwall/England; Altai, Urals/Russia; DR Congo; Arizona, Idaho/USA; Mexico; Chile. **Similar to**: variscite, aurichalcite, turquoise, malachite.

Chlorite
$(Fe,Mg,Al)_6[(OH)_2 \,|\, (Si,Al)_4O_{10}]$

④ Zermatt/Switzerland
⑤ Bavarian Forest/Germany

Streak green to brown. **Mohs' hardness** 2–3. **Specific gravity** 2.6–3.3. **Characteristics**: green to greenish black, brown, seldom pink, violet, white. Luster: vitreous, on cleavage face mother-of-pearl, also dull; translucent, in very thin blades transparent. Cleavage: complete. Fracture: foliated, mild, cleavage flakes nonelastic malleable. Crystals: (monoclinic) thin to thick tabular, columnar; mostly with hexagonal contours; twinning, pseudomorphic. **Aggregates**: rough, scaly, fibrous, granular, dense, botryoidal, as surface covering; present in metamorphic rocks, sedimentary rocks, in crevices. **Accompanied by**: garnet, rutile, titanite, diopside, idocrase, feldspars, quartz. **Found in**: Rheinpfalz, Saxony/Germany; Tauern/Austria; Wallis/Switzerland; Cornwall/England; Sweden; Urals/Russia; Massachusetts, Pennsylvania/USA; Transvaal/South Africa. **Similar to**: serpentine, talc, mica, brucite.

annabergite p. 48, tyrolite p. 136, liroconite p. 210

Torbernite

$Cu[UO_2 | PO_4]_2 \cdot 8-12\ H_2O$

① Poppenreuth, Oberpfalz/Germany

Streak pale green. **Mohs' hardness** 2–2½. **Specific gravity** 3.3–3.7. **Characteristics**: grass to emerald green. Luster: on cleavage face mother-of-pearl; translucent to transparent. Cleavage: complete. Fracture: uneven, brittle to mild; thin blades elastic; soluble in nitric acid. Highly radioactive. Crystals: (tetragonal) thin and thick tabular, less often pyramidal; usually small; surface growth. **Aggregates**: scaly, crumbly, powdery, as crust, dusting; present in oxidized zones of uranium deposits, crevices. **Accompanied by**: autunite, zeunerite, uranocircite, uraninite, fluorite, barite, limonite, quartz. **Found in**: Black Forest, Erzgebirge, Oberpfalz/Germany; Czech Republic; Cornwall/ England; Massif Central/France; Portugal; Sardinia/Italy; DR Congo; North Carolina, Utah/USA; Mexico; southern Australia. **Similar to**: autunite, zeunerite, uranocircite.

Zeunerite

$Cu[UO_2 | AsO_4]_2 \cdot 10-16\ H_2O$

② Wheal Edward, Cornwall/England 1:2

Streak green. **Mohs' hardness** 2–2½. **Specific gravity** 3.4–3.8. **Characteristics**: emerald green to yellow-green. Luster: vitreous, on cleavage face mother-of-pearl; transparent to translucent. Cleavage: complete. Fracture: uneven, brittle to mild; highly radioactive. Crystals: (tetragonal) tabular, less often pyramidal. **Aggregates**: bladed, crusty; present in oxidized zones of uranium and arsenic-rich deposits. **Accompanied by**: torbernite, uranocircite, uranophane, uraninite, sphalerite, galena, limonite, quartz, barite, fluorite, calcite. **Found in**: Black Forest, Erzgebirge, Rheinland Pfalz/Germany; Czech Republic; Cornwall/ England; Colorado, Utah/USA. **Similar to**: torbernite.

Devilline

$CaCu_4[(OH)_6 | (SO_4)_2] \cdot 3\ H_2O$

③ Richelsdorf/Germany 1:6

Streak light green. **Mohs' hardness** 2½. **Specific gravity** 3.13. **Characteristics**: emerald green to blue-green. Luster: vitreous, mother-of-pearl; transparent to translucent. Cleavage: complete. Fracture: conchoidal, bladed; thin blades malleable. Crystals: (monoclinic) thin tabular with hexagonal contours, also bladed, acicular. **Aggregates**: rough, crusty, rosette-shaped, bladed, dendritic; present in oxidized zones of copper deposits. **Accompanied by**: malachite, azurite, tyrolite, calcite, gypsum, quartz. **Found in**: Czech Republic; Cornwall/England; Corsica/France; Kazakhstan; Pennsylvania/USA. **Similar to**: chalcophyllite.

Tyrolite

$Ca_2Cu_9[(OH)_{10} | (AsO_4)_4] \cdot 10\ H_2O$

④ Brixlegg, Tyrol/Austria 1:4

Streak light green to blue-green, also blue. **Mohs' hardness** 1½–2. **Specific gravity** 3.0–3.2. **Characteristics**: light green to blue-green, sky blue. Luster: vitreous, cleavage face mother-of-pearl; translucent. Cleavage: perfect. Fracture: bladed, mild; in thin blades elastically malleable; soluble in acid. Crystals: (rhombic) thin bladed, pseudohexagonal; rare. **Aggregates**: rosette-shaped, scaly, radial, fibrous, rough, crusty, botryoidal, crumbly, dense, foamy; present in oxidized zones of copper deposits. **Accompanied by**: chalcophyllite, brochantite, malachite, azurite, schwazite, freibergite, tetrahedrite. **Found in**: Erzgebirge, Hesse, Thüringen/Germany; Tyrol/Austria; Czech Republic; Romania; Nevada/USA. **Similar to**: azurite, brochantite.

annabergite p. 48, chlorite p. 134, aurichalcite p. 212, caledonite p. 212

Brochantite
$Cu_4[(OH)_6 | SO_4]$

① Mina Raphaola/Chile 1:6

Streak light green. **Mohs' hardness** $3\frac{1}{2}$–4. **Specific gravity** 3.97. **Characteristics:** emerald green to greenish black. Luster: vitreous, cleavage faces mother-of-pearl; translucent to transparent. Cleavage: complete. Fracture: uneven, brittle; soluble in diluted acid. Crystals: (monoclinic) short prismatic, acicular, less often tabular, vertically striped; small; surface growth; occasional twinning. **Aggregates:** rough, radial, botryoidal, crusty, granular, dense, crumbly; present in oxidized zones of copper deposits. **Accompanied by:** malachite, azurite, atacamite. **Found in:** Lahn region/Germany; Urals/Russia; Banat/Romania; Sardinia/Italy; Spain; Attica/Greece; Algeria; Namibia; Arizona, New Mexico/USA; Chile. **Similar to:** malachite, atacamite, tyrolite.

Cronstedtite
$Fe_4^{2+}Fe_2^{3+}[(OH)_8 | Fe_2^{3+}Si_2O_{10}]$

② on pyrite; Cornwall/England 1:3

Streak dark green. **Mohs' hardness** $3\frac{1}{2}$. **Specific gravity** 3.3–3.4. **Characteristics:** deep black to greenish black, in thin blades deep green. Luster: vitreous; transparent to translucent. Cleavage: complete. Fracture: cannot be determined, brittle; thin cleavage blades elastically malleable. Crystals: (trigonally hexagonic or monoclinic) narrow pyramidal with triangular or hexagonal contours; rare. **Aggregates:** radial, botryoidal; present in ore veins. **Accompanied by:** pyrite, sphalerite, limonite, calcite. **Found in:** Czech Republic, Cornwall/England; Minas Gerais/Brazil.

Euchroite
$Cu_2[OH | AsO_4] \cdot 3 H_2O$

③ Libethen/Czech Republic 1:5

Streak light green. **Mohs' hardness** $3\frac{1}{2}$–4. **Specific gravity** 3.34–3.47. **Characteristics:** emerald green to leek green. Luster: vitreous; transparent to translucent. Cleavage: incomplete. Fracture: conchoidal to uneven, brittle; soluble in hydrochloric and nitric acid. Crystals: (rhombic) short prismatic, less often thick tabular, vertically striped. **Aggregates:** crystal groups in drusy cavities and crusts; present in oxidized zones of copper deposits, mica schist. **Accompanied by:** olivinite, azurite, libethenite, cacoxenite. **Found in:** Slovakia; Bulgaria; France. **Similar to:** dioptase, malachite, olivinite, libethenite.

Malachite
$Cu_2[(OH)_2 | CO_3]$

④ Shaba/DR Congo

Streak green. **Mohs' hardness** $3\frac{1}{2}$–4. **Specific gravity** 3.6–4.0. **Characteristics:** emerald green to greenish black. Luster: vitreous, fibrous aggregates silky, also dull; transparent to translucent. Cleavage: complete. Fracture: conchoidal, brittle; strong pleochroism; easily soluble in hydrochloric acid (effervescence). Crystals: (monoclinic) long prismatic, acicular, filamentary; very rare; frequent twinning, pseudomorphic. **Aggregates:** clumps of acicular crystals, botryoidal, stalactitic, radially fibrous, crumbly, dense, glass bead-shaped, agate-like banding, dusting; present in oxidized zones of copper deposits, as impregnation in sandstone. **Accompanied by:** azurite, limonite, cuprite, chalcopyrite, chalcosite, bornite. **Found in:** Erzgebirge, Siegerland/Germany; Lyon/France; Cornwall/England; Urals/Russia; DR Congo; Arizona, New Mexico/USA; New South Wales/Australia; Chile. **Similar to:** pseudomalachite, chrysocolla, atacamite, brochantite, dioptase.

chlorite p. 134, chrysocolla p. 134, garnierite p. 134

Atacamite

① Lafarola/Chile 1:4

$Cu_2(OH)_3Cl$

Streak apple green. **Mohs' hardness** 3–3½. **Specific gravity** 3.76. **Characteristics**: grass green to greenish black. Luster: vitreous, adamantine; translucent to transparent. Cleavage: complete. Fracture: conchoidal, brittle. Flame test: blue-green. Readily soluble in hydrochloric acid and ammonia. Crystals: (rhombic) prismatic, acicular, seldom tabular, often vertically striped. **Aggregates**: rough, radial, bladed, granular, dense, as dusting present in oxidized zones of copper deposits, seldom as a volcanic sublimation product. **Accompanied by**: malachite, cuprite, brochantite, hematite, limonite, gypsum. **Found in**: Sardinia, Vesuvius/Italy; Kazakhstan; Namibia; Arizona, California/USA; Baja California/Mexico; Peru; Bolivia; Atacama/Chile; southern Australia. **Similar to**: malachite, dioptase, brochantite, libethenite.

Scorodite

② Black Forest/Germany 1:3

$Fe^{3+}[AsO_4] \cdot 2\,H_2O$

Streak greenish white. **Mohs' hardness** 3½–4. **Specific gravity** 3.1–3.3. **Characteristics**: light to dark green, seldom gray, violet, white, colorless. Luster: vitreous to resinous, dull; transparent to translucent. Cleavage: incomplete. Fracture: splintery, conchoidal to uneven, brittle. Flame test: blue. Easily soluble in hydrochloric acid. Garlic odor when fractured. Crystals: (rhombic) dipyramidal, short columnar, tabular; usually small. **Aggregates**: botryoidal, crusty, fibrous, dense, granular, as dusting; present in oxidized zones of arsenic nonferrous metal deposits. **Accompanied by**: limonite, arsenopyrite, olivinite, adamantine, pyrite. **Found in**: Erzgebirge, Westerwald/Germany; England; Urals/Russia; Uzbekistan; Namibia; Ontario/Canada; South Dakota, Utah/USA; Mexico; Brazil. **Similar to**: strengite, dufrenite.

Libethenite

③ Cornwall/England 1:4

$Cu_2[OH\,|\,PO_4]$

Streak olive green. **Mohs' hardness** 4. **Specific gravity** 3.8–3.97. **Characteristics**: leek, olive green, greenish black, often black tarnish. Luster: vitreous, greasy; transparent to translucent. Cleavage: none. Fracture: conchoidal to uneven, brittle. Crystals: (rhombic) short prismatic to octahedral; surface growth; usually small. **Aggregates**: radial, fibrous, spheroidal, reniform, crusty, dense; present in oxidized zones of copper deposits. **Accompanied by**: malachite, pseudomalachite, euchroite, limonite, quartz. **Found in**: Czech Republic; France; Cornwall/England; Urals/Russia; Shaba/DR Congo; Nevada/USA. **Similar to**: malachite, pseudomalachite, olivenite, euchroite.

Dufrenite

④ Cornwall/England 1:5

$Ca_{0.5}Fe^{2+}Fe_5^{3+}[(OH)_6\,|\,(PO_4)_4] \cdot 2\,H_2O$

Streak yellow-green. **Mohs' hardness** 3½–4½. **Specific gravity** 3.1–3.5. **Characteristics**: leek green, greenish black, sometimes brown covering. Luster: greasy, vitreous, dull; transparent to opaque. Cleavage: complete. Fracture: uneven, brittle; soluble in hydrochloric acid. Crystals: (monoclinic) pseudocubic, also thick tabular; very rare and small. **Aggregates**: radially fibrous, botryoidal, glass-bead shaped, crusty and powdery; present in oxidized zones of iron ore deposits, in phosphate pegmatites. **Accompanied by**: limonite, wavellite, cacoxenite, strengite. **Found in**: Siegerland, Thüringen/Germany; England; Portugal; Alabama, Virginia/USA. **Similar to**: scorodite.

beudantite p. 142, pseudomalachite p. 142

Olivenite

$Cu_2[OH\,|\,AsO_4]$

① Cornwall/England 1:4

Streak olive green, also brownish. **Mohs' hardness** 3. **Specific gravity** 4.3–4.5. **Characteristics:** greenish black, olive green to brown. Luster: vitreous, silky, adamantine; translucent to opaque. Cleavage: incomplete. Fracture: conchoidal to uneven, brittle; soluble in acid and ammonia. Crystals: (rhombic) prismatic to acicular, tabular; small. **Aggregates:** radial, botryoidal, reniform, fibrous, granular, crumbly, present in oxidized zones of arsenic-rich copper deposits. **Accompanied by:** malachite, azurite, arsenopyrite, zeunerite. **Found in:** Black Forest/Germany; Czech Republic; Var/France; Cornwall, Cumberland/ England; Attica/Greece; Urals/Russia; Namibia; Nevada, Utah/USA; Chile. **Similar to:** adamite, euchroite, libethenite.

Pseudomalachite

$Cu_5[(OH)_2\,|\,PO_4]_2$

② Lichtenberg,
Franken/Germany 1:3

Streak green. **Mohs' hardness** 4–5. **Specific gravity** 4.0–4.3. **Characteristics:** green to greenish black, often spotted. Luster: greasy to vitreous; translucent. Cleavage: incomplete. Fracture: conchoidal, brittle. Crystals: (monoclinic) short prismatic, tabular; very small, single crystals rare. **Aggregates:** radial, fibrous, botryoidal, crusty, also rough and crumbly; present in oxidized zones of copper deposits. **Accompanied by:** malachite, azurite, chalcopyrite, cuprite, tenorite, chrysocolla, limonite, chalcedony. **Found in:** Rheinland, Vogtland/ Germany; Czech Republic, Cornwall/England; Portugal; Urals/Russia; western Australia. **Similar to:** malachite, libethenite.

Mottramite

$Pb(Cu,Zn)[OH\,|\,VO_4]$

③ Tsumeb/Namibia 1:2

Streak green. **Mohs' hardness** 3½. **Specific gravity** 5.7–6.2. **Characteristics:** light green, olive green to greenish black. Luster: vitreous, adamantine, resinous; transparent to opaque. Cleavage: none. Fracture: conchoidal to uneven, brittle. Crystals: (rhombic) pyramidal, prismatic, tabular; rare and small. **Aggregates:** radial, wart-like, dendritic, stalactitic, crusty; present in oxidized zones of ore deposits. **Accompanied by:** descloizite, vanadinite, pyromorphite, mimetite, cerussite, wulfenite, azurite, malachite, calcite. **Found in:** Kärnten/Austria; Cheshire/England; Namibia; Arizona, Montana, New Mexico/ USA; Bolivia; Argentina. **Similar to:** descloizite, malachite.

Beudantite

$PbFe_3^{3+}[(OH)_6\,|\,SO_4\,|\,AsO_4]$

④ Tsumeb, Namibia 1:5

Streak greenish, also yellowish. **Mohs' hardness** 3½–4½. **Specific gravity** 4.0–4.3. **Characteristics:** green, yellow to brown and black. Luster: vitreous and resinous, transparent to opaque. Cleavage: incomplete. Fracture: conchoidal to uneven, brittle. Crystals: (trigonal) rhombohedral, pseudocubic, tabular. **Aggregates:** rough, crusty, crumbly; present in oxidized zones of ore deposits. **Accompanied by:** mimetite, jarosite, limonite. **Found in:** Westerwald/ Germany; Haute Vienne/France; Attica/Greece; Namibia; Arizona/USA; Sonora/Mexico; western Australia. **Similar to:** jarosite.

chalcopyrite p. 162, millerite p. 164, uraninite p. 178, carnotite p. 198, powellite p. 200, caledonite p. 212, boleite p. 214

Allanite

$Ca(Ce,La)Fe^{2+}(Al,Fe^{3+})_2[O\,|\,OH\,|\,SiO_4\,|\,Si_2O_7]$

① Arriege/France 1:10

Streak greenish gray. **Mohs' hardness** 6–6½. **Specific gravity** 3.1–4.2. **Characteristics:** gray to black, brown, seldom yellow. Luster: vitreous, greasy, resinous; opaque, thin splinters translucent. Cleavage: none. Fracture: conchoidal to uneven, brittle; strong pleochroism; soluble in hydrochloric acid. Occasionally radioactive Crystals: (monoclinic) thick tabular, long prismatic; rare; twinning. **Aggregates:** rough, granular, dendritic; present in acidic plutonic rocks, metamorphic rocks, products of volcanic eruptions. **Accompanied by:** feldspars, epidote, biotite, monazite, gadolinite, quartz. **Found in:** Eifel, Saxony/Germany; Switzerland; Norway; Sweden; Urals/Russia; California/USA; Queensland/Australia. **Similar to:** fergusonite, gadolinite, columbite.

Gadolinite

$Y_2Fe^{2+}Be_2[O\,|\,SiO_4]_2$

② Birkeland/Norway 1:2

Streak greenish gray. **Mohs' hardness** 6½–7. **Specific gravity** 4.0–4.7. **Characteristics:** green, brown, black. Luster: vitreous, resinous, greasy; translucent to opaque. Cleavage: none. Fracture: conchoidal, splintery, brittle; soluble in acid; mostly radioactive. Crystals: (monoclinic) short columnar, thick tabular; rare. **Aggregates:** rough, dense, granular, crumbly; present in granite pegmatites, in alpine crevices. **Accompanied by:** fluorite, epidote, titanite, feldspars, quartz. **Found in:** Harz mountains/Germany; Austria; central Switzerland; Norway; Sweden; Greenland; Arizona, Texas/USA. **Similar to:** fergusonite, allanite.

Ludwigite

$Mg_2Fe^{3+}[O_2\,|\,BO_3]$

③ Brosso, Piemonte/Italy 1:3

Streak greenish black, blue-green, black. **Mohs' hardness** 5. **Specific gravity** 3.6–4.2. **Characteristics:** black to greenish black. Luster: vitreous, fibrous aggregates silky; opaque. Cleavage: complete. Fracture: fibrous, brittle; very strong pleochroism; easily soluble in hydrochloric acid. Crystals: (rhombic) prismatic, acicular, fibrous; very rare. **Aggregates:** rough to dense, radial, fine-grained, matted, tough; present in dolomite and limestone, in magnetite deposits. **Accompanied by:** magnetite, phlogopite, cassiterite, quartz. **Found in:** Erzgebirge/Germany; Romania; Sweden; Norway; Nevada/USA; Korea. **Similar to:** tourmaline, hedenbergite, ilvaite.

Actinolite

$Ca_2(Mg,Fe^{2+})_5[(OH)\,|\,Si_4O_{11}]_2$

④ Tyrol/Austria

Streak greenish, white. **Mohs' hardness** 5½–6. **Specific gravity** 2.9–3.3. **Characteristics:** green, gray, also white, nearly colorless. Luster: vitreous, silky; opaque, thin splinters translucent. Cleavage: complete. Fracture: uneven, splintery, brittle; thin blades malleable. Crystals: (monoclinic) linear prisms with a cleavage angle of approximately 120°, also acicular; frequent twinning. **Aggregates:** rough, dendritic, acicular, radial (amianthus), acicular matted (mountain leather), microcrystalline matted (nephrite); present in metamorphic rocks, alpine crevices, less often magmatites. **Accompanied by:** talc, serpentine, chlorite, epidote, mica. **Found in:** Erzgebirge, Thüringen/Germany; Tyrol/Austria; Graubünden/Switzerland; Sondrio/Italy; Baikal Lake region/Russia; Turkestan; Wyoming/USA; New Zealand. **Similar to:** jadeite, epidote, tourmaline, augite, aegirine.

fassaite p. 102, pseudomalachite p. 142, thortveitite p. 170, marcasite p. 174, pyrite p. 174

Augite

(1) Lochkov, Bohemia/Czech Republic 1:2

(2) in volcanic tuff; Vesuvius/Italy

$(Ca,Na)(Mg,Fe^{2+},Al,Fe^{3+},Ti)[(Si,Al)_2O_6]$

Streak green, white. **Mohs' hardness** 5–6. **Specific gravity** 3.2–3.6. **Characteristics**: leek green to greenish black, pitch-black, brownish, rarely almost colorless. Luster: vitreous; opaque, edges transparent. Cleavage: incomplete. Fracture: conchoidal to uneven, brittle; weak pleochroism. Crystals: (monoclinic) short prismatic with octahedral contours and a cleavage angle of approximately 90°; also thick tabular, acicular; frequent twinning, occasionally pseudomorphic. **Aggregates**: rough, radial, granular to dense; present as a component of magmatites, less often in metamorphic rocks. **Accompanied by**: hornblende, feldspars, biotite, olivine. **Found in**: Eifel/Germany; Czech Republic; Auvergne/France; Liparian Island/Italy; Urals/Russia; Ontario/Canada; Colorado/USA. **Similar to**: hornblende, tourmaline, actinolite.

Dioptase

(3) Tsumeb/Namibia 1:2

$Cu_6[Si_6O_{18}] \cdot 6\,H_2O$

Streak green. **Mohs' hardness** 5. **Specific gravity** 3.3. **Characteristics**: emerald green to dark green. Luster: vitreous; transparent to translucent. Cleavage: incomplete. Fracture: conchoidal to uneven, brittle; soluble in hydrochloric and nitric acid, ammonia. Crystals: (trigonal) short prismatic. **Aggregates**: crystal groups as crusts; present in oxidized zones of copper deposits. **Accompanied by**: malachite, chrysocolla, azurite, limonite, calcite. **Found in**: Shaba/DR Congo; Namibia; Kazakhstan; Arizona, California/USA; Chile; Peru. **Similar to**: atacamite, emerald, malachite, euchroite.

Hornblende

(4) Schima, Bohemia/Czech Republic

$Ca_2Fe_4^{2+}(Al,Fe^{3+})[(OH,F)\,|\,Al_{0.5}Si_{3.5}O_{11}]_2$

Streak gray-green to gray-brown. **Mohs' hardness** 5–6. **Specific gravity** 2.9–3.4. **Characteristics**: green to black. Luster: vitreous, silky; opaque; thin splinters transparent. Cleavage: complete. Fracture: uneven, brittle; strong pleochroism, Crystals: (monoclinic) prismatic, mostly short columnar with hexagonal contours, cleavage angle of approximately 120°; also long columnar and acicular; twinning; pseudomorphic. **Aggregates**: rough, dendritic, fibrous, less often granular; present as a constituent of magmatites, metamorphic rocks, magnetite deposits. **Accompanied by**: augite, garnet, biotite, feldspars, epidote. **Found in**: Eifel, Thüringer Forest/Germany; Czech Republic; Norway; Finland; Urals/Russia; Ontario/Canada; Idaho/USA; Japan. **Similar to**: augite, tourmaline, epidote, aegirine, idocrase.

Hedenbergite

(5) Nordmark/Sweden 1:½

$CaFe^{2+}[Si_2O_6]$

Streak greenish, brownish, gray, also colorless. **Mohs' hardness** 5–6. **Specific gravity** 3.5–3.6. **Characteristics**: dark green, greenish black, brownish black, black. Luster: vitreous; transparent to translucent. Cleavage: incomplete. Fracture: conchoidal to uneven, brittle. Crystals: (monoclinic) short prismatic with almost rectangular cross sections, cleavage angle of approximately 90°; frequent twinning. **Aggregates**: rough, spar-like, radial, dendritic, granular; present in iron ore deposits, calc-silicate rocks. **Accompanied by**: magnetite, hematite, ilmenite, andradite, epidote, calcite, sphalerite. **Found in**: Erzgebirge/Germany; Elba, Tuscany/Italy; Sweden; Norway; Kazakhstan; Algeria; New Jersey/USA; Australia. **Similar to**: ludwigite.

thorianite p. 178, uraninite p. 178, aegirine p. 202, fergusonite p. 206

Molybdenite
MoS$_2$

① in quartz; Nevada/USA
② on quartz; Australia

Streak dark gray, finely pulverized dirty-green. **Mohs' hardness** 1–1$\frac{1}{2}$. **Specific gravity** 4.7–4.8. **Characteristics**: lead gray with violet tint. Luster: metallic; opaque. Cleavage: perfect. Fracture: cannot be determined, soft; thin layers nonelastically malleable; greasy to the touch; will color paper; soluble in nitric acid and aqua regia. Flame test: greenish. Crystals: (hexagonal) flat tubular to bladed with hexagonal contours; rare. **Aggregates**: rough, bladed, scaly, as impregnation, granular, dense; present in quartz veins, pegmatites. **Accompanied by**: wolframite, scheelite, cassiterite, sphalerite, arsenopyrite, chalcopyrite, pyrite, magnetite, quartz. **Found in**: Erzgebirge/Germany; Kärnten/Austria; Sweden; Norway; Cornwall/England; Caucasus/Russia; Quebec/Canada; Colorado, New Jersey/USA; Queensland/Australia. **Similar to**: graphite, galena, hematite, ilmenite, nagyagite, tetradymite.

Polybasite
(Ag,Cu)$_{16}$Sb$_2$S$_{11}$

③ Yukon/Canada 1:2

Streak black to deep red. **Mohs' hardness** 1$\frac{1}{2}$–2. **Specific gravity** 6.0–6.2. **Characteristics**: iron black. Luster: metallic; thin splinters red translucent. Cleavage: complete. Fracture: uneven, soft. Crystals: (monoclinic) thin tabular, with hexagonal contours. **Aggregates**: rough, scaly, granular; present in silver ore veins. **Accompanied by**: stephanite, pyrargyrite, proustite, argentite. **Found in**: Erzgebrige, Harz mountains/Germany; Czech Republic; Colorado, Nevada/USA; Mexico; Bolivia; Chile. **Similar to**: stephanite, argentite, pyrargyrite, hematite, miargyrite.

Covellite
CuS

④ Bor/Serbia

Streak blue-black. **Mohs' hardness** 1$\frac{1}{2}$–2. **Specific gravity** 4.68. **Characteristics**: blue-black. Luster: metallic, greasy, dull, opaque, very thin blades translucent. Cleavage: perfect. Fracture: conchoidal, soft. Flame test: blue. Soluble in nitric acid. Color: violet in water, red in oil. Crystals: (hexagonal) tubular to bladed; rare. **Aggregates**: rough, spar-like, bladed; fine-grained, dense, powdery, as covering or crust; present in weathered zones of copper-ore deposits; also as volcanic sublimation product. **Accompanied by**: chalcopyrite, bornite, chalcosite, pyrite. **Found in**: Harz mountains/Germany; Sardinia/Italy; Serbia; Alaska, Montana/USA; Bolivia; Chile. **Similar to**: bornite.

Boulangerite
Pb$_5$Sb$_4$S$_{11}$

⑤ Ramsback, Sauerland/Germany 1:4
⑥ Müsen, Westphalia/Germany

Streak black. **Mohs' hardness** 2$\frac{1}{2}$–3. **Specific gravity** 5.8–6.2. **Characteristics**: lead gray to gray-black. Luster: metallic; opaque. Cleavage: complete. Fracture: uneven, brittle; thin fibres malleable; soluble in warm nitric or hydrochloric acid. Crystals: (rhombic) long prismatic to acicular; very rare. **Aggregates**: rough, fine-grained, dense, fibrous, radial; present in lead-ore deposits. **Accompanied by**: galena, sphalerite, stibnite, arsenopyrite, pyrite, quartz. **Found in**: Sauerland/Germany; Urals/Russia; Czech Republic; Serbia; South Dakote/USA. **Similar to**: stibnite, jamesonite, bournonite, tetrahedrite, galena.

chalcosite p. 164, pyrolusite p. 176. berthierite p. 194

Jamesonite

$Pb_4FeSb_6S_{14}$

① in quartz; Neumühle, Thüringen/Germany
② with pyrite; Zacatecas/Mexico

Streak black to gray. **Mohs' hardness** $2\frac{1}{2}$. **Specific gravity** 5.63. **Characteristics**: lead gray, often colored tarnish. Luster: metallic, silky; opaque. Cleavage: complete. Fracture: cannot be detected, brittle. Crystals: (monoclinic) acicular to filamentary. **Aggregates**: rough, radial, fibrous, dense; present in veins. **Accompanied by**: galena, bournonite, sphalerite, arsenopyrite. **Found in**: Erzgebirge, Harz mountains/Germany; Czech Republic; Romania; Cornwall/England; Utah/USA; Bolivia. **Similar to**: boulangerite, stibnite.

Bournonite

$PbCuSbS_3$

③ with siderite; Horhausen/Germany

Streak gray. **Mohs' hardness** $2\frac{1}{2}$–3. **Specific gravity** 5.7–5.9. **Characteristics**: steel gray to iron black. Luster: metallic, dull; opaque. Cleavage: incomplete. Fracture: conchoidal, brittle; soluble in nitric acid. Crystals: (rhombic) thick tabular, short columnar; rare; twinning. **Aggregates**: rough, spar-like, granular, dense; present in lead and zinc deposits. **Accompanied by**: stibnite, tetrahedrite, galena, sphalerite, chalcopyrite, quartz. **Found in**: Harz mountains, Siegerland/Germany; Kärnten/Austria; Slovenia; Czech Republic; Cornwall/England; Ukraine; Transbaikal region/Russia; Arkansas, Colorado/USA; Mexico; Bolivia; Chile. **Similar to**: boulangerite, tennantite, freibergerite, schwazite, tetrahedrite.

Graphite

C

④ Trieben, Steiermark/Austria

Streak gray to black. **Mohs' hardness** 1. **Specific gravity** 2.1–2.3. **Characteristics**: steel gray, dark gray to black. Luster: metallic, dull; opaque, very thin blades translucent. Cleavage: perfect. Fracture: bladed, uneven; non-elastically malleable; good heat conductor; greasy to the touch, color brushes off when touched. Crystals: (hexagonal) tabular with hexagonal contours. **Aggregates**: bladed, scaly, dendritic, fine-grained to dense; present in pegmatites, metamorphic rocks, by-product in magmatites. **Accompanied by**: wollastonite, garnet, spinel, calcite. **Found in**: Bavarian Forest/Germany; Steiermark/Austria; Finland; Ukraine; middle Siberia/Russia; Quebec/Canada; New York/USA; Mexico; Madagascar; Sri Lanka. **Similar to**: molybdenite, nagyagite, tetradymite.

Stibnite antimonite

Sb_2S_3

⑤ Pribram/Czech Republic

Streak gray. **Mohs' hardness** 2. **Specific gravity** 4.6–4.7. **Characteristics**: blue-gray to black, often colorful tarnish. Luster: metallic, dull; opaque. Cleavage: perfect. Fracture: conchoidal, soft; very thin blades nonelastically malleable; soluble in hydrochloric and nitric acid, potassium leach; will melt in the flame of a candle with a pale blue-green color. Crystals: (rhombic) columnar, spar-like, acicular; usually surface growth. **Aggregates**: radial, acicular, spheroidal, also rough, densely matted; present in quartz veins, in lead, silver and cinnabar deposits. **Accompanied by**: gold, cinnabar, realgar, orpiment, galena, barite, quartz. **Found in**: Harz mountains, Westphalia/Germany; Czech Republic; Kärnten/Austria; Auvergne/France; Ukraine; China; Japan; South Africa; Nevada/USA; Bolivia. **Similar to**: bismuthinite, galena, pyrolusite, manganite, boulangerite.

Argentite
Ag₂S

① Oberschlema/Germany
② with calcite;
   Czech Republic

Streak lead gray to black, usually shiny. **Mohs' hardness** 2–2½. **Specific gravity** 7.2–7.4. **Characteristics:** lead gray, usually black tarnish. Luster: on fresh surfaces metallic, otherwise dull; opaque. Cleavage: complete. Fracture: conchoidal to uneven; elastic, can be cut and shaped; soluble in acid. Crystals: (cubic: argentite; monoclinic: acanthite) cubes, octahedral, prismatic, tabular, acicular; frequently pseudomorphic; also twinning. **Aggregates:** rough, granular, scattered, skeletal, dendritic, filamentary, powdery; present in silver-ore veins. **Accompanied by:** pyrargyrite, proustite, chlorargyrite, polybasite, stephanite, pure silver, galena, cerussite, sphalerite, fluorite, barite, calcite. **Found in:** Erzgebirge/Germany; Czech Republic; Norway; Siebenbürgen/ Romania; Altai/ Russia; Nevada, Utah/USA; Mexico; Bolivia; Peru. **Similar to:** polybasite, silver, argyrodite, stephanite, chalcosite, galena.

Krennerite
(Au,Ag)Te₂

③ Sacaramb/Romania 1:4

Streak yellowish gray. **Mohs' hardness** 2–3. **Specific gravity** 8.6. **Characteristics:** silver-white to brass yellow. Luster: metallic; opaque. Cleavage: complete. Fracture: uneven. Crystals: (rhombic) short prismatic, horizontally striped; small and very rare. **Aggregates:** rough, coarse, spar-like, granular and scattered; present in gold deposits. **Accompanied by:** sylvanite, calaverite, nagyagite, quartz. **Found in:** Transylvania/Romania; Quebec/Canada; Colorado/ USA; western Australia. **Similar to:** sylvanite, pure tellurium, calaverite, pyrite.

Bismuthinite
Bi₂S₃

④ with pyrite; Vogtland/Germany

Streak lead gray, shiny. **Mohs' hardness** 2. **Specific gravity** 6.8–7.2. **Characteristics:** lead gray to pewter white, often multicolored or yellowish tarnish. Luster: metallic; opaque. Cleavage: perfect. Fracture: splintery, soft; thin blades nonelastically malleable; will melt in the flame of a candle; easily soluble in warm hydrochloric acid. Crystals: (rhombic) columnar, acicular; seldom well-developed. **Aggregates:** rough, radial, dendritic, bladed, granular, scattered; present in veins, pegmatites, as volcanic exhalation products. **Accompanied by:** pure bismuth, chalcopyrite, arsenopyrite, cassiterite, wolframite, quartz. **Found in:** Erzgebirge/Germany; Romania; Cornwall/England; South Dakota/USA; Mexico; Bolivia; Peru; New South Wales/ Queensland/Australia. **Similar to:** stibnite, emplectite.

Meneghinite
Cu(Pb₁₃Sb₇)S₂₄

⑤ Bottino/Italy 1:2

Streak black. **Mohs' hardness** 2½. **Specific gravity** 6.3–6.4. **Characteristics:** lead gray to black. Luster: metallic; opaque. Cleavage: complete. Fracture: conchoidal, brittle; soluble in nitric acid. Crystals: (rhombic) long acicular, vertically striped; rare. **Aggregates:** rough, granular to dense, fibrous; present in zinc-bearing deposits. **Accompanied by:** sphalerite, galena, jamesonite, boulangerite, stannite. **Found in:** northern Bavaria, Erzgebirge/Germany; Tuscany/Italy; Sweden; California/USA; Ontario/ Canada; New South Wales/ Australia. **Similar to:** stibnite, jamesonite.

boulangerite p. 148, polybasite p. 148, galena p. 166

Sylvanite
(Au,Ag)$_2$Te$_4$

① Siebenbürgen/Romania 1:8
② yellowish crystals; USA 1:2

Streak gray. **Mohs' hardness** 1$^1/_2$–2. **Specific gravity** 8.0–8.3. **Characteristics:** steel gray to silver-white; also brass yellow, occasionally yellow tarnish. Luster: metallic; opaque. Cleavage: complete. Fracture: uneven, soft; soluble in nitric acid and aqua regia. Crystals: (monoclinic) tabular, prismatic, often vertically striped; usually small and rare; occasionally pseudomorphic; frequent twinning. **Aggregates:** skeletal crystals mimic closely spaced written characters; also occurs scattered, as dust, less often rough, granular; present in gold-ore veins. **Accompanied by:** argentite, nagyagite, calaverite, krennerite, pure gold, sphalerite, pyrite, tetrahedrite, quartz, calcite, fluorite. **Found in:** Siebenbürgen/Romania; California, Colorado/USA; Sumatra; Java/Indonesia; western Australia. **Similar to:** krennerite, calaverite, nagyagite, tetrahedrite, tellurium.

Emplectite
CuBiS$_2$

③ Mackenheim/Germany 1:2

Streak black. **Mohs' hardness** 2. **Specific gravity** 6.38. **Characteristics:** pewter white to steel gray, often yellow tarnish. Luster: metallic; opaque. Cleavage: complete. Fracture: uneven to conchoidal, brittle; soluble in acid. Crystals: (rhombic) prismatic to acicular, vertically striped; usually surface growth; rare. **Aggregates:** rough, dendritic, granular, scattered; present in bismuth-bearing veins. **Accompanied by:** pure bismuth, skutterudite, chalcopyrite, fluorite, quartz, barite. **Found in:** Black Forest, Erzgebirge/Germany; Czech Republic; Norway; Peru; Chile. **Similar to:** stibnite, bismuthinite.

Argyrodite
Ag$_8$GeS$_6$

④ Colquechara/
Bolivia 1:5

Streak gray to black. **Mohs' hardness** 2$^1/_2$. **Specific gravity** 6.1–6.3. **Characteristics:** steel gray with a reddish tint, often black tarnish. Luster: metallic; opaque. Cleavage: none. Fracture: conchoidal to uneven, brittle. Crystals: (rhombic) octahedral, rhombododecahedral; usually very small; sometimes twinning. **Aggregates:** rough, reniform, botryoidal, dense; present in silver-ore veins. **Accompanied by:** argentite, pyrargyrite, proustite, galena, sphalerite, pyrite, siderite. **Found in:** Erzgebirge/Germany; Bolivia; Argentinia. **Similar to:** argentite, germanite.

Bismuth, pure
Bi

⑤ Hertenstein, Saxony/Germany 1:10
⑥ Mackenheim, Odenwald/Germany 1:5

Streak gray. **Mohs' hardness** 2–2$^1/_2$. **Specific gravity** 9.7–9.8. **Characteristics:** silver-white with reddish tint, often colorful or brass-yellow tarnish. Luster: metallic; opaque. Cleavage: complete. Fracture: hook-shaped, uneven, brittle; can be cut; soluble in nitric acid. Crystals: (trigonal) cubes, rare; twinning with characteristic stripes. **Aggregates:** knitted, dendritic, bladed, granular, scattered; present in ore veins, pegmatites. **Accompanied by:** bismuthinite, niccolite, chloanthite, cassiterite, stannite, molybdenite, wolframite, galena, arsenopyrite, pyrite, quartz. **Found in:** Black Forest, Erzgebirge/Germany; Czech Republic; Cornwall/England; Spain; California, South Dakota/USA; Ontario/Canada; Bolivia; New South Wales, Queensland/Australia. **Similar to:** linneite, niccolite, breithauptite.

bismuthite p. 168, calaverite p. 168

Tellurium, pure
Te

① Hope Mine/USA 1:2

Streak gray. **Mohs' hardness** 2–2½. **Specific gravity** 6.1–6.3. **Characteristics:** pewter white. Luster: metallic; opaque. Cleavage: complete. Fracture: uneven, brittle. Flame test: green. Soluble in concentrated sulfuric acid. Crystals: (trigonal) prismatic; rare, usually small. **Aggregates:** rough, scattered, dendritic, fine-grained; present in gold-ore veins. **Accompanied by:** pure gold, nagyagite, sylvanite, galena, pyrite, quartz. **Found in:** Siebenbürgen/Romania; Cornwall/ England; California, Colorado/USA; Sonora/Mexico; Hokkaido/Japan; western Australia. **Similar to:** krennerite, sylvanite.

Tetradymite
Bi_2Te_2S

② Schemnitz/Czech Republic 1:3

Streak gray, shiny. **Mohs' hardness** 1½–2. **Specific gravity** 7.1–7.9. **Characteristics:** lead gray, steel gray to pewter white, often dark tarnish. Luster: on fresh cleavage face metallic, otherwise dull; opaque. Cleavage: complete. Fracture: uneven, soft, nonelastically malleable; leaves color on paper. Crystals: (trigonal) narrow pyramidal, tabular; very rare; quadrupling is characteristic. **Aggregates:** rough, bladed, also granular; present in gold deposits. **Accompanied by:** gold, pure bismuth, bismuthinite, tetrahydrite, molybdenite, galena, chalcopyrite, arsenopyrite, pyrite, quartz. **Found in:** Carpathian mountains/Romania; Czech Republic; Sweden; Urals/Russia; Colorado, Montana/USA; Canada; Japan; western Australia. **Similar to:** molybdenite, graphite.

Nagyagite
$AuPb_5(Sb,Bi)Te_2S_6$

③ with rhodochrosite;
Nagyag/Romania 1:4

Streak gray, black. **Mohs' hardness** 1–1½. **Specific gravity** 7.4–7.5. **Characteristics:** dark lead-gray and iron black. Luster: metallic; opaque. Cleavage: complete. Fracture: hook-shaped, soft; thin blades malleable; soluble in nitric acid and aqua regia. Crystals: (rhombic) thin tabular; rare. **Aggregates:** rough, bladed, granular, present in gold-ore veins. **Accompanied by:** pure gold, sylvanite, calaverite, argentite, tellurium, pyrite, calcite, rhodochrosite, quartz. **Found in:** Siebenbürgen/Romania; Colorado, North Carolina/USA; Canada; western Australia; New Zealand; Japan. **Similar to:** sylvanite, molybdenite, graphite.

Stephanite
Ag_5SbS_4

④ Freiberg, Saxony/Germany 1:3
⑤ with silver; Aue, Saxony/Germany

Streak black, shiny. **Mohs' hardness** 2–2½. **Specific gravity** 6.2–6.4. **Characteristics:** lead gray to black, often black tarnish. Luster: metallic, dull; opaque. Cleavage: incomplete. Fracture: conchoidal to uneven, brittle; soluble in nitric acid. Crystals: (rhombic) short prismatic, thick tabular; frequent twinning. **Aggregates:** rosette-shaped, scattered, seldom rough and as dusting; present in silver-ore veins. **Accompanied by:** argentite, pyrargyrite, polybasite, pure silver, galena, pyrite, barite, fluorite, calcite. **Found in:** Erzgebirge/ Germany; Czech Republic; Sardinia/Italy; Cornwall/England; Ontario/Canada; Nevada, Virginia/USA; Mexico; Peru; Chile. **Similar to:** argentite, polybasite, miargyrite, pyrargyrite, chalcosite.

Tetrahedrite series with tennantite

① Pasto Bueno/Peru

$Cu_{12}Sb_4S_{13}$

Streak black, gives off brown color when rubed vigorously. **Mohs' hardness** 3–4½. **Specific gravity** 4.6-5.2. **Characteristics:** steel gray to black with olive-colored tint. **Luster:** on cleavage face metallic, otherwise dull; opaque. **Cleavage:** none. **Fracture:** conchoidal to uneven, brittle; soluble in nitric acid and aqua regia. **Crystals:** (cubic) tetrahedral, seldom dodecahedral, cubes, often edge-parallel striped; frequent twinning. **Aggregates:** rough, scattered, granular to dense; present in lead and copper deposits. **Accompanied by:** chalcopyrite, bournonite, galena, pyrargyrite, sphalerite, arsenopyrite, pyrite. **Found in:** Erzgebirge, Harz mountains, Siegerland/Germany; Czech Republic; England; Sweden; Montana/USA; Peru; Bolivia; Namibia. **Similar to:** tennantite, bournonite, galena, sphalerite, sylvanite.

Germanite

② with blue-gray chalcosite; Kolaazi/DR Congo

$Cu_{13}Fe_2Ge_2S_{16}$

Streak black. **Mohs' hardness** 3–4. **Specific gravity** 4.4–4.6. **Characteristics:** violet to pink, usually dark violet tarnish. **Luster:** metallic; opaque. **Cleavage:** none. **Fracture:** not determined, brittle; soluble in nitric acid. **Crystals:** (cubic) micoscopically small. **Aggregates:** rough, granular, scattered; present in ore veins. **Accompanied by:** tennantite, tetrahedrite, sphalerite, pyrite, enargite, chalcosite, galena, azurite, malachite. **Found in:** only Tsumeb/ Namibia. **Similar to:** argyrodite.

Tennantite series with tetrahedrite

③ Mandeln, Hesse/Germany

$(Cu,Fe)_{12}As_4S_{13}$

Streak black, in powder form red-brown. **Mohs' hardness** 3–4½. **Specific gravity** 4.6–5.2. **Characteristics:** steel gray, lead gray with olive-colored tint. **Luster:** on fresh surface metallic; otherwise dull; opaque; thin layers red, translucent. **Cleavage:** none. **Fracture:** conchoidal to uneven, brittle; soluble in sulfuric acid. **Crystals:** (cubic) tetrahedral, seldom dodecahedral, cubes, often edge-parallel striped; frequent twinning. **Aggregates:** rough, scattered, granular to dense; present in lead and copper deposits. **Accompanied by:** chalcopyrite, enargite, bournonite, galena, sphalerite, arsenopyrite, pyrite. **Found in:** Erzgebirge, Harz mountains/Germany; Czech Republic; Sweden; Montana/USA; Peru; Bolivia; Namibia; Japan; Queensland/Australia. **Similar to:** tetrahedrite, freibergite, enargite, bournonite, galena, arsenopyrite.

Schwazite

④ Schwaz, Tyrol/Austria
⑤ Rudnany/Czech Republic

$(CuHg)_3SbS_4$

Streak gray to black. **Mohs' hardness** 3–4½. **Specific gravity** 4.6–5.2. **Characteristics:** dark steel-gray to black. **Luster:** on fresh surfaces metallic, otherwise dull; opaque. **Cleavage:** none. **Fracture:** conchoidal to uneven, brittle; soluble in nitric acid. **Crystals:** (cubic) tetrahedral, seldom dodecahedral, cubic; frequent twinning. **Aggregates:** rough, scattered, granular to dense; present in lead and copper deposits. **Accompanied by:** cinnabar, mercury, chalcopyrite, bournonite, galena, sphalerite, arsenopyrite, pyrite, barite. **Found in:** Rheinpfalz/Germany; Tyrol/Austria; Czech Republic; Cornwall/ England; Sweden; Idaho, Montana/USA; Namibia. **Similar to:** tannantite, tetrahedrite, sphalerite, bournonite.

ankerite p. 68, dolomite p, 68, betafite p. 74, triphylite p. 74

Arsenic, pure
As

① St. Andreasberg/Germany

Streak black. **Mohs' hardness** 3–4. **Specific gravity** 5.4–5.9. **Characteristics:** pale lead-gray to pewter white, copper to black tarnish. Luster: on fresh surfaces metallic, otherwise dull; opaque. Cleavage: complete. Fracture: uneven, brittle; garlic odor when fractured. Crystals: (trigonal) rhombohedral, cubic, acicular; rare and small. **Aggregates:** rough, fine-grained, botryoidal, glass bead-like; present in arsenic-rich ore veins. **Accompanied by:** dyscrasite, proustite, antimony, galena, calcite. **Found in:** Erzgebirge, Harz mountains/ Germany; Czech Republic; Vogesen/France; Norway; New Jersey/USA; Chile; West Australia; Japan. **Similar to:** antimony, silver.

Tenorite
CuO

② Nickenich, Eifel/Germany 1:4

Streak black. **Mohs' hardness** 3–4. **Specific gravity** 5.8–6.4. **Characteristics:** steel gray to black. Luster: metallic, dull; opaque; very fine blades brown, translucent. Cleavage: indeterminable. Fracture: conchoidal to uneven, brittle; elastically malleable when very thin; easily soluble in acid. Crystals: (monoclinic) tabular with hexagonalcontours, paper thin; rare. **Aggregates:** rough, crumbly, fine-grained, crusty; present in oxidized zones of copper deposits, occasionally as a volcanic exhalation product. **Accompanied by:** chalcosite, cuprite, malachite, limonite. **Found in:** Erzgebirge, northern Bavaria/Germany; Vesuvius/Italy; Shaba/DR Congo; Namibia; Michigan, Tennessee/USA; Chile. **Similar to:** pyrolusite.

Pentlandite
$(Ni,Fe)_9S_8$

③ Ontario/Canada

Streak white. **Mohs' hardness** $3\frac{1}{2}$–$4\frac{1}{2}$. **Specific gravity** 4.5–5.0. **Characteristics:** bronze yellow. Luster: metallic; opaque. Cleavage: complete. Fracture: conchoidal, brittle; soluble in nitric acid. Crystals: (cubic) rare, usually with irregularly shaped contours. **Aggregates:** rough, scattered, usually intergrowth with pyrrhotite; present in basic magmatites. **Accompanied by:** pyrrhotite, chalcopyrite, pyrite, magnetite, ilmenite. **Found in:** Black Forest/Germany; Norway; Finland; Kola, Siberia/Russia; South Africa; Ontario/Canada; California/ USA. **Similar to:** pyrrhotite, cubanite.

Pyrrhotite
FeS

④ with siderite; Trepca/Serbia

Streak gray to black. **Mohs' hardness** $3\frac{1}{2}$–$4\frac{1}{2}$. **Specific gravity** 4.6–4.7. **Characteristics:** bronze-colored with brownish tint, often dark brown tarnish. Luster: metallic, dull; opaque. Cleavage: incomplete. Fracture: conchoidal to uneven, brittle; strongly magnetic; solubility in acid difficult. Crystals: (hexagonal) usually tabular with hexagonal contours, isolated prismatic; rare. **Aggregates:** rough, scattered, granular to dense, rosette-shaped; present as a by-product in magmatites, less often in metamorphic rocks, sedimentary rocks, in sulfide deposits. **Accompanied by:** chalcopyrite, chalcosite, pyrite, arsenopyrite, pentlandite, sphalerite, galena. **Found in:** Erzgebirge, northen Bavaria, Siegerland/Germany; Serbia; Sweden; Norway; Urals/Russia; Namibia; Tennessee/USA; Mexico; Brazil. **Similar to:** niccolite, bornite, cubanite, chalcopyrite, pyrite.

boulangerite p. 148, bournonite p. 150, linneite p. 172, pyrolusite p. 176

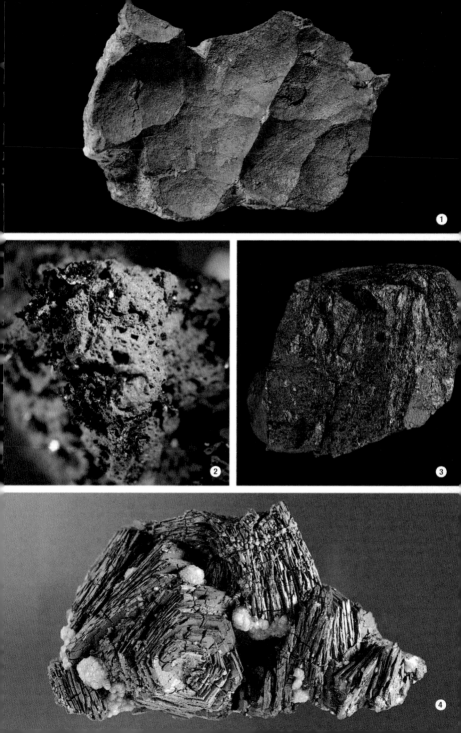

Cubanite

(1) Marro Velho/Brazil 1:4

CuFe₂S₃

Streak black. **Mohs' hardness** 3½–4. **Specific gravity** 4.0–4.2. **Characteristics**: bronze yellow. Luster: metallic; opaque. Clevage: incomplete. Fracture: conchoidal, brittle; strongly magnetic. Crystals: (rhombic) columnar, acicular, vertically striped; rare; frequent twinning. **Aggregates**: rough; present in copper deposits. **Accompanied by**: chalcopyrite, pyrrhotite, pyrite, siderite, magnetite. **Found in**: Erzgebirge/Germany; Czech Republic; Sweden; Transvaal/South Africa; Ontario/Canada; Alaska/USA; Cuba; Minas Gerais/Brazil. **Similar to**: pyrrhotite, chalcopyrite, pentlandite.

Chalcopyrite

(2) Siegen,
Westfalen/Germany

CuFeS₂

Streak greenish black to black. **Mohs' hardness** 3½–4. **Specific gravity** 4.1–4.3. **Characteristics**: brass yellow with greenish tint, often colorful or black tarnish. Luster: metallic; opaque. Cleavage: incomplete. Fracture: conchoidal to uneven, brittle; soluble in nitric acid. Crystals: (tetragonal) pseudo-octahedral, pseudododecahedral, often distorted with rough faces; usually surface growth, twinning. **Aggregates**: rough, fine-grained, crystalline crusts, botryoidal; present in magmatites, pegmatites, copper deposits. **Accompanied by**: pyrrhotite, pyrite, sphalerite, galena, tetrahedrite, pentlandite. **Found in**: Harz mountains, Thüringen/Germany; Alsace/France; Cornwall, Devonshire/ England; Urals/Russia; Kazakhstan; Ontario/Canada; New York/USA; Transvaal/South Africa; Namibia; Japan. **Similar to**: gold, bornite, marcasite, pyrrhotite.

Enargite

(3) Pasto Bueno/Peru 1:2

Cu₃AsS₄

Streak black. **Mohs' hardness** 3–3½. **Specific gravity** 4.4–4.5. **Characteristics**: steel gray to iron black with violet tint. Luster: metallic; opaque. Cleavage: complete. Fracture: uneven, brittle; soluble in nitric acid and aqua regia. Crystals: (rhombic) prismatic; often vertically striped, also tabular; frequent twinning. **Aggregates**: rough, spar-like, radial, fine-grained, scattered; present in arsenic-rich copper deposits. **Accompanied by**: chalcosite, covellite, bornite, pyrite, tennantite. **Found in**: Baden/Germany; Hungary; Tyrol/Austria; Serbia; Namibia; Montana, Utah/USA; Chile; Luzon/Phillipines. **Similar to**: tennantite, freibergite, sphalerite, manganite, arsenopyrite.

Stannite

(4) in zinnwaldite; Erzgebirge/Germany
(5) San José Mine/Bolivia

Cu₂FeSnS₄

Streak black. **Mohs' hardness** 3–4. **Specific gravity** 4.3–4.5. **Characteristics**: steel gray with olive tint. Luster: metallic; opaque. Cleavage: incomplete. Fracture: uneven, brittle; soluble in nitric acid. Crystals: (tetragonal) pseudo-octahedral; pseudocubic, tabular, rare, usually small; twinning. **Aggregates**: rough, fine-grained to dense; scattered, often intergrowth with chalcopyrite, sphalerite, fahl ore; present in zinc-ore deposits. **Accompanied by**: sphalerite, chalcopyrite, cassiterite, wolframite, arsenopyrite, tetrahedrite, galena, quartz. **Found in**: Erzgebirge/Germany; Czech Republic; England; eastern Siberia/Russia; South Dakota/USA; Bolivia; Tasmania/Australia. **Similar to**: chalcopyrite, arsenopyrite.

berthierite p. 194, manganite p. 200

Millerite

① Belmunt, Tarragona/Spain 1:3

NiS

Streak greenish black. **Mohs' hardness** 3–3½. **Specific gravity** 5.3–5.6. **Characteristics**: brass yellow, greenish gray, brownish to blackish. Luster: metallic, silky, dull; opaque. Cleavage: complete. Fracture: uneven, brittle; soluble in nitric acid and aqua regia. Crystals: (trigonal) acicular, filamentary, often striped; twinning. **Aggregates**: radial, filamentary tuffs, matted, seldom rough or granular; present in niccolite deposits, as volcanic exhalation products. **Accompanied by**: linneite, gersdorffite, pentlandite, galena, sphalerite, pyrrhotite, calcite. **Found in**: Erzgebirge, Siegerland/Germany; Czech Republic; Quebec/Canada; New York, Pennsylvania/USA. **Similar to**: marcasite, pyrite.

Freibergite

② Cavnic/Romania 1:3

$Cu_6(Ag,Fe)_6(Sb,As)_4S_{13}$

Streak gray to black. **Mohs' hardness** 3–4½. **Specific gravity** 4.6–5.2. **Characteristics**: lead gray to steel gray. Luster: on fresh surfaces metallic, otherwise dull; opaque. Cleavage: none. Fracture: conchoidal to uneven, brittle; soluble in nitric acid. Crystals: (cubic) tetrahedral; seldom dodecahedral, cubic. **Aggregates**: rough, scattered, granular to dense; present in lead and copper deposits. **Accompanied by**: argentite, pure silver, polybasite, argyrodite, stephanite. **Found in**: Erzgebirge/Germany; Czech Republic; Idaho/USA. **Similar to**: bournonite, enargite, sphalerite.

Bornite

③ Neue Hart Mines, Siegerland/Germany

Cu_5FeS_4

Streak gray-black. **Mohs' hardness** 3. **Specific gravity** 4.9–5.3. **Characteristics**: on fresh surfaces reddish to bronze-brown, often multicolored tarnish. Luster: metallic; opaque. Cleavage: incomplete. Fracture: conchoidal, soft; soluble in nitric acid and concentrated hydrochloric acid. Crystals: (cubic) cubes, also pseudo-octahedral; very rare. **Aggregates**: rough, scattered, granular to dense, as covering and dusting; present in magmatites, veins, pegmatites, alpine crevices and as impregnation. **Accompanied by**: chalcosite, chalcopyrite, enargite, pyrite, malachite, magnetite, galena. **Found in**: Saxony, Siegerland, Thüringen/Germany; Silesia/Poland; Cornwall/England; Transvaal/South Africa; Namibia; Connecticut/USA; Chile. **Similar to**: covellite, pyrrhotite, niccolite, chalcopyrite.

Chalcocite

④ Camborne, Cornwall/England 1:3

Cu_2S

Streak gray to black. **Mohs' hardness** 2½–3. **Specific gravity** 5.5–5.8. **Characteristics**: dark lead-gray, usually black tarnish. Luster: on fresh surfaces, metallic, otherwise dull; opaque. Cleavage: incomplete. Fracture: conchoidal, soft; soluble in nitric acid. Crystals: (monoclinic, tetragonal or hexagonal) thick tabular, short columnar, also pyramidal; rare; twinning, pseudomorphic. **Aggregates**: rough, crumbly, scattered, as dusting; present in copper-ore veins, as impregnations. **Accompanied by**: chalcopyrite, enargite, bornite, covellite, malachite, tetrahedrite, magnetite. **Found in**: Siegerland, Thüringen/Germany; Czech Republic; Selesia/Poland; Cornwall/England; Siberia/Russia; DR Congo; Transvaal/South Africa; Namibia; Arizona, Montana/USA. **Similar to**: argenite, stephanite, bournonite, fahl ore.

Streak

gray and
black

Dyscrasite
Ag₃Sb

① St. Andreasberg/Germany

Streak gray. **Mohs' hardness** 3½–4. **Specific gravity** 9.4–10. **Characteristics:** silver-white, cream-white, often gray or with yellow-brown tarnish. Luster: metallic; opaque. Cleavage: complete. Fracture: uneven, soft; can be cut; soluble in nitric acid. Crystals: (rhombic) pyramidal, prismatic, often vertically striped; frequent twinning. **Aggregates:** rough, spar-like, granular, bladed, scattered, as dusting; present in ore-deposits, particularly silver-ore veins. **Accompanied by:** pure arsenic, pure silver, pyrargyrite, galena, calcite. **Found in:** Black Forest, Harz mountains/Germany; Vogesen/France; Sweden; Ontario/Canada; Colorado, Nevada/USA; Chile; New South Wales/Australia. **Similar to:** antimony, silver.

Mohs' h.

Antimony, pure
Sb

② Torrington,
New South Wales/Australia

Streak lead gray. **Mohs' hardness** 3–3½. **Specific gravity** 6.6–6.7. **Characteristics:** pewter white, often gray tarnish. Luster: metallic; opaque. Cleavage: complete. Fracture: uneven, brittle. Flame test: bluish green. Soluble in aqua regia. Crystals: (trigonal) thick tabular, cubes; rare; usually small. **Aggregates:** rough, spar-like, bladed, granular, scattered, botryoidal; present in ore veins. **Accompanied by:** stibnite, arsenic, sphalerite, galena, pyrite, calcite. **Found in:** Harz mountains, Germany; Czech Republic; Portugal; Sardinia/Italy; Sweden; Quebec/Canada; California/USA; Borneo/Indonesia; Australia. **Similar to:** arsenic, silver, dyscrasite.

Jordanite
Pb₁₄(As,Sb)₆S₂₃

③ Binntal/Switzerland 1:2

Streak black. **Mohs' hardness** 3. **Specific gravity** 6.4. **Characteristics:** lead gray, sometimes multicolored tarnish. Luster: metallic; opaque. Cleavage: complete. Fracture: uneven to conchoidal, brittle. Crystals: (monoclinic) tabular, often with rounded edges and striped, multifaceted, usually small; twinning, pseudomorphic. **Aggregates:** rough, botryoidal, spheroidal, scaly; present in lead-zinc deposits, dolomite marble. **Accompanied by:** sphalerite, realgar, galena, pyrite, barite. **Found in:** Baden/Germany; Selesia/Poland; Wallis/Switzerland; Romania; Japan. **Similar to:** galena, bournonite.

S. gravity

Galena
PbS

④ Siegen,
Westfalen/Germany

Streak gray-black. **Mohs' hardness** 2½–3. **Specific gravity** 7.2–7.6. **Characteristics:** reddish gray with reddish tint, often dark gray and bluish tarnish. Luster: on fresh surfaces strongly metallic, otherwise dull; opaque. Cleavage: perfect. Fracture: conchoidal, soft; soluble in nitric acid. Crystals: (cubic) cubic, octahedral, rhombododecahedral; occasionally edge-parallel striped; usually surface growth; often twinning, pseudomorphic. **Aggregates:** rough, coarsely spar-like, granular, less often botryoidal, fibrous, dendritic; present in veins and as replacement. **Accompanied by:** sphalerite, wurtzite, chalcopyrite, tetrahydrite, bournonite, proustite, pyrite, marcasite, barite, quartz, calcite. **Found in:** Erzgebirge, Harz mountains, Siegerland/Germany; Serbia; Kärnten/Austria; Zambia; Caucasus, eastern Siberia/Russia; Ontario/Canada; Colorado, Idaho/USA. **Similar to:** antimonite, boulangerite, molybdenite, tetrahydrite, argentite, sphalerite.

boulangerite p. 148, krennerite p. 152, tenorite p. 160

Bismutite

$Bi_2[O_2 \,|\, CO_3]$

(1) Namibia 1:3

Streak gray to whitish. **Mohs' hardness** $2\frac{1}{2}$–$3\frac{1}{2}$. **Specific gravity** 6.1–7.7. **Characteristics**: straw yellow to brown, greenish, also gray to black, seldom blue. Luster: vitreous, mother-of-pearl, dull; transparent to opaque. Cleavage: indeterminable. Fracture: conchoidal to uneven. Crystals: (tetragonal) microscopically small. **Aggregates**: rough, crumbly, botryoidal, radial, crusty, powdery; present in oxidized zones of bismuth-ore deposits. **Accompanied by:** bismuthinite, pure bismuth, wolframite. **Found in:** Erzgebirge/Germany; Cornwall/England; Madagascar; Arizona, Colorado/USA; Mexico; Peru; Bolivia; Australia. **Similar to:** greenockite, all ochre types such as hematite.

Calaverite

$AuTe_2$

(2) Cripple Creek, Colorado/USA 1:5

Streak yellowish gray. **Mohs' hardness** $2\frac{1}{2}$–3. **Specific gravity** 9.3. **Characteristics**: light brass yellow. Luster: metallic; opaque. Cleavage: none. Fracture: conchoidal to uneven, brittle. Flame test: blue-green. Crystals: (monoclinic) columnar, vertically striped, multifaceted; rare; frequent twinning. **Aggregates**: rough, granular, scattered, bladed, dense; present in old ore veins. **Accompanied by:** sylvanite, gold, nagyagite, krennerite, pyrite, quartz. **Found in:** Siebenbürgen/Romania; California, Colorado/USA; Ontario/Canada; Mexico; western Australia. **Similar to:** sylvanite, krennerite, pyrite.

Platinum, pure

Pt

(3) Urals/Russia

Streak steel gray to silver-white. **Mohs' hardness** 4–$4\frac{1}{2}$. **Specific gravity** 14.0–21.4. Characteristics: steel gray to silver-white, often dark tarnish. Luster: metallic; opaque. Cleavage: none. Fracture: hook-shaped, elastically malleable, ductile, can be formed with a hammer; soluble in hot aqua regia; sometimes magnetic. Crystals: (cubic) cubes, mostly distorted; very rare. **Aggregates**: irregular or rounded nuggets, blades and leaves; present in in basic rocks and alluvial deposits. **Accompanied by:** sperrylite, gold, chromite, magnetite, ilmenite, pyrrhotite. **Found in:** middle Siberia, Urals/Russia; Bushveld/South Africa; Ontario/Canada; Alaska/USA; Columbia; Peru; New Zealand. **Similar to:** silver, iron, sperrylite.

Iron, pure

Fe

(4) meteoric iron; Arizona/USA
(5) widmannstett figures; Toluca/Mexico
(6) iron meteorite; Arizona/USA

Streak steel gray, shiny. **Mohs' hardness** 4–5. **Specific gravity** 7.3–7.9. **Characteristics**: steel gray to iron black. Luster: metallic; opaque. Cleavage: none. Fracture: hook-shaped, elastic. Crystals: (cubic) unknown. **Aggregates**: terrestrial: rough, scattered, granular, clumps, nuggets; meteoric: rough and granular, nuggets, usually with black melted crusts; if polished often take on "beam" structures (widmannstett figures); always combined with niccolite; terrestrial iron occurs in many formations; meteoric iron occurs in some matter from the solar system that reaches the surface of the earth. **Accompanied by:** pyrrhotite, pentlandite, graphite. **Found in:** terrestrial iron in Hesse/Germany; Ireland; Auvergne/France; Greenland; Missouri/USA; Meteoric iron in Arizona/USA; Mexico; Namibia; Siberia/Russia. **Similar to:** platinum.

uranite p. 178, safflorite p. 182

Epidote

Ca$_2$(Fe^{3+},Al)Al$_2$[O | OH | SiO$_4$ | Si$_2$O$_7$]

① Baja California/Mexico
② Valle Magia, Tessin/Switzerland

Streak gray. **Mohs' hardness** 6–7. **Specific gravity** 3.3–3.5. **Characteristics:** green, less often yellow, gray. Luster: vitreous; transparent to opaque. Cleavage: complete. Fracture: conchoidal, uneven, splintery, brittle; strong pleochroism. Crystals: (monoclinic) long columnar, broadly dendritic to acicular, often striped, multifaceted; frequent twinning, pesudomorphic. **Aggregates:** rough, radial, bunched, acicular, as dusting; present in metamorphic rocks, magmatites, pegmatites, alpine crevices. **Accompanied by:** actinolite, idocrase, augite, hornblende, apatite, quartz, garnet, feldspars. **Found in:** Salzburg, Tyrol/Austria; Dauphené/France; Alba, Piemonte/Italy; Norway; Urals/Russia; California, Michigan/USA; Mexico. **Similar to:** actinolite, hornblende, idocrase, tourmaline, willemite.

Thortveitite

(Sc,Y)$_2$[Si$_2$O$_7$]

③ Hiltvert/Norway 1:2

Streak light gray, gray green. **Mohs' hardness** 6½. **Specific gravity** 3.6–3.8. **Characteristics:** dirty green to almost black. Luster: vitreous; transparent to opaque. Cleavage: incomplete. Fracture: conchoidal to uneven, brittle. Occasionally radioactive. Crystals: (monoclinic) long columnar; always intergrowth; frequent twinning. **Aggregates:** radial, rosette-shaped; present in granite pegmatites. **Accompanied by:** monazite, zircon, beryl, euxenite, fergusonite, magnetite, ilmenite, quartz, feldspars. **Found in:** Norway; Urals/Russia; Kazakhstan; Madagascar; Japan. **Similar to:** monazite.

Riebeckite

Na$_2$(Fe^{2+},Mg)$_3$Fe$_2$$^{3+}$[OH | Si$_4O_{11}$]$_2$

④ Rosswald, Wallis/Switzerland 1:2

Streak blue-gray. **Mohs' hardness** 5–6. **Specific gravity** 3.0–3.4. **Characteristics:** blue to blue-black. Luster: vitreous, silky; translucent to opaque. Cleavage: complete. Fracture: uneven to brittle. Flame test: yellow. Crystals: (monoclinic) long prismatic, vertically striped; rare. **Aggregates:** radial, fibrous (asbestos form crocidolite), dendritic, bladed, granular; present in acidic magmatites, schist. **Accompanied by:** quartz, orthoclase, albite, epidote, hematite, magnetite. **Found in:** Corsica/France; Shetland Island/Scotland; Ukraine; Madagascar; South Africa; Massachussetts, Rhode Island/USA; western Australia. **Similar to:** tourmaline, amianthus.

Hypersthene

(Fe,Mg)$_2$[Si$_2$O$_6$]

⑤ Quebec/Canada

Streak gray, brownish, whitish. **Mohs' hardness** 5–6. **Specific gravity** 3.3–3.8. **Characteristics:** dark green, dark brown, black, often metallized, sometimes with copper-red luster. Luster: vitreous; transparent to opaque. Cleavage: incomplete. Fracture: uneven to brittle; distinct pleochroism. Crystals: (rhombic) short prismatic, tabular, mostly small, multifaceted. **Aggregates:** rough, granular, bladed; present in basic magmatites, as a volcanic exhalation product. **Accompanied by:** olivine, augite, hornblende, feldspars, diopside, pyrrhotite. **Found in:** Eifel, Harz mountains/Germany; Romania; Massif Central/France; Baikal Lake region/Russia; Labrador/Canada; Colorado/USA. **Similar to:** enstatite, bronzite, diallage.

betafite p. 74, triphyline p. 74, millerite p. 94, clinozoisite p. 106, perovskite p. 112, boracite p. 116, allanite p. 144, ludwigite p. 144, hedenbergite p. 146, hornblende p. 146, ilvaite p. 176

Bixbyite, sitaparite
$(Mn^{3+},Fe^{3+})_2O_3$

① Thomas Range, Utah/USA 1:4

Streak black. **Mohs' hardness** 6–6½. **Specific gravity** 4.9–5.0. **Characteristics:** black with bronze-colored tint. Luster: metallic; opaque. Cleavage: incomplete. Fracture: uneven, brittle. Crystals: (cubic) cubes. **Aggregates:** rough, fine-grained; present in rhyolite, manganese deposits. **Accompanied by:** topaz, garnet, manganite, psilomelane, hausmannite, braunite, hollandite. **Found in:** Sweden, Gerona/Spain; South Africa; India; Utah, New Mexico/USA. Argentina. **Similar to:** braunite, magnetite.

Magnetite
$Fe^{2+}Fe_2^{3+}O_4$

② in chlorite-slate; Tyrol/Austria

Streak black. **Mohs' hardness** 5½–6½. **Specific gravity** 5.2. **Characteristics:** iron-black. Luster: metallic; opaque. Cleavage: incomplete. Fracture: conchoidal, brittle; highly magnetic; as powder soluble in hydrochloric acid. Crystals: (cubic) octahedral, rhombododecahedral; rarely hexahedral, often striped; intergrowth and surface growth; frequent twinning, pseudomorphic. **Aggregates:** rough, scattered, granular to dense, sometimes scoriaceous, individual rounded grains; present in magmatites, alpine crevices, as isolated deposits, in sand and alluvial deposits. **Accompanied by:** ilmenite, hematite, hedenbergite, spinel, garnet, chalcopyrite, pyrite, apatite, olivine, calcite. **Found in:** Siegerland, Erzgebirge, Thüringen/Germany; Sweden; Norway; Finland; Lothringen/France; Ukraine; Urals, Altai/Russia; India; Transvaal/South Africa; Michigan, Utah/USA. **Similar to:** chromite, hematite, hausmannite, ilmenite, betafite, descloizite.

Arsenopyrite
FeAsS

③ with calcite; Trepca/Serbia

Streak gray to black. **Mohs' hardness** 5–6. **Specific gravity** 5.9–6.2. **Characteristics:** pewter white to steel gray; often yellowish or dark gray tarnish. Luster: metallic; opaque. Cleavage: incomplete. Fracture: uneven, brittle; garlic odor when fractured; soluble in nitric acid. Crystals: (monoclinic) columnar, dendritic, often striped; frequent twinning. **Aggregates:** rough, radial, fibrous, botryoidal, granular; present in ore veins. **Accompanied by:** gold, chalcopyrite, pyrite, pyrrhotite, magnetite, sphalerite, apatite, rutile, tourmaline, quartz. **Found in:** Harz mountains, northern Bavaria, Erzgebirge/Germany; Czech Republic; Cornwall/England; Sweden; Urals, eastern Siberia/Russia; Transvaal/South Africa; California/USA; Tasmania/Australia. **Similar to:** tennantite, loellingite, pyrite, marcasite, chloanthite, skutterudite.

Linneite
$Co^{2+}Co_2^{3+}S_4$

④ Stahlberg, Siegerland/Germany 1:4
⑤ Luttfeld, Siegerland/Germany

Streak gray to black. **Mohs' hardness** 4½–5½. **Specific gravity** 4.8–5.8. **Characteristics:** silver-white with reddish or yellowish tint, sometimes steel-gray, copper-red or violet-blue tarnish. Luster: metallic; opaque. Cleavage: incomplete. Fracture: uneven, brittle; soluble in nitric acid. Crystals: (cubic) octahedral; sometimes twinning. **Aggregates:** rough, granular, scattered; present in ore deposits. **Accompanied by:** siderite, tetrahedrite, pyrite, cobaltite, galena, barite. **Found in:** Siegerland/Germany; Sweden; Shaba/DR Congo; Zambia; Missouri/USA. **Similar to:** cobaltite, niccolite, pure bismuth, skutterudite, gersdorffite, ullmanite.

betafite p. 74, perovskite p. 112, allanite p. 144, ludwigite p. 144

Pyrite
FeS$_2$

① Calais/France
② Elba/Italy

Streak greenish black. **Mohs' hardness** 6–6½. **Specific gravity** 5.0–5.2. **Characteristics:** brass yellow, golden yellow, frequent multicolored tarnish, sometimes rust-colored, weathered crust. Luster: metallic; opaque. Cleavage: none. Fracture: conchoidal, brittle. Flame test: bluish; soluble in nitric acid. On fracturing sulfuric odor and sparkling. Crystals: (cubic) cubes with striped faces, octahedral, pentagondodecahedral; intergrowth and surface growth frequent twinning, pseudomorphic. **Aggregates:** rough, granular to dense, scattered; radial, tuberous, botryoidal, oolitic; present in isolated deposits, sulphur-ore mines, as by-product in magmatites. **Accompanied by:** pyrrhotite, chalcopyrite, arsenopyrite, sphalerite, galena, quartz, calcite. **Found in:** Westfalen, Harz mountains, Erzgebirge/Germany; Piemonte, Elba/Italy; Huelva/Spain; Norway; Sweden; Chalkidice/Greece; Urals/Russia; Transvaal/South Africa; Colorado, Tennessee/USA; Tasmania/Australia. **Similar to:** marcasite, pyrrhotite, chalcopyrite, arsenopyrite, gold, millerite.

Marcasite
FeS$_2$

③ Indiana/USA
④ Brüx/Czech Republic

Streak greenish black. **Mohs' hardness** 6–6½. **Specific gravity** 4.8–4.9. **Characteristics:** brass yellow with greenish tint; often multicolored tarnish, sometimes with rust-colored, weathered crust. Luster: metallic. Cleavage: incomplete. Fracture: uneven, brittle; when fracturing sulfuric odor and sparkling; soluble in hydrochloric acid. Crystals: (rhombic) tabular, columnar, acicular, intergrowth and surface growth, sometimes striped; twinning very frequent; dimorph of pyrite; spear-like and cockscomb-like; also pseudomorphic. **Aggregates:** as crystal groups, rough, coarse-radial to fine-fibrous, dense, botryoidal, tuberous, crusty, as dusting; present in veins in limestone, as concretion in argillaceous and carbonaceous rocks, as weathering product. **Accompanied by:** pyrite, pyrrhotite, sphalerite, galena. **Found in:** Westfalen, Erzgebirge/Germany; Czech Republic; Champagne/France; Urals/Russia; Missouri/USA; Bolivia. **Similar to:** pyrite, chalcopyrite, arsenopyrite, pyrrhotite, gold.

Ilmenite
Fe^{2+}TiO$_3$

⑤ Norway

Streak black with brownish tint, in powder form dark brown. **Mohs' hardness** 5–6. **Specific gravity** 4.5–5.0. **Characteristics:** black with violet tint. Luster: metallic, often dull tarnish; opaque, very thin blades translucent. Cleavage: none. Fracture: conchoidal to uneven, brittle; sometimes slightly magnetic; lively pleochroism; in powder form soluble in concentrated hydrochloric acid. Crystals: (trigonal) tabular, rhombohedral; intergrowth and surface growth; frequent twinning. **Aggregates:** rough, granular, scattered; individual grains; rosette-shaped (iron rose); present in magmatites, their pegmatites, sand alluvial deposits, alpine crevices. **Accompanied by:** magnetite, hematite, rutile, monazite, apatite, feldspars, quartz. **Found in:** Norway; Sweden; St. Gotthard/Switzerland; Urals/Russia; India; Natal/South Africa; Quebec/Canada; Wyoming, New York/USA; Queensland/Australia. **Similar to:** chromite, rutile, hematite, magnetite, columbite.

columbite p. 180, cobaltite p. 180, hematite p. 190, braunite p. 204

Ilvaite

① Elba/Italy 1:3

$CaFe_2^{2+}Fe^{3+}[OH\,|O\,|Si_2O_7]$

Streak black with greenish or brownish tint. **Mohs' hardness** 5½–6. **Specific gravity** 3.8–4.1. **Characteristics:** black with brownish or greenish tint. Luster: on fresh cleavage face vitreous, otherwise metallic or greasy; opaque. Cleavage: incomplete. Fracture: uneven to conchoidal, brittle; distinct pleochroism; easily soluble in hydrochloric acid. Crystals: (rhombic) long columnar to acicular, vertically striped. **Aggregates:** rough, radial, dendritic, granular; present in metamorphic rocks, ore deposits. **Accompanied by:** hedenbergite, garnet, magnetite, arsenopyrite, pyrite. **Found in:** Harz mountains/Germany; Elba/Italy; Serbia; Serifos/Greece; Urals/Russia; Idaho/USA. **Similar to:** ludwigite, tourmaline, actinolite.

Pyrolusite

② California/USA

MnO_2

Streak black. **Mohs' hardness** in crystals 6–7, in rough form 2–6. **Specific gravity** 4.5–5.0. **Characteristics:** gray to black. Luster: metallic, dull; opaque. Cleavage: complete. Fracture: uneven, fibrous, crumbly; brittle; color rubs off when touched; soluble in hydrochloric acid. Crystals: (tetragonal) columnar, acicular; rare; twinning; pseudomorphic. **Aggregates:** rough, radial, glass bead-like; crusty, fine-grained to dense, crumbly (wad); present in oxidized zones of manganese deposits, as separate deposits, as tubers on deep ocean floor. **Accompanied by:** magnetite, psilomelane, hausmannite. **Found in:** Siegerland, Harz mountains/Germany; Ukraine; South Africa; Arkansas/USA; Brazil. **Similar to:** manganite, stibnite, psilomelane.

Gersdorffite

③ Montana/USA
④ Heimberg, Harz mountains/Germany 1:3

NiAsS

Streak gray-black. **Mohs' hardness** 5–5½. **Specific gravity** 5.6–6.2. **Characteristics:** silver-white to steel gray, usually dark gray tint. Luster: metallic, dull; opaque. Cleavage: complete. Fracture: uneven, brittle; soluble in nitric acid. Crystals: (cubic or orthorhombic) cubes, octahedral; intergrowth or on geodes; rare and small. **Aggregates:** rough, spar-like, granular, scattered; present in siderite veins and silver-cobalt-nickel deposits. **Accompanied by:** siderite, niccolite, chalcopyrite, galena, quartz, calcite. **Found in:** Siegerland/Germany; Vogtland/France; Steiermark, Salzburg/Austria; Ontario/Canada; Colorado/USA; Bolivia; Tasmania/Australia. **Similar to:** ullmannite, cobaltite, skutterudite, linneite.

Psilomelane wad, romanechite

⑤ Rauback, Westerwald/Germany

$(Ba,H_2O)_2(Mn^{4+},Mn^{3+})_5O_{10}$

Streak brownish black. **Mohs' hardness** 5–6. **Specific gravity** 4.4–4.7. **Characteristics:** black, brownish black, gray. Luster: metallic, dull; opaque. Cleavage: none. Fracture: conchoidal to uneven, brittle; soluble in hydrochloric acid. Crystals: (monoclinic) unknown; microcrystalline to amorphous. **Aggregates:** rough, fine-grained to dense; radial, dendritic, botryoidal, glass bead-like, crumbly; present in oxidized zones of manganese deposits, as concretions in sedimentary rocks. **Accompanied by:** pyrolusite, manganite, hausmannite, calcite, barite. **Found in:** Black Forest, Siegerland, Erzgebirge/Germany; Sweden; Belgium; Saone/France; Ukraine/Russia; India; Virginia/USA. **Similar to:** pyrolusite, hausmannite.

euxenite p. 206, fergusonite p. 206

Ullmannite series with Willyamite
NiSbS

Streak black. **Mohs' hardness** 5–5½. **Specific gravity** 6.6–6.7. **Characteristics**: silver-white to steel gray; sometimes multicolored tarnish. Luster: metallic; opaque. Cleavage: complete. Fracture: uneven, brittle. Crystals: (cubic) cubes with striped faces, octahedral, pentagondodecahedral; rare. **Aggregates**: rough, granular, scattered; present in ore deposits. **Accompanied by**: gerddorffite, linneite, sphalerite, galena, siderite, calcite. **Found in**: Siegerland, Harz mountains/Germany; Kärnten/Austria; Sardinia/Italy; Colorado/USA. **Similar to**: gersdorffite, chloanthite, linneite.

Sperrylite
PtAs₂

Streak dark gray to black. **Mohs' hardness** 6–7. **Specific gravity** 10.4–10.6. **Characteristics**: pewter white. Luster: strongly metallic. Cleavage: incomplete. Fracture: conchoidal, brittle. Crystals: (cubic) cubes, octahedral; usually small and intergrown, sometimes multifaceted. **Aggregates**: individual grains; present in sulfide and alluvial deposits. **Accompanied by**: chalcopyrite, pyrrhotite, pentlandite, niccolite, pure platinum, pure gold. **Found in**: Transvaal/South Africa; eastern Siberia/Russia; Ontario/Canada; North Carolina, Wyoming/USA. **Similar to**: cobaltite, platinum.

Thorianite
ThO₂

Streak gray, gray-green to black. **Mohs' hardness** 6½–7. **Specific gravity** 9.7–10.0. **Characteristics**: dark gray, brownish black to black. Luster: metallic, resinous; often dull tarnish; opaque; very thin blades translucent. Cleavage: incomplete. Fracture: conchoidal to uneven, brittle; usually radioactive; soluble in nitric acid. Crystals: (cubic) cubes, intergrowth, twinning. **Aggregates**: rounded grains; present in pegmatites, marble, alluvial deposits. **Accompanied by**: monazite, diopside, scapolite, pitchblende. **Found in**: South Africa; Madagascar; Transbaikal region/Russia; Ontario/ Canada; Pennsylvania/USA. **Similar to**: pitchblende.

Uraninite
UO₂

Streak black, brownish black, greenish. **Mohs' hardness** 4–6. **Specific gravity** 7.5–10.6. **Characteristics**: pitch black to gray, sometimes with brownish or greenish tint; weathered yellowish to reddish. Luster: on fresh surfaces pitch black and greasy, otherwise dull, opaque; only occasionally in very thin splinters reddish brown, translucent. Cleavage: none. Fracture: conchoidal, brittle; easily soluble in warm nitric and sulfuric acid. Strongly radioactive. Crystals: (cubic) octahedral, less often dodecahedral; occasional twinning, pseudomorphic. **Aggregates**: rough (pitchblende), granular to dense, scattered, botryoidal, spheroidal; present in acidic magmatites, pegmatites, and ore veins, in ancient placer deposits and sandstone. **Accompanied by**: fluorite, apatite, barite, monazite, zircon, feldspars, quartz, pyrite. **Found in**: Black Forest, eastern Bavaria, Erzgebirge/Germany; Czech Republic; Vendée/France; Shaba/ DR Congo; Transvaal/South Africa; Ontario/Canada; Northern Territory/Australia; Turkestan. **Similar to**: betafite, thorianite, psilomelane.

iron p. 168, arsenopyrite p. 172, gersdorffite p. 176

Streak

gray and
black

Mohs' h.

1
2
3
4
5
6
7
8
9
10

S. gravity

1
2
3
4
5
6
7

Rammelsbergite
NiAs$_2$

① Bou Azzer/Morocco 1:3

Streak gray to black. **Mohs' hardness** 5½–6. **Specific gravity** 7.0–7.1. **Characteristics**: pewter to white with reddish tint, usually dark tarnish; occasional green covering (annabergite). Luster: metallic, opaque. Cleavage: incomplete. Fracture: uneven, brittle; garlic odor when fractured. Crystals: (rhombic) short prismatic, tabular; small, rare; occasional twinning. **Aggregates**: rough, radial, granular; occasionally intergrown with skutterudite; present on nickel- and cobalt-rich ore deposits. **Accompanied by**: niccolite, chloanthite, skutterudite, maucherite, loellingite. **Found in**: Harz mountains/Germany; Wallis/Switzerland; Ontario/Canada; Michigan/USA. **Similar to**: chloanthite, safflorite, skutterudite, loellingite, maucherite.

Cobaltite cobaltine
CoAsS

② Tunaberg/Sweden 1:3

Streak gray to black. **Mohs' hardness** 5½. **Specific gravity** 6.0–6.4. **Characteristics**: silver-white with reddish or steel-gray tint, often reddish-gray tarnish, sometimes reddish covering (erythrite). Luster: metallic; opaque. Cleavage: incomplete. Fracture: conchoidal to uneven, brittle; soluble in hot nitric acid. Crystals: (rhombic) cubes with striped faces, octahedral, dodecahedral; always intergrowth. **Aggregates**: rough, granular, scattered; present in ore veins, in metamorphic rocks. **Accompanied by**: pyrrhotite, chalcopyrite, pyrite, cubanite, skutterudite, linneite, erythrine. **Found in**: Siegerland, Erzgebirge/German; Sweden; Caucasus/Russia; Ontario/Canada; Colorado, Idaho/USA; Mexico; New South Wales/Australia. **Similar to**: arsenopyrite, gersdorffite, linneite, ullmannite.

Columbite combination of niobite and tantalite
niobite (Mn^{2+},Fe^{2+})Nb$_2$O$_6$
tantalite (Mn^{2+},Fe^{2+})(Ta,Nb)$_2$O$_6$

 ③ black crystals; Oberpfalz, Bavaria/Germany

Streak brown to black. **Mohs' hardness** 6–6½. **Specific gravity** 5.1–8.2. **Characteristics**: black to brown. Luster: pitch and metallic; transparent to opaque. Cleavage: incomplete. Fracture: conchoidal, brittle. Occasionally radioactive. Crystals: (rhombic) tabular, columnar, occasionally striped, usually intergrown; frequent twinning. **Aggregates**: rough, scattered, rounded grains; present in granite and granite pegmatites, alluvial deposits. **Accompanied by**: cassiterite, spodumene, beryl, tourmaline, lepidolite, quartz. **Found in**: eastern Bavaria/Germany; Sweden; Norway; Urals/Russia; Nigeria; Namibia; South Dakota/USA; Brazil; western Australia. **Similar to**: wolframite, ilmenite, allanite, euxenite.

Loellingite
FeAs$_2$

④ in rhodonite; Australia
⑤ Reichenstein, Silesia/Poland

Streak gray to black. **Mohs' hardness** 5–5½. **Specific gravity** 7.1–7.5. **Characteristics**: silver-white, often gray tarnish. Luster: metallic; opaque. Cleavage: incomplete. Fracture: uneven, brittle; soluble in nitric acid. Crystals: (rhombic) prismatic, acicular, mostly small; usually intergrown. **Aggregates**: rough, scattered, granular, dendritic; present in veins, pegmatites, as impregnation. **Accompanied by**: arsenopyrite, chloanthite, magnetite, siderite, galena, sphalerite, pyrite. **Found in**: Harz mountains, Erzgebirge/Germany; Kärnten/Austria; Sweden; Siberia/Russia; Ontario/Canada; South Dakota/USA. **Similar to**: arsenopyrite, chloanthite, safflorite.

Chloanthite
① Schneeberg, Saxony/Germany

(Ni,Co)As₃

Streak gray to black. **Mohs' hardness** 5½–6. **Specific gravity** 6.4–6.6. **Characteristics:** pewter white to steel gray, often dark-gray tarnish; reddish or green surface covering. Luster: metallic; opaque. Cleavage: none. Fracture: uneven, brittle; arsenic odor when fractured; soluble in nitric acid. Crystals: (cubic) cubes with warped faces, also octahedral, dodecahedral; usually surface growth; frequent twinning. **Aggregates:** rough, scattered, granular, dense, botryoidal; present in cobalt deposits. **Accompanied by:** niccolite, safflorite, skutterudite, maucherite, fluorite, quartz. **Found in:** Black Forest, Erzgebirge, Thüringen/Germany; Czech Republic; Alsace/France; Morocco; Ontario/Canada; New Jersey/USA. **Similar to:** arsenopyrite, skutterudite, loellingite, rammelsbergite.

Maucherite
② Zinkwand, Salzburg/Austria 1:3

Ni₁₁As₈

Streak brownish to gray-black. **Mohs' hardness** 5. **Specific gravity** 8.0. **Characteristics:** silver-gray with reddish tint, often reddish-gray tarnish. Luster: metallic; opaque. Cleavage: none. Fracture: uneven, brittle; soluble in concentrated nitric acid. Crystals: (tetragonal) thin tabular, narrow pyramidal; small and rare. **Aggregates:** rough, bladed, radial, granular; present in ore veins. **Accompanied by:** niccolite, chloanthite, cobaltite, calcite. **Found in:** Thüringen/Germany; Steiermark/Austria; Spain; Morocco; Ontario/Canada. **Similar to:** niccolite, breithauptite, rammelsbergite.

Safflorite
③ Niederschlema,
Saxony/Germany 1:4

CoAs₂

Streak gray to black. **Mohs' hardness** 4½–5½. **Specific gravity** 6.9–7.3. **Characteristics:** pewter white, usually dark-gray tarnish. Luster: metallic; opaque. Cleavage: none. Fracture: uneven to conchoidal, brittle; emits garlic odor when fractured. Crystals: (orthorhombic): prismatic, tabular; very small, rare; often star-shaped tripling. **Aggregates:** rough, radial, fibrous, botryoidal, crusty, fine-grained to dense; present in cobalt-rich veins. **Accompanied by:** skutterudite, erythrite, niccolite, chloanthite, rammelsbergite, pure bismuth, silver, arsenic. **Found in:** Black Forest, Erzgebirge/Germany; Czech Republic; Ontario/Canada; Mexico. **Similar to:** skutterudite, chloanthite, rammelsbergite, arsenopyrite.

Skutterudite
④ Schneeberg, Saxony/Germany

CoAs₃

Streak black. **Mohs' hardness** 6. **Specific gravity** 6.8. **Characteristics:** pewter white to steel gray; occasionally red-tinted tarnish, also greenish (annabergite) or pinkish-red (erythrite) surface crusts. Luster: metallic; opaque. Cleavage: none. Fracture: conchoidal to uneven, brittle; soluble in nitric acid. Crystals: (cubic) octahedral, often with curved faces. **Aggregates:** rough, scattered, granular to dense, also reniform and knitted; present in cobalt-nickel deposits. **Accompanied by:** cobaltite, safflorite, chloanthite, rammelsbergite, niccolite, bismuthite, silver. **Found in:** Harz mountains, Black Forest, Erzgebirge/Germany; Czech Republic; Steiermark/Austria; Norway; Morocco; Ontario/Canada; Colorado/USA. **Similar to:** arsenopyrite, gersdorffite, chloanthite, rammelsbergite, safflorite.

Copper, pure
Cu

① Santa Vita/Mexico 1:2

Streak copper red, metallic. **Mohs' hardness** 2½–3. **Specific gravity** 8.93. **Characteristics**: copper red, darkly tarnished to brown, black or green crust. Luster: metallic; opaque; very thin layers green, translucent. Cleavage: none. Fracture: hook-like, soft, very elastic; excellent heat conductor; easily soluble in nitric acid. Crystals: (cubic) cubic, octahedral, severely distorted; twinning, pseudomorphic. **Aggregates**: rough, as grains, nuggets, foliated, skeletal, dendritic; present in oxidized zones of copper deposits, pore space of magmatites, alluvial deposits. **Accompanied by**: cuprite, cobaltite, malachite, azurite, calcite. **Found in**: Siegerland, Saxony/Germany; Corsica/France; Sweden; Zambia; Michigan, Arizona/USA; Urals/Russia. **Similar to**: silver.

Erythrite
$CO_3[AsO_4]_2 \cdot 8\,H_2O$

② Bou Azzer/Morocco

Streak pink. **Mohs' hardness** 2. **Specific gravity** 3.07. **Characteristics**: peach-blossom red. Luster: vitreous, adamantine, on cleavage faces mother-of-pearl; transparent to translucent. Cleavage: perfect. Fracture: uneven, soft; thin blades elastic; strong pleochroism; soluble in hydrochloric acid. Crystals: (monoclinic) prismatic, acicular, tabular. **Aggregates**: acicular, dendritic, bladed, spheroidal, reniform, crumbly, as dusting, also rough; present in oxidized zones of cobalt-rich deposits. **Accompanied by**: skutterudite, cobaltite, annabergite, malachite, azurite. **Found in**: Black Forest, Erzgebirge/Germany; Cornwall/England; Azerbaijan; Morocco; Ontario/Canada; Idaho/USA; Mexico. **Similar to**: cinnabar.

Proustite
Ag_3AsS_3

③ Erzgebirge, Saxony/Germany 1:3

Streak scarlet-red. **Mohs' hardness** 2½. **Specific gravity** 5.5–5.7. **Characteristics**: cinnabar-to scarlet-red, quickly darkens when exposed to light. Luster: adamantine; translucent. Cleavage: complete. Fracture: conchoidal, brittle; soluble in nitric acid. Crystals: (trigonal) prismatic, pyramidal; multifaceted, mostly surface growth. **Aggregates**: rough, dendritic, as dusting; present in ore veins. **Accompanied by**: pyrargyrite, argentite, polybasite, stephanite, galena, rhodochrosite, pyrite, calcite, quartz. **Found in**: Black Forest, Erzgebirge, Harz mountains/Germany; Vogesen/France; Czech Republic; Sardinia/Italy; Ontario/Canada; Colorado, Nevada/USA; Mexico; Chile. **Similar to**: pyrargyrite; miargyrite, cuprite, cinnabar, hematite.

Kermesite
Sb_2S_2O

④ Pribram, Bohemia/Czech Republic 1:10

Streak red, brownish red, in powder form yellow-orange. **Mohs' hardness** 1–1½. **Specific gravity** 4.7. **Characteristics**: dark red to violet. Luster: vitreous to adamantine; translucent to opaque. Cleavage: complete. Fracture: fibrous, soft; can be cut; thin splinters elastic. Crystals: (triclinic) acicular, filamentary; surface growth; rare, scattered. **Aggregates**: radial, tangled-fibrous, as surface covering; present in oxidized zones of antimony (stibnite) deposits. **Accompanied by**: stibnite, valentinite, senarmontite, berthierite. **Found in**: Erzgebirge/Germany; Hungary; Czech Republic; Tuscany/Italy; Algeria; Quebec/Canada; California, Idaho/USA; Sonora/Mexico.

polybasite p. 148, realgar p. 194

Pyrargyrite

Ag₃SbS₃

① Quiruvilca/Peru 1:2
② Sonora/Mexico 1:2

Streak cherry red. **Mohs' hardness** 2½–3. **Specific gravity** 5.8. **Characteristics**: dark red to gray-black. Luster: metallic; transparent. Cleavage: incomplete. Fracture: conchoidal to splintery, brittle; soluble in nitric acid. Crystals: (trigonal) prismatic, pyramidal, rhombohedral, multifaceted; usually surface growth; twinning, pseudomorphic. **Aggregates**: rough, dendritic, as surface covering; present in ore veins. **Accompanied by**: proustite, argentite, stephanite, galena, rhodochrosite, calcite, quartz. **Found in**: Harz mountains, Erzgebirge/Germany; Czech Republic; Sardinia/Italy; Spain; Ontario/Canada; Colorado, Nevada/USA; Mexico; Bolivia; Peru; Chile. **Similar to**: proustite, miargyrite, cuprite, cinnabar, hematite.

Crocoite

Pb[CrO₄]

② Tasmania/Australia

Streak orange. **Mohs' hardness** 2½–3. **Specific gravity** 5.9–6.1. **Characteristics**: yellowish red, orange. Luster: adamantine; translucent. Cleavage: complete. Fracture: conchoidal to uneven, soft; strong double refraction; soluble in hydrochloric acid. Crystals: (monoclinic) long prismatic with parallel stripes, often hollow; also acicular, spear-like; multi-faceted, many shapes; surface growth or dispersed. **Aggregates**: rough, surface covering; present in oxidized zones of lead deposits. **Accompanied by**: galena, cerussite, mimetesite. **Found in**: Erzgebirge/Germany; Urals/Russia; California, Arizona/USA; Brazil; Tasmania/Australia. **Similar to**: realgar, cinnabar, cuprite, vanadanite.

Miargyrite

AgSbS₂

④ St. Andreasberg/Germany 1:10

Streak cherry red. **Mohs' hardness** 2–2½. **Specific gravity** 5.2. **Characteristics**: steel gray, lead gray to black. Luster: metallic, adamantine; opaque; red, translucent in thin layers. Cleavage: incomplete. Fracture: small conchoidal to uneven, brittle. Crystals: (monoclinic) thick tabular, spear-like, multifaceted; mostly small; surface growth or dispersed. **Aggregates**: rough; present in silver-ore veins. **Accompanied by**: pyrargyrite, proustite, stephanite, polybasite, galena. **Found in**: Harz mountains, Erzgebirge/Germany; Czech Republic; Spain; Romania; Idaho, Colorado/USA; Mexico; Bolivia; Chile. **Similar to**: pyrargyrite, proustite, stephanite, polybasite, freibergite, tennantite.

Cinnabar

HgS

⑤ with mercury;
Almaden/Spain

Streak scarlet red. **Mohs' hardness** 2–2½. **Specific gravity** 8.0–8.2. **Characteristics**: scarlet red, brownish red, often bluish tarnish. Luster: adamantine, dull; transparent to translucent. Cleavage: complete. Fracture: splintery, brittle; strong double-refraction; soluble in aqua regia. Crystals: (trigonal) prismatic, thick tabular, rhombohedral, dipyramidal, multifaceted; rare, small; twinning. **Aggregates**: rough, granular, crumbly, powdery, as impregnation; present in veins and pore space of sedimentary rocks, volcanic hot springs, less often in alluvial deposits. **Accompanied by**: pyrite, marcasite, stibnite, realgar, galena, hematite, fluorite, chalcedony. **Found in**: Rheinland Pfalz/Germany; Sierra Morena/Spain; Serbia; Tuscany/Italy; Ukraine; China; Japan; California, Texas/USA; Mexico; Peru. **Similar to**: crocoite, proustite, realgar, cuprite, hematite.

Purpurite

① Sandamab/Namibia

$(Mn^{3+},Fe^{3+})[PO_4]$

Streak purple. **Mohs' hardness** 4–4½. **Characteristics**: pink to purplish red, often black or brown tarnish. Luster: vitreous, metallic, on fresh surfaces silky, also dull; translucent to opaque. Cleavage: complete. Fracture: uneven, brittle; strong pleochroism. Crystals: (rhombic) very small; always intergrowth. **Aggregates**: rough, coarse-grained to dense, crusty; present in pegmatites. **Accompanied by**: heterosite. **Found in**: Sweden; France; Portugal; Namibia; California/USA; western Australia. **Similar to**: heterosite.

Heterosite

② Namibia

$(Fe^{3+},Mn^{3+})[PO_4]$

Streak brownish red. **Mohs' hardness** 4–4½. **Specific gravity** 3.2–3.4. **Characteristics**: pink to purplish red, often brown or black tarnish. Luster: vitreous, on fresh surfaces silky, also dull; translucent to opaque. Cleavage: complete. Fracture: spar-like, uneven, brittle; strong pleochroism. Crystals (rhombic): always pseudomorphic after triphylite; intergrowth. **Aggregates**: rough, spear-like, spar-like, coarse-grained, crusty; present in pegmatites. **Accompanied by**: purpurite, triphylite, vivianite. **Found in**: Bavarian Forest/Germany; Limoges/France; Portugal; Sweden; Namibia; South Dakota/USA; Australia. **Similar to**: purpurite.

Cuprite

③ on cerussite;
Tsumeb/Namibia

Cu_2O

Streak brownish red. **Mohs' hardness** 3½–4. **Specific gravity** 5.8–6.2. **Characteristics**: deep red, carmine red, red-brown, often gray-black tarnish. Luster: metallic on crystal and fresh cleavage faces, aggregates are dull; opaque, in thin splinters translucent. Cleavage: complete. Fracture: conchoidal to uneven, brittle; soluble in hydrochloric acid (effervescence). Flame test: green. Crystals: (cubic) octahedral, dodecahedral, less often cubed, acicular; usually surface growth; frequently pseudomorphic. **Aggregates**: rough, granular, scattered, powdery, filamentary (chalcotrichite); sometimes mixed with powdery limonite, also in a thick mixture with limonite and silica (copper pitch ore); present in oxidized zones of copper deposits, rarely as volcanic exhalation product. **Accompanied by**: copper, malachite, azurite, chrysocolla, tenorite, limonite. **Found in**: Siegerland/Germany; Vesuvius, Etna/Italy; Lyon/France; Cornwall/England; Urals/Russia; Arizona/USA; Peru; Chile; Namibia. **Similar to**: proustite, pyrargyrite, cinnabar, crocoite, realgar, hematite.

Roselite

④ Bou Azzer/Morocco 1:5

$Ca_2(Co,Mg)[AsO_4]_2 \cdot 2\,H_2O$

Streak reddish. **Mohs' hardness** 3½. **Specific gravity** 3.5–3.7. **Characteristics**: pink to rose-red, dark red. Luster: vitreous; transparent to translucent. Cleavage: complete. Fracture: uneven to brittle. Crystals: (monoclinic) short prismatic, thick tabular, usually small; frequent twinning. **Aggregates**: crystal groups nodular or in drusy cavities; also rough and crusty; present in oxidized zones of cobalt-rich deposits. **Accompanied by**: erythrite. **Found in**: Black Forest, Saxony/Germany; Morocco.

tennantite p. 158, copper p. 184, crocoite p. 186, pyrargyrite p. 186, hauerite p. 196, zincite p. 198, huebnerite p. 208

Hematite
Fe$_2$O$_3$

① iron glass; Elba/Italy
② red iron ore; Hunsrück/Germany
③ red glass bead; Cumberland/England
④ iron-rose; Tessin/Switzerland

Streak red, red-brown, seldom black. **Mohs' hardness** 5½–6½. **Specific gravity** 5.2–5.3. **Characteristics**: color of coarse-crystalline types are steel gray to iron black, often with bluish tint; crystal faces sometimes colorfully tarnished; fine-grained types are red to red-brown. Luster: on fresh surfaces metallic, otherwise dull; opaque; thin layers red, translucent. Cleavage: none. Fracture: conchoidal, brittle; slowly soluble in hydrochloric acid. Crystals: (trigonal) dipyramidal, cubelike-rhombohedral, thick and thin tabular, often striped; intergrowth and surface growth; frequent twinning, pseudomorphic. **Aggregates**: coarse-crystalline, granular or scaly (iron glass, specularite); rough, fine-grained, dense; dense and usable for jewelry (blood stone); radial-fibrous with smooth surface (red glass bead); thin-bladed (iron glass); rosette-like scaly (iron rose); crumbly-powdery (red iron ochre); crumbly-powdery with color rubbing off (red chalk); present as a by-product in many rocks, also as isolated deposits, and in alpine crevices, rarely as a sublimation product. **Accompanied by**: magnetite, pyrite, siderite, limonite, calcite, quartz. **Found in**: eastern upper Bavaria, Siegerland, Lahn-Dill region, Thüringen, Erzgebirge/Germany; Elba/Italy; Auvergne/France; Romania; Sweden; Ukraine; Urals/Russia; Newfoundland/ Canada; upper Great Lakes region/USA; Minas Gerais/Brazil; India; southern Australia. **Similar to**: magnetite, ilmenite, pyrargyrite, cinnabar, cuprite.

Lepidocrocite
Fe^{3+}O(OH)

⑤ Hartenstein, Saxony/Germany 1:2

Streak reddish, brownish. **Mohs' hardness** 5. **Specific gravity** 4.0. **Characteristics**: ruby red, dark red, yellow to red. Luster: adamantine; translucent; thin layers transparent. Cleavage: complete. Fracture: uneven, brittle; strong double refraction; soluble in hydrochloric acid. Crystals: (rhombic) tabular, acicular; usually surface growth; rare. **Aggregates**: rosette-shaped crystals, rough, fibrous, scaly, glass bead-like, crumbly, powdery; present as a formation on many rock surfaces, in oxidized zones of sulfur-ore deposits, and combined with limonite. **Accompanied by**: goethite, hematite, pyrolusite, calcite, quartz. **Found in**: Siegerland/Germany; Kärnten/Austria; Lothringen/France; Luxemburg; Attica/Greece; Crimea/Ukraine; Pennsylvania, California/USA; Mexico; India; Japan. **Similar to**: goethite, hematite, limonite.

Piemontite
Ca$_2$(Mn^{3+},Fe^{3+})(Al,Mn^{3+})$_2$[O |OH |SiO$_4$ |Si$_2$O$_7$]

⑥ Valle d'Aosta/Italy

Streak cherry red. **Mohs' hardness** 6-6½. **Specific gravity** 3.4-3.5. **Characteristics**: red, brownish red, reddish black to black. Luster: vitreous; translucent to opaque. Cleavage: complete. Fracture: uneven, brittle; strong pleochroism. Crystals: (monoclinic) prismatic, acicular. **Aggregates**: rough, radial, granular, dense; present in manganese deposits, schist, seldom in pegmatites and volcanic rocks. **Accompanied by**: quartz, glaucophane, braunite, rhodonite, rhodochrosite. **Found in**: Piemonte/Italy; Graubünden/Switzerland; Bretagne/France; Sweden; Scotland; Egypt; California, Arizona/USA; Japan; New Zealand.

zincite p. 198, franklinite p. 204, hausmannite p. 206,
breithauptite p. 208, huebnerite p. 208

Uranocircite

Ba[UO₂ | PO₄]₂ · 10 H₂O — $Ba[UO_2 | PO_4]_2 \cdot 10\,H_2O$

① Menzenschwand,
Black Forest/Germany

Streak yellowish. **Mohs' hardness** 2½. **Specific gravity** 3.5. **Characteristics**: yellowish green to yellow. Luster: vitreous, mother-of-pearl; translucent. Cleavage: complete. Fracture: uneven, brittle to soft; thin blades malleable; blue-green fluorescence under ultraviolet light. Strongly radioactive. Crystals: (tetragonal) thin tabular with rectangular contours, acicular, pyramidal. **Aggregates**: bladed, dusting; present in oxidized zones of uranium deposits, quartz veins. **Accompanied by**: autunite, torbernite, quartz. **Found in**: Black Forest, eastern Bavaria, Vogtland/Germany; France. **Similar to**: autunite, torbernite, carnotite.

Autunite lime uranite

Ca[UO₂ | PO₄]₂ · 10–12 H₂O — $Ca[UO_2 | PO_4]_2 \cdot 10\text{–}12\,H_2O$

② on quartz; Erzgebirge/Germany

Streak yellowish, colorless. **Mohs' hardness** 2–2½. **Specific gravity** 3.2. **Characteristics**: yellow with greenish tint. Luster: vitreous, on cleavage surfaces mother-of-pearl; translucent. Cleavage: complete. Fracture: uneven, brittle; thin blades malleable; soluble in hydrochloric acid; yellow-green fluorescence under ultraviolet light. Highly radioactive. Crystals (tetragonal) tabular; usually surface growth. **Aggregates**: clusters, crusty, dense, as dusting; present in oxidized zones of uranium deposits. **Accompanied by**: torbernite, uranocircite, fluorite, barite, quartz. **Found in**: eastern Bavaria, Erzgebirge/Germany; France; England; Czech Republic; DR Congo; Washington/USA; southern Australia. **Similar to**: torbernite, uranocircite, carnotite, chalcophyllite, auripigment.

Uranophane

Ca[UO₂ | SiO₃(OH)]₂ · 5 H₂O — $Ca[UO_2 | SiO_3(OH)]_2 \cdot 5\,H_2O$

③ New Mexico/USA

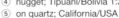

Streak pale yellow. **Mohs' hardness** 2½. **Specific gravity** 3.8–3.9. **Characteristics**: yellow. Luster: vitreous, mother-of-pearl on cleavage faces; transparent to translucent. Cleavage: complete. Fracture: conchoidal, brittle; soluble in acid. Strongly radioactive. Crystals: (monoclinic) prismatic, acicular. **Aggregates**: radial, crumbly, botryoidal, as dusting; present in oxidized zones of uranium deposits, in pegmatites. **Accompanied by**: torbernite, autunite, uranocircite, uraninite, fluorite. **Found in**: Eastern Bavaria/Germany; Czech Republic; DR Congo; New Mexico/USA; Canada; Australia. **Similar to**: sulfur.

Gold, pure

Au

④ nugget; Tipuani/Bolivia 1:3
⑤ on quartz; California/USA

Streak yellow. **Mohs' hardness** 2½.–3. **Specific gravity** 15.5.–19.3. **Characteristics**: gold-yellow to brass yellow, in powder form brown (mustard gold). Luster: metallic; opaque, very thin layers green translucent. Cleavage: none. Fracture: hook-like, soft; can be cut with a knife and flattened to the very thinnest of sheets; soluble in aqua regia and mercury. Crystals: (cubic) octahedral, cubes, dodecahedral; frequent twinning. **Aggregates**: rough, springy, wire-and moss-shaped, dendritic; as grains, nuggets, dusting; often with high silver content (electrum); present in veins (mountain gold) or alluvial deposits (placer gold). **Accompanied by**: pyrite, pyrrhotite, chalcopyrite, sphalerite, magnetite, quartz, tourmaline. **Found in**: Hohe Tauern/Austria; Romania; Altai, Siberia/Russia; India; western Australia; Transvaal/South Africa; British Columbia/Canada; California/USA. **Similar to**: pyrite, chalcopyrite, biotite, marcasite.

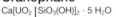

ozocerite p. 32, chlorite p. 134; krennerite p. 152, calaverite p. 168

Realgar
AsS

① on limestone;
Washington/USA 1:2

Streak yellow-orange. **Mohs' hardness** 1½–2. **Specific gravity** 3.5–3.6. **Characteristics**: red, red-orange; Luster: adamantine, on cleavage face greasy; translucent. Cleavage: incomplete. Fracture: conchoidal, soft to brittle; can be cut; thin blades malleable; soluble in aqua regia. Flame test: bluish white. Crystals: (monoclinic) short prismatic, vertically striped. **Aggregates**: rough, bladed, fine-grained, as dusting; present as volcanic sublimation product. **Accompanied by**: orpiment, stibnite, pyrite, sphalerite, barite, calcite. **Found in**: Wallis/Switzerland; Macedonia; Siebenbürgen/Romania; Czech Republic; Caucasus/Russia; Utah, Wyoming/USA; Mexico. **Similar to**: crocoite, cinnabar, orpiment, proustite, sulfur, cuprite.

Berthierite
FeSb₂S₄

② Herja/Romania

Streak brownish, also gray. **Mohs' hardness** 2–3. **Specific gravity** 4.6. **Characteristics**: dark steel-gray, often colorful tarnish. Luster: metallic, opaque. Cleavage: incomplete. Fracture: uneven, brittle. Crystals: (rhombic) prismatic; dendritic, acicular, filamentary, vertically striped. **Aggregates**: radial, fibrous, granular to dense; present in antimony-ore deposits. **Accompanied by**: stibnite, quartz, arsenopyrite, pyrite. **Found in**: Saxony/Germany; Auvergne/France; Czech Republic; England; Romania; South Africa; Ontario/Canada; Colorado/USA; Mexico; Bolivia. **Similar to**: stibnite.

Calomel
Hg₂Cl₂

③ with cinnabar; Nevada/USA

Streak light yellow, white. **Mohs' hardness** 1–2. **Specific gravity** 6.4–7.1. **Characteristics**: gray, yellowish brown, colorless. Luster: adamantine; transparent to translucent. Cleavage: incomplete. Fracture: conchoidal, soft, can be cut; strong double refraction; soluble in aqua regia; dark red fluorescence under ultraviolet light. Crystals: (tetragonal) prismatic, tabular, acicular, pyramidal; very small. **Aggregates**: crusty; rough, crumbly; hornlike; present in oxidized zones of mercury deposits. **Accompanied by**: cinnabar, mercury, schwazite, barite, quartz. **Found in**: Rheinpfalz/Germany; Spain; Slovenia; Texas, California/USA; Mexico. **Similar to**: chlorargyrite.

Orpiment
As₂S₃

④ Khorassan/Iran
⑤ Goyaz/Brazil

Streak light yellow to orange. **Mohs' hardness** 1½–2. **Specific gravity** 3.48. **Characteristics**: lemon yellow to orangish-yellow. Luster: adamantine, greasy, on cleavage faces mother-of-pearl; transparent to translucent. Cleavage: perfect. Fracture: bladed, soft; can be cut; thin cleavage blades inelastically malleable; soluble in nitric acid, aqua regia, potassium leach. Crystals: (monoclinic) short prismatic; tabular; very rare. **Aggregates**: rough, dendritic, reniform, crusty, as dusting; present in deposits of arsenic-rich ore, in clay and marlstone, as volcanic sublimation product. **Accompanied by**: realgar, stibnite, pyrite, sphalerite, calcite. **Found in**: Harz mountains/Germany; Macedonia; eastern Anatolia/Turkey; Hungary; Romania; Tuscany/Italy; Wallis/Switzerland; Caucasus/Russia; Utah, Nevada/USA. **Similar to**: realgar, sulfur, greenockite, autunite.

kermesite p. 184, vivianite p. 210

Cacoxenite

① Svappavara/Sweden 1:4

$(Fe^{3+},Al)_{25}[O_6 | (OH)_{12} | (PO_4)_{17}] \cdot 75\ H_2O$

Streak straw yellow. **Mohs' hardness** 3–4. **Specific gravity** 2.2–2.4. **Characteristics:** yellow to brownish, seldom greenish. Luster: silky, waxy; translucent. Cleavage: indeterminable. Fracture: fibrous, brittle; soluble in hydrochloric acid. Flame test: bluish green. Crystals: (hexagonal) prismatic, acicular, filamentary, occasionally with hexagonal contours, small. **Aggregates:** fibrous, clusters, reniform, as dusting; present in limonite deposits, pegmatites. **Accompanied by:** hematite, limonite, siderite, strengite. **Found in:** Hesse, northern Bavaria, Thüringen/Germany; Czech Republic; France; Sweden; Arkansas, Alabama/USA. **Similar to:** all types of ochre, such as hematite.

Jarosite

② Laurion/Greece

$KFe_3^{3+}[(OH)_6 | (SO_4)_2]$

Streak yellow. **Mohs' hardness** 3–4. **Specific gravity** 2.9–3.3. **Characteristics:** ochre-yellow, brown to blackish brown. Luster: vitreous, adamantine, dull; translucent. Cleavage: incomplete. Fracture: conchoidal to uneven, brittle; greasy to the touch when rubbed; soluble in acid. Crystals: (trigonal) tabular, rhombohedral, very small; occasionally pseudomorphic. **Aggregates:** rough, scaly, fibrous, botryoidal, crusty, granular, crumbly; present in oxidized zones of sulfide deposits. **Accompanied by:** limonite, hematite, alunite, quartz. **Found in:** Erzgebirge/Germany; Spain; Greece; Urals/Russia; South Dakota/Russia; Chile. **Similar to:** limonite, beudantite, all types of ochre such as hematite.

Wurtzite

③ Pibram/Czech Republic 1:½
④ Wiesloch, Baden/Germany

ZnS

Streak light brown. **Mohs' hardness** 3½–4. **Specific gravity** 4.0. **Characteristics:** light to dark brown. Luster: vitreous, resinous; translucent. Cleavage: complete. Fracture: uneven, brittle; soluble in hydrochloric acid; occasionally orange fluorescence under ultraviolet light. Crystals: (hexagonal) prismatic to pyramidal, also tabular, mostly horizontally striped; rare and small; twinning; quadrupling. **Aggregates:** rough, crusty, finely fibrous to dense; polymorph of sphalerite often combined in banded intergrowth with protruding surfaces; present in veins, in sedimentary rocks. **Accompanied by:** sphalerite, galena; pyrite; siderite; marcasite; quartz. **Found in:** Erzgebirge/Germany; Czech Republic; Upper Silesia/Poland; Slovenia; Montana, Missouri/USA; Bolivia; Peru. **Similar to:** sphalerite.

Hauerite

⑤ Sicily/Italy

MnS_2

Streak reddish brown. **Mohs' hardness** 4. **Specific gravity** 3.5. **Characteristics:** brownish to red to brownish black. Luster: metallic, adamantine, dull; opaque, thin layers transparent. Cleavage: complete. Fracture: conchoidal to uneven, brittle; soluble in hydrochloric acid. Crystals: (cubic) octahedral or cubo-octahedral; usually intergrowth. **Aggregates:** dendritic, spheroidal; crusty, granular to dense; present in clay and gypsum stone, on salt and sulfur deposits, also in schist. **Accompanied by:** gypsum, calcite, sulfur, pyrite. **Found in:** Czech Republic; Sicily/Italy; Louisiana/USA; New Zealand.

ankerite p. 68, astrophyllite p. 72, betafite p. 74, chlorite p. 134, dufrenite p. 140, beudanite p. 142, heterosite p. 188, sphalerite p. 198, limonite p. 202

Sphalerite zincblende
① Trepca/Kosovo
ZnS

Streak brown, white. **Mohs' hardness** 3½–4. **Specific gravity** 3.9–4.2. **Characteristics**: yellow, brown to black, seldom red, green. Luster: adamantine, greasy, metallic; transparent to translucent. Cleavage: complete. Fracture: conchoidal, brittle; soluble in nitric acid; foul-smelling odor when rubbed on streak plate. Crystals: (cubic) tetrahedral, dodecahedral, hexahedral, often distorted and striped; twinning, pseudomorphic. **Aggregates**: rough, spar-like, granular, dense, radial; partially intergrown with wurtzite; present in plutonic rocks, in ore veins, schist, as petrification medium. **Accompanied by**: galena, chalcopyrite, pyrrhotite, arsenopyrite, pyrite, marcasite, barite, fluorite. **Found in**: western Westfalia, Erzgebirge/Germany; Czech Republic; Upper Silesia/Poland; Serbia; eastern Siberia/Russia; Idaho/USA. **Similar to**: galena, sulfur, tennanite, tetrahedrite, wolframite, garnet.

Zincite
② New Jersey/USA 1:3
ZnO

Streak orange to yellow. **Mohs' hardness** 4–5. **Specific gravity** 5.4–5.7. **Characteristics**: red to reddish brown. Luster: adamantine, greasy; transparent to translucent. Cleavage: complete. Fracture: conchoidal, brittle; soluble in acid. Crystals: (hexagonal) pyramidal; very rare. **Aggregates**: rough, spar-like, granular, scattered; present in marble. **Accompanied by**: franklinite, willemite, calcite, garnet. **Found in**: Tuscany/Italy; Poland; Spain; New Jersey, Colorado/USA; Tasmania/Australia. **Similar to**: rutile, cinnabar.

Carnotite
③ Arizona/USA
K₂[(UO₂)₂|V₂O₈] · 3 H₂O

$K_2[(UO_2)_2|V_2O_8] \cdot 3\,H_2O$

Streak yellow, greenish. **Mohs' hardness** approximately 4. **Specific gravity** 4.5–4.7. **Characteristics**: canary yellow to greenish yellow, seldom red, green. Luster: adamantine, greasy; transparent to translucent. Cleavage: complete. Fracture: bladed, brittle; powder exposed to hydrochloric acid will turn blood-red; not readily soluble in acid. Strongly radioactive. Crystals: (monoclinic) tabular, bladed; small and rare. **Aggregates**: crusty, reniform, granular, crumbly, as impregnation; present in sedimentary rocks, in uranium deposits. **Accompanied by**: pitchblende; pyrite, chalcopyrite, bornite. **Found in**: England; Morocco; DR Congo; Uzbekistan; southern Australia; Colorado/USA. **Similar to**: uranocircite, autunite.

Vanadinite
④ Mibladen/Morocco
Pb₅[Cl|(VO₄)₃]

$Pb_5[Cl|(VO_4)_3]$

Streak yellowish, white. **Mohs' hardness** 3. **Specific gravity** 6.5–7.1. **Characteristics**: yellow, brown, orangish red. Luster: adamantine, greasy; translucent to opaque. Cleavage: none. Fracture: conchoidal, brittle; readily soluble in nitric acid. Crystals: (hexagonal) short columnar, tabular, pyramidal, sometimes barrel-shaped; pseudomorphic. **Aggregates**: rough, radial, fibrous, reniform, spheroidal; present in oxidized zones of lead deposits. **Accompanied by**: descloizite, pyromorphite, wulfenite, mottramite, calcite. **Found in**: Kärnten/Austria; Karawanken/Slovenia; Morocco; Zambia; Kazakhstan; Arizona/USA; Argentina; Chihuahua/Mexico. **Similar to**: pyromorphite, mimetite, apatite, crocoite, descloizite.

betafite p. 74, beudantite p. 142, olivenite p. 142, krennerite p. 152, tennantite p. 158, tetrahedrite p. 158, calaverite p. 168, uraninite p. 178

Powellite

① Poona, India

Ca[MoO₄]

Streak yellowish to white, greenish. **Mohs' hardness** 3½–4. **Specific gravity** 4.2–4.3. **Characteristics:** greenish yellow, gray, brown, blue to blue-black. Luster: adamantine, vitreous, greasy; transparent. Cleavage: incomplete. Fracture: uneven, brittle; soluble in hydrochloric acid; yellow to orange fluorescence under ultraviolet light. Crystals: (tetragonal) dipyramidal, flat tabular; small; pseudomorphic. **Aggregates:** rough, scaly, dendritic, crusty, crumbly, as dusting; present in oxidized zones of ore deposits. **Accompanied by:** molybdenite, scheelite, laumontite, calcite, quartz. **Found in:** Turkey; Morocco; Caucasus/Russia; Michigan/USA. **Similar to:** scheelite, wulfenite.

Greenockite

② Mittenwald/Germany 1:3

CdS

Streak yellow. **Mohs' hardness** 3–3½. **Specific gravity** 4.8–5.0. **Characteristics:** yellow to orange, brown. Luster: greasy-adamantine, resinous; translucent. Cleavage: complete. Fracture: conchoidal, brittle; soluble in hydrochloric acid; sometimes orange fluorescence under ultraviolet light. Crystals: (hexagonal) pyramidal, prismatic, thick tabular, often horizontally striped; rare and small; twinning. **Aggregates:** powdery covering; present in oxidized zones of sphalerite-bearing deposits. **Accompanied by:** sphalerite, smithsonite, natrolite, quartz, calcite. **Found in:** Erzgebirge/Germany; Czech Republic; Scotland; Urals/Russia; Bolivia; Missouri, Arkansas/USA. **Similar to:** orpiment, realgar, wulfenite, and all types of ochre.

Manganite

③ Illfeld/Germany

Mn³⁺O(OH)

Streak dark brown, black. **Mohs' hardness** 4. **Specific gravity** 4.3–4.4. **Characteristics:** brownish black, weathered steel gray. Luster: metallic; opaque, very thin splinters red, translucent. Cleavage: complete. Fracture: uneven, brittle; soluble in hydrochloric acid. Crystals: (monoclinic) prismatic, vertically striped, rarely tabular; twinning, pseudomorphic. **Aggregates:** rough, radial tangles, crumbly, granular, oolitic; present in magmatite veins, also as weathering on sedimentary deposits. **Accompanied by:** barite, pyrolusite, psilomelane, braunite, hausmannite, limonite, calcite. **Found in:** Harz mountains, Thüringer Forest/Germany; Cornwall/England; Ukraine; Sardinia/Italy; Vogesen/France; Nova Scotia/Canada; California, Arizona/USA; India. **Similar to:** stibnite, pyrolusite, goethite, enargite.

Descloizite

④ Ankas/Namibia 1:2

Pb(Zn,Cu)[OH | VO₄]

Streak light brown. **Mohs' hardness** 3½. **Specific gravity** 5.5–6.2. **Characteristics:** brown, brownish red, brownish black. Luster: resinous, adamantine, on cleavage face greasy; transparent to opaque. Cleavage: none. Fracture: conchoidal, brittle; soluble in acid. Crystals: (rhombic) prismatic, dipyramidal, tabular. **Aggregates:** rough, radial, botryoidal, crusty; present in oxidized zones of nonferrous metal deposits. **Accompanied by:** vanadanite, pyromorphite, cerussite, wulfenite, limonite, quartz. **Found in:** Rheinpfalz/Germany; Kärnten/Austria; Algeria; DR Congo; Zambia; Arizona, New Mexico/USA; Argentina. **Similar to:** mottramite, magnetite, wulfenite, vanadanite.

cuprite p. 188, gold p. 192, berthierite p. 194, limonite p. 202, huebnérite p. 208

Aegirine acmite
NaFe^{3+}[Si$_2$O$_6$]

① Eker/Norway

Streak yellow to brownish, greenish. **Mohs' hardness** 6–6½. **Specific gravity** 3.5–3.6. **Characteristics**: dark green, greenish black, brownish. Luster: vitreous, resinous; opaque, on edges greasy, translucent. Cleavage: complete. Fracture: uneven, brittle. Flame test: yellow. Pleochroic. Crystals: (monoclinic) columnar, acicular, tabular, vertically striped; usually intergrowth; often twinning. **Aggregates**: rough, fibrous, radial, granular; present in magmatites, pegmatites, seldom in metamorphic rocks. **Accompanied by**: arfvedsonite, feldspars, nepheline, sodalite, zircon. **Found in**: Norway; Sweden; Portugal; Sardinia/Italy; Kola/Russia; Quebec/Canada; Arkansas, Montana/USA. **Similar to**: hornblende, arfvedsonite, actinolite.

Neptunite
KNa$_2$Li(Fe^{2+},Mg,Mn^{2+})$_2$Ti$_2^{4+}$[O | Si$_4$O$_{11}$]$_2$

② California/USA 1:3

Streak brown. **Mohs' hardness** 5½. **Specific gravity** 3.2. **Characteristics**: black to dark brown, as splinter red. Luster: strong vitreous; opaque to translucent. Cleavage: complete. Fracture: conchoidal, brittle; strong pleochroism. Crystals: (monoclinic) prismatic. **Aggregates**: none; only individual crystals, intergrowth and surface growth; present in pegmatites, natrolite deposits. **Accompanied by**: benitoite, natrolite, aegirine. **Found in**: Ireland; Kola/Russia; Greenland; Canada; California/USA.

Goethite
Fe^{3+}O(OH)

③ Freisen, Saarland/Germany 1:8
④ Chihuahua/Mexico

Streak brown to yellow. **Mohs' hardness** 5–5½. **Specific gravity** 3.8–4.3. **Characteristics**: brown to yellow. Luster: strong vitreous; opaque, thin splinters translucent. Cleavage: complete. Fracture: uneven, brittle; soluble in hydrochloric acid. Crystals: (rhombic) prismatic, acicular, tabular, horizontally striped; rare, pseudomorphic. **Aggregates**: rough, radial, crusty, dense, crumbly, acicular, velvet-like; present in oxidized zones of sulfide-ore deposits. **Accompanied by**: lepidocrocite, hematite, pyrite, calcite, quartz. **Found in**: Siegerland/Germany; Czech Republic; England; Lothringen/France; Crimea/Ukraine; Canada; Alabama/USA; Cuba. **Similar to**: manganite, lepidocrocite, hematite.

Limonite
FeOOH · nH$_2$O

⑤ ochre; Auerbach, Oberpfalz/Germany
⑥ Westerwald/Germany

Mixture of goethite and lepidocrocite. **Streak** brown. **Mohs' hardness** 4–5½. **Specific gravity** 2.7–4.3. **Characteristics**: yellow (yellow iron ore, ochre) to brown, black. Luster: vitreous, adamantine, dull; translucent to opaque. Cleavage: indeterminable. Fracture: conchoidal, uneven, fibrous, brittle, soluble in hydrochloric acid. Crystals: (rhombic) cryptocrystalline, usually amorphous; often pseudomorphic. **Aggregates**: rough, crumbly, powdery, reniform; tuberous, bean-shaped, oolitic; present in oxidized zones of iron-ore deposits, as petrification medium. **Accompanied by**: pyrite, hematite, pyrolusite, psilomelane, calcite, quartz. **Found in**: Lower Saxony/Germany; Lothringen/France; Luxembourg; Elba/Italy; Ukraine; Urals/Russia; Utah, Arizona/USA; Cuba; Brazil; DR Congo; India. **Similar to**: hematite and other ochre.

betafite p. 74, bronzite p. 110, allanite p. 144, hedenbergite p. 146, hornblende p. 146, hypersthene p. 170, lepidocrocite p. 190, pyrochlore p. 204

Franklinite

$(Zn,Mn^{2+},Fe^{2+})(Fe^{3+},Mn^{3+})_2O_4$

① Franklin,
New Jersey/USA

Streak reddish brown. **Moh's hardness** 6–6½. **Specific gravity** 5.0–5.2.
Characteristics: iron-black. Luster: metallic; opaque; very thin splinters deep
red, translucent. Cleavage: incomplete. Fracture: conchoidal to uneven, brittle; slightly magnetic; soluble in hydrochloric acid. Crystals: (cubic) octahedral, edges mostly rounded; intergrowth. **Aggregates**: rough, granular to
dense; present in zinc-ore deposits. **Accompanied by**: zincite, willemite,
rhodonite, garnet, axinite, magnetite. **Found in**: New Jersey/USA. **Similar to**:
magnetite, chromite, braunite, hausmannite.

Pyrochlore

$(Na,Ca)_2Nb_2O_6(OH,F)$

② Minas Gerais/Brazil 1:3

Streak pale yellow to brown. **Mohs' hardness** 5–5½. **Specific gravity** 3.5–4.6.
Characteristics: light yellow to dark brown, reddish. Luster: vitreous, greasy,
adamantine; translucent to opaque. Cleavage: none. Fracture: conchoidal to
uneven, brittle. Often radioactive. Crystals: (cubic) octahedral; seldom cubes,
mostly intergrowth. **Aggregates**: rough, granular to dense; present in foyaite
(syenite), carbonatite, pegmatites, by-product of volcanic eruptions.
Accompanied by: zircon, feldspars, nepheline, calcite, biotite, apatite,
fluorite. **Found in**: Eifel/Germany; Norway; Sweden; Urals, Kola/Russia;
Tanzania; Uganda; Greenland; Ontario/Canada; Colorado/USA. **Similar to**:
befatite, zircon, scheelite.

Rutile

TiO_2

③ Namibia 1:2
④ in quartz crystals; Brazil

Streak yellowish brown. **Mohs' hardness** 6–6½. **Specific gravity** 4.2–4.3.
Characteristics : brownish red, red, yellowish, iron-black. Luster: metallic-like,
adamantine; transparent to opaque. Cleavage: complete. Fracture: conchoidal to uneven, brittle; strong double-refraction. Crystals: (tetragonal)
prismatic, dipyramidal; dendritic, acicular; thick columnar, often vertically
striped; intergrowth and surface growth; twinning, polycrystalline sometimes
with net-like intergrowth (sagenite). **Aggregates**: rough, granular, acicular, often intergrown with quartz; present in basic magmatites, pegmatites, metamorphic rocks, alpine crevices, alluvial deposits. **Accompanied by**: apatite,
hematite, brookite, anatase, titanite. **Found in**: Tyrol/Austria; southern
Tirol/Italy; Wallis/Switzerland; Norway; Urals/Russia; Virginia/USA; Mexico;
Brazil; Namibia. **Similar to**: zincite, cassiterite, magnetite, zircon, tourmaline.

Braunite

$Mn^{2+}Mn_6^{3+}[O_8 \mid SiO_4]$

⑤ Langban/Sweden 1:8

Streak dark brown, black-brown. **Mohs' hardness** 6–6½. **Specific gravity**
4.7–4.8. **Characteristics**: black to brownish black. Luster: metallic; opaque.
Cleavage: complete. Fracture: uneven, brittle; solubility in hydrochloric acid
difficult. Crystals: (tetragonal) octahedroid, dipyramidal, usually very small;
twinning. **Aggregates**: crystalline crusts, rough, granular, dense; present in
manganese deposits. **Accompanied by**: hausmannite, manganite, pyrolusite,
psilomelane, magnetite, barite, calcite, quartz. **Found in**: Thüringen/Germany;
Piemonte/Italy; Sweden; Griqualand West/South Africa; Namibia; Kazakhstan,
Urals/Russia; Texas, California/USA; Minas Gerais/Brazil; Chile. **Similar to**:
hausmannite, magnetite, bromite, franklinite, bixbyite.

---

betafite p. 74, brookite p. 114, allanite p. 144, ilmenite p. 174,
psilomelane p. 176, columbite p. 180

Streak

gold and
brown

Mohs' h.
— 1 ◄
2 ◄
3 ◄
4 ◄
— 5 ◄
6 ◄
7 ◄
8 ◄
9 ◄
— 10 ◄

S. gravity
— 1 ◄
2 ◄
3 ◄
4 ◄
5 ◄
6 ◄
7 ◄

Euxenite
$(Y,Ca,Ce,U,Th)(Nb,Ta,Ti)_2O_6$

① Madagascar 1:5

Streak yellowish to brownish, gray. **Mohs' hardness** $5\frac{1}{2}$–$6\frac{1}{2}$. **Specific gravity** 4.3–5.9. **Characteristics**: black, greenish brown, often with a greenish cover. Luster: metallic, resinous, greasy; opaque, thin splinters translucent. Cleavage: none. Fracture: conchoidal, brittle. Soluble in powder form in hot hydrochloric and sulfuric acid. Radioactive. Crystals: (rhombic) short prismatic, tabular, often striped, frequent twinning. **Aggregates**: rough, granular, fan-shaped; present in granite pegmatites, alluvial deposits. **Accompanied by**: monazite, ilmenite, magnetite, beryl, zircon, gadolinite. **Found in**: Hohe Tauern/Austria; Norway; Finland; Madagascar; Ontario/Canada; North Carolina/USA. **Similar to**: columbite, monazite, fergusonite, betafite.

Fergusonite
$YNbO_4$

② Madagascar 1:3

Streak light brown, gray-green. **Mohs' hardness** 5–$6\frac{1}{2}$. **Specific gravity** 4.7–6.3. **Characteristics**: black to brownish. Luster: vitreous, dull, on fresh surfaces greasy and metallic; opaque, thin splinters translucent. Cleavage: none. Fracture: conchoidal to uneven, brittle. Occasionally radioactive. Crystals: (tetragonal) prismatic, dipyramidal; always intergrowth. **Aggregates**: rough, granular to dense; present in granite pegmatites, alluvial deposits. **Accompanied by**: monazite, euxenite, gadolinite. **Found in**: Norway; Sweden; Finland; Urals/Russia; Tanzania; Zimbabwe; Madagascar; Greenland; Texas, California/USA; Sri Lanka. **Similar to**: columbite, gadolinite, monazite.

Chromite
$Fe^{2+}Cr_2O_4$

③ Guleman/Turkey

Streak brown. **Mohs' hardness** $5\frac{1}{2}$. **Specific gravity** 4.5–4.8. **Characteristics**: black to brownish black. Luster: greasy to metallic; opaque; thin splinters brown, translucent. Cleavage: none. Fracture: uneven to conchoidal, brittle; sometimes slightly magnetic. Crystals: (cubic) octahedral; rare and small. **Aggregates**: rough, granular, in clumps, dense, scattered; present in peridotite, serpentinite, banded complexes. **Accompanied by**: olivine, bronzite, uvarovite, magnetite, pure platinum, kämmererite. **Found in**: Steiermark/Austria; Silesia/Poland; Serbia; Turkey; Norway; Transvaal/South Africa; Urals, Altai/ Russia; California, Oregon/USA; New Zealand. **Similar to**: magnetite, franklinite, braunite, ilmenite.

Hausmannite
$Mn^{2+}Mn^{3+}_2O_4$

④ Langban/Sweden

Streak brown to reddish. **Mohs' hardness** $5\frac{1}{2}$. **Specific gravity** 4.7–4.8. **Characteristics**: iron-black with brownish tint. Luster: metallic; opaque; thin splinters deep red, translucent. Cleavage: complete. Fracture: uneven, brittle; soluble in hydrochloric acid. Crystals: (tetragonal) pseudo-octahedral, pyramidal, often horizontally striped; intergrowth and surface growth; frequent twinning, particularly quintupling, pseudomorphic. **Aggregates**: rough, granular, dense; present in manganese deposits. **Accompanied by**: braunite, pyrolusite, psilomelane, manganite, piemontite, magnetite, barite. **Found in**: Harz mountains, Thüringer Forest/Germany; Graubünden/Switzerland; Sweden; Bulgaria; England; Urals/Russia; Nevada, California/USA; Brazil; India. **Similar to**: braunite, magnetite, franklinite, psilomelane.

hematite p. 190, zincite p. 198, goethite p. 202, limonite p. 202

Huebnerite

① Silverton, California/USA 1:7

$Mn^{2+}WO_4$

Streak reddish brown. **Mohs' hardness** 4–5½. **Specific gravity** 7.2–7.3. **Characteristics**: yellow, red to dark brown, brownish black. Luster: metallic, resinous; transparent to opaque. Cleavage: complete. Fracture: uneven, brittle. Crystals: (monoclinic) short to long columnar, tabular, vertically striped; rare; twinning, pseudomorphic. **Aggregates**: parallel or radial arranged crystals; present in pegmatites, veins. **Accompanied by**: wolframite, scheelite, rhodochrosite, fluorite, quartz. **Found in**: Erzgebirge/Germany; Czech Republic; France; Transbaikal region/Russia; Colorado, New Mexico/USA; Peru; Australia. **Similar to**: goethite.

Wolframite

② Erzgebirge/Germany

$(Fe^{2+},Mn^{2+})WO_4$

Streak brown to black. **Mohs' hardness** 5–5½. **Specific gravity** 7.1–7.6. **Characteristics**: dark brown to black. Luster: metallic, greasy; transparent to opaque. Cleavage: complete. Fracture: uneven, brittle; soluble in hydrochloric acid; powder will turn blue in concentrated sulfuric acid. Crystals: (monoclinic) thick tabular, prismatic, acicular, mostly vertically striped; surface growth and intergrowth; twinning, pseudomorphic. **Aggregates**: rough, bladed, radial, as impregnation; present in veins, pegmatites, alluvial deposits. **Accompanied by**: cassiterite, zinnwaldite, molybdenite, fluorite, apatite, quartz. **Found in**: Erzgebirge/Germany; Spain; Portugal; England; China; Malaysia; Burma; Canada; Colorado/USA; Bolivia; Queensland/Australia. **Similar to**: sphalerite, columbite, cassiterite.

Niccolite nickeline

③ St. Joachimsthal/ Czech Republic

NiAs

Streak brownish black. **Mohs' hardness** 5–5½. **Specific gravity** 7.5–7.8. **Characteristics**: bright copper-red, often tinted grayish black or with a green crust (anabergite). Luster: metallic, dull; opaque. Cleavage: incomplete. Fracture: conchoidal to uneven, brittle; gives off garlic odor when fractured; soluble in nitric acid with a green color. Crystals: (hexagonal) tabular, pyramidal; very rare and small; occasionally twinning. **Aggregates**: rough, botryoidal, knitted, dense, scattered; present in ore veins, gabbros. **Accompanied by**: chloanthite, skutterudite, bismuth, silver, proustite, arsenic, galena, barite. **Found in**: Black Forest, Erzgebirge, Harz mountains/Germany; Czech Republic; Ontario/Canada; California/USA; Japan. **Similar to**: breithauptite, maucherite, pyrrhotite, linneite, pure bismuth.

Breithauptite

④ St. Andreasberg/Germany 1:10

NiSb

Streak reddish brown. **Mohs' hardness** 5½. **Specific gravity** 7.5–8.5. **Characteristics**: bright copper-red, tinted blue-violet. Luster: metallic; opaque. Cleavage: incomplete. Fracture: uneven to conchoidal, brittle; soluble in nitric acid and aqua regia; Crystals: (hexagonal) thin tabular, columnar, acicular; rare; twinning. **Aggregates**: rough, granular, bladed, dendritic; present in ore veins. **Accompanied by**: chloanthite, niccolite, ullmannite, pyrargyrite, silver. **Found in**: Harz mountains/Germany; Sardinia/Italy; Sweden; Norway; Ontario/Canada. **Similar to**: maucherite, niccolite, bismuth.

cassiterite p. 132, uraninite p. 178, columbite p. 180, maucherite p. 182, fergusonite p. 206

Liroconite

① Cornwall/England 1:2

$Cu_2Al[(OH)_4 | AsO_4] \cdot 4\,H_2O$

Streak blue, blue-green. **Mohs' hardness** 2–2½. **Specific gravity** 2.9–3.0. **Characteristics:** sky blue to greenish. Luster: vitreous, greasy; transparent to translucent. Cleavage: incomplete. Fracture: conchoidal to uneven, brittle; soluble in acid. Crystals: (monoclinic) pseudohexagonal, lens-shaped; small and rare. **Aggregates:** rough, granular; present in oxidized zones of copper deposits. **Accompanied by:** azurite, malachite, chalcophyllite, olivenite. **Found in:** Saxony/Germany; Czech Republic; England; Urals/Russia; California/USA. **Similar to:** azurite, malachite, chalcanthite.

Vivianite

② Trepca/Kosovo

$Fe_3^{2+}[PO_4]_2 \cdot 8\,H_2O$

Streak light blue, white, brownish. **Mohs' hardness** 1½–2. **Specific gravity** 2.6–2.7. **Characteristics:** white, blue when exposed to air, black, brown. Luster: vitreous, on cleavage face mother-of-pearl; transparent to translucent. Cleavage: complete. Fracture: bladed, fibrous, soft; thin blades malleable; strong pleochroism; readily soluble in hydrochloric and nitric acid. Flame test: blue-green. Crystals: (monoclinic) long prismatic to tabular; surface growth; usually small, rare. **Aggregates:** radial, fibrous, spheroidal, botryoidal, crumbly to powdery; present in ore-deposit sediments, on pegmatites, in clay, bogs, brown coal deposits, as impregnation, in bones and teeth of fossils (e.g., odontolite). **Accompanied by:** pyrrhotite, pyrite, siderite, triphylite. **Found in:** eastern Bavaria, Thüringen/Germany; Cornwall/England; Serbia; Crimea/Ukraine; Colorado/USA; Bolivia; Cameroon. **Similar to:** azurite, lazulite, turquoise.

Chalcanthite

③ Laurion/Greece 1:3

$Cu[SO_4] \cdot 5\,H_2O$

Streak blue, also colorless. **Mohs' hardness** 2½. **Specific gravity** 2.2–2.3. **Characteristics:** light to dark blue, greenish blue. Luster: vitreous; transparent to translucent. Cleavage: incomplete. Fracture: conchoidal, brittle; readily soluble in water; repulsive taste. Crystals: (triclinic) short prismatic; thick tabular; many different shapes; rare and small. **Aggregates:** rough, stalactitic, fibrous, crusty, botryoidal, surface growth, also granular and dense; present in oxidized zones of copper deposits in arid climates, in old mines. **Accompanied by:** chalcopyrite, atacamite, bronchantite, malachite, pyrite. **Found in:** Harz mountains, Erzgebirge/Germany; Slovakia; Spain; England; Ireland; Chile; California, Arizona/USA. **Similar to:** azurite, liroconite.

Cyanotrichite

④ La Garone, Var/France 1:5

$Cu_4Al_2[(OH)_{12} | SO_4] \cdot 2\,H_2O$

Streak blue. **Mohs' hardness** 1–3, difficult to determine. **Specific gravity** 2.7–2.9. **Characteristics:** sky blue to dark blue. Luster: silky to vitreous; transparent to translucent. Cleavage: incomplete. Fracture: uneven; soluble in acid. Crystals: (rhombic) filamentary, acicular, long tabular; rare. **Aggregates:** radial tufts, velvet-like; present in oxidized zones of copper deposits. **Accompanied by:** brochantite, malachite, azurite, smithsonite. **Found in:** Var/France; Elba/Italy; Attica/Greece; Romania; Scotland; Urals/Russia; Namaqualand/South Africa; Arizona, Nevada/USA. **Similar to:** azurite, aurichalcite, connelite.

annabergite p. 48, tyrolite p. 136

Linarite

PbCu[(OH)₂|SO₄]

① New Mexico/USA

Streak light blue. **Mohs' hardness** 2½. **Specific gravity** 5.3–5.5. **Characteristics**: azure blue. Luster: adamantine; translucent. Cleavage: complete. Fracture: conchoidal, brittle; when touched with hydrochloric acid color turns light blue to white; soluble in diluted nitric acid. Crystals: (monoclinic) prismatic, less often tabular; often multifaceted; surface growth, usually small; frequent twinning. **Aggregates**: in crystal groups and crusts, also radial, fibrous, matted, crumbly, powdery; present in oxidized zones of copper-lead deposits. **Accompanied by**: galena, cerussite, anglesite, brochantite, chalcopyrite, malachite, azurite, calcite. **Found in**: Black Forest, Harz mountains/Germany; Sierra Moraina/Spain; Kärnten/Austria; Sardinia/Italy; Cumberland/England; Namibia; Arizona, Utah/USA; Argentina; New South Wales/Australia. **Similar to**: azurite, caledonite, lapis lazuli, serpierite.

Diaboleite

Pb₂[Cu(OH)₄Cl₂]

② Mendip Hills/Wales 1:2

Streak blue. **Mohs' hardness** 2½. **Specific gravity** 5.42. **Characteristics**: light blue to deep blue. Luster: vitreous; transparent to translucent. Cleavage: complete. Fracture: conchoidal to bladed, brittle. Crystals: (tetragonal) tabular, prismatic, usually with square contours, small. **Aggregates**: rough, granular, bladed; present in oxidized zones of copper-lead deposits. **Accompanied by**: boleite, linarite, cerrussite, phosgenite. **Found in**: Summerset/England; Attica/Greece; Arizona/USA. **Similar to**: boleite.

Caledonite

Pb₅Cu₂[(OH)₆|CO₃|(SO₄)₃]

③ Lead Hills/England 1:12

Streak blue, also white, greenish. **Mohs' hardness** 2½–3. **Specific gravity** 5.6–5.7. **Characteristics**: blue, light green to bluish green. Luster: vitreous, greasy; transparent to translucent. Cleavage: complete. Fracture: uneven, brittle. Crystals: (rhombic) prismatic, fibrous, acicular; rare, small. **Aggregates**: tuft-like, as surfaces covering, rough; present in oxidized zones of copperlead deposits. **Accompanied by**: anglesite, leadhillite, linarite, malachite, cerussite. **Found in**: Scotland; Cumberland/England; Sardinia/Italy; Romania; Urals/Russia; Namibia; Arizona, California/USA; Chile; Japan. **Similar to**: linarite.

Aurichalcite

(Zn,Cu)₅[(OH)₆|(CO₃)₂]

④ Mapimi, Durango/Mexico

Streak light blue, also white and blue-green. **Mohs' hardness** 2. **Specific gravity** 3.6–4.2. **Characteristics**: pale green to sky blue, greenish blue. Luster: mother-of-pearl, silky; translucent. Cleavage: complete. Fracture: bladed, soft; soluble in acid and ammonia. Flame test: green. Crystals: (monoclinic) finely fibrous, acicular, tabular, indistinct faces; very rare and small. **Aggregates**: bladed, rosette-shaped, crumbly, dense, as crusts, surface covering; present in oxidized zones of nonferrous deposits. **Accompanied by**: malachite, azurite, smithsonite, sphalerite, hemimorphite, chalcopyrite, cuprite, limonite. **Found in**: Attica/Greece; Sardinia/Italy; Romania; Santander/Spain; Lyon/France; Altai/Russia; Namibia; Arizona, Utah/USA; Mexico. **Similar to**: chrysocolla, cyanotrichite.

annabergite p. 48, tyrolite p. 136, covellite p. 148

Azurite

Cu$_3$[OH | CO$_3$]$_2$

① on malachite; Arizona/USA

Streak light blue. **Mohs' hardness** 3½–4. **Specific gravity** 3.7–3.9. **Characteristics**: deep blue. Luster: vitreous, adamantine; transparent to almost opaque. Cleavage: complete. Fracture: conchoidal to uneven, brittle; soluble in ammonia and nitric acid (effervescence). Crystals: (monoclinic) mostly short columnar to thick tabular; intergrowth and surface growth; often multifaceted, pseudomorphic; seldom twinning. **Aggregates**: rough, radial, reniform, stalactitic, spheroidal, dense; crumbly, as dusting; present in oxidized zones of copper deposits, in porous sandstones. **Accompanied by**: malachite, chalcocite, cuprite, enargite, chrysocolla, chalcopyrite, pure copper, cerussite, anglesite, limonite, calcite, aragonite. **Found in**: Eifel, Spessart/Germany; Lyon/France; Cornwall/England; Attica/Greece; Sardinia/Italy; Urals/Russia; Namibia; Arizona, New Mexico/USA; Chile, New South Wales/Australia. **Similar to**: linarite, vivianite, lapis lazuli, cyanotrichite, liroconite, chalcanthite, charoite, tyrolite.

Boleite

Pb$_{26}$Ag$_9$Cu$_{24}$(OH)$_{48}$Cl$_{62}$

② Baja California/Mexico 1:4

Streak blue, also greenish. **Mohs' hardness** 3–3½. **Specific gravity** 5.10. **Characteristics**: deep blue. Luster: vitreous, on cleavage faces mother-of-pearl; transparent to translucent. Cleavage: complete. Fracture: conchoidal, brittle; soluble in nitric acid. Crystals: (cubic) cubic, or octahedroid. **Aggregates**: botryoidal, rare; present in oxidized zones of copper-ore deposits. **Accompanied by**: malachite, azurite, diaboleite, cuprite, atacamite. **Found in**: Baja California/Mexico; Chile; Arizona/USA; New South Wales/Australia. **Similar to**: diaboleite.

Serpierite

Ca(Cu,Zn)$_4$[(OH)$_6$ | SO$_4$]$_2$ · 3 H$_2$O

③ Bad Elms/Germany 1:4

Streak bluish, also white. **Mohs' hardness** 3½–4. **Specific gravity** 2.5–3.1. **Characteristics**: sky blue. Luster: vitreous, on cleavage faces mother-of-pearl; transparent. Cleavage: complete. Fracture: uneven, brittle; soluble in acid. Crystals: (monoclinic) thin tabular to acicular; only very rare. **Aggregates**: tuft-shaped, crusty, botryoidal; present in oxidized zones of sulfide deposits. **Accompanied by**: smithsonite, cyanotrichite, linarite. **Found in**: Sauerland/Germany; Attica/Greece; Ireland; Kazakhstan; Ross Island/Antarctica. **Similar to**: linarite.

Connellite

Cu$_{19}$[Cl$_4$(OH)$_{32}$ | SO$_4$] · 2 H$_2$O

④ Cornwall/England 1:15

Streak light blue. **Mohs' hardness** 3. **Specific gravity** 3.41. **Characteristics**: greenish blue, blue-green, azure blue. Luster: vitreous; translucent. Cleavage: indeterminable. Fracture: conchoidal, brittle. Crystals: (hexagonal) finely acicular, horizontally striped. **Aggregates**: bark-like, tuft-shaped, matted; present in oxidized zones of copper-ore deposits. **Accompanied by**: azurite, malachite. **Found in**: Cornwall/England; Sardinia/Italy; Algeria; Namaqualand/South Africa; California, Utah, Arizona/USA. **Similar to**: cyanotrichite.

cyanotrichite p. 210, caledonite p. 212

Glaucophane

① Valle d'Aosta/Italy 1:2

$Na_2(Mg,Fe^{2+})_3Al_2[OH \mid Si_4O_{11}]_2$

Streak light blue. **Mohs' hardness** 5½–6½. **Specific gravity** 3.0–3.3. **Characteristics**: blue-gray, blue-lavender, blue-black. Luster: vitreous; translucent. Cleavage: complete. Fracture: conchoidal to uneven, brittle; strong pleochroism. Crystals: (monoclinic) prismatic, acicular; intergrowth; end-faces seldom well-developed. **Aggregates**: rough, dendritic, fibrous, granular; present in metamorphic rocks. **Accompanied by**: chlorite, muscovite, biotite, paragonite, clinozoisite, jadeite, epidote, garnet, albite, calcite, quartz. **Found in**: Piemonte/Italy; Walls/Switzerland; Bretagne/France; Euböa/Greece; Ukraine; Kazakhstan; California, Colorado/USA; Japan. **Similar to**: kyanite.

Arfvedsonite

② Macedonia 1:2

$Na_3(Fe^{2+},Mg)_4Fe^{3+}[OH \mid Si_4O_{11}]_2$

Streak gray to blue, also colorless. **Mohs' hardness** 5–6. **Specific gravity** 3.0–3.5. **Characteristics**: blue to greenish black, black. Luster: vitreous; opaque to translucent. Cleavage: complete. Fracture: uneven, brittle; strong pleochroism. Flame test: yellow. Crystals: (monoclinic) long columnar, tabular; rare. **Aggregates**: rough, dendritic, granular; intergrowth; present in basic plutonic rocks, less often in schist. **Accompanied by**: aegirine, nepheline, sodalite, eudialyte, zircon. **Found in**: Odenwald/Germany; Norway; Finland; Pantelleria/Italy; Ukraine; Kola/Russia; Greenland; Quebec/Canada; Colorado, New Hampshire/USA. **Similar to**: aegirine.

Odontolite

③ Kitzbühl, Tyrol/Austria 1:½

Mixture of apatite, calcite, organic substances, and vivianite.

Streak blue, white. **Mohs' hardness** 5. **Specific gravity** 3.0–3.5. **Characteristics**: turquoise blue, in artificial light blue-gray. Luster: waxy; translucent to opaque. Cleavage: indeterminable. Fracture: conchoidal; light effervescence when in contact with hydrochloric acid. Crystals: microcrystalline; present as fossil teeth and bone substances of extinct prehistoric animals (mammoth, mastodon, dinosaurs) in sedimentary rocks. **Found in**: Siberia/Russia; Gascogne/France; has become very rare. **Similar to**: turquoise, colored ivory.

Lapis Lazuli lazurite

④ Chile 1:2

$Na_6Ca_2[(S,SO_4,Cl_2)_2 \mid Al_6Si_6O_{24}]$

Streak pale blue. **Mohs' hardness** 5–6. **Specific gravity** 2.4–2.9. **Characteristics**: glazed blue, also greenish, violet, often spotted. Luster: vitreous, on cleavage faces greasy, dull; opaque, edges translucent. Cleavage: incomplete. Fracture: conchoidal to uneven, brittle; soluble in hydrochloric acid with a foul odor; white fluorescence under ultraviolet light. Crystals: (cubic) rhombododecahedral, also octahedral; very rare; only intergrowth. **Aggregates**: rough, fine-grained, dense; always in combination with other minerals, such as pyrite, sodalite, calcite, haüynite; present in limestone, sometimes in lava and as a by-product of volcanic eruptions. **Accompanied by**: scapolite, enstatite, augite, hornblende, diopside, mica, humite. **Found in**: Alban hills, Vesuvius/Italy; Afghanistan; Baikal Lake region/Russia; Burma; Pakistan; Labrador/Canada; California, Colorado/USA; Chile; Angola. **Similar to**: sodalite, haüynite, lazulite, azurite, linarite, dumortierite.

ludwigite p. 144, riebeckite p. 170

Bibliography

Anderson, B. W., and Jobbins, E. A. 1990. *Gem Testing*. Butterworths, London.

Arem, J.E. 1987. *Color Encyclopedia of Gemstones*. 2nd ed. Van Nostrand Reinhold, New York.

Bruton, E. 1977. *Diamonds*. 2nd ed. NAG, London.

Copeland, L. L. 1960. *The Diamond Dictionary*. Los Angeles.

Dake, H.C. 1950. *Northwest Gem Trails*. Portland, OR, U.S.

Fisher. P. J. 1966. *The Science of Gems*. Charles Scribner's Sons, New York.

Fleischer, M., and Mandarino, J. A. 1995. *Glossary of Mineral Species 1995*. The Mineralogical Record, Tucson, AZ, U.S.

Ford, W. E. 1932. *Dana's Textbook of Mineralogy*. John Wiley and Sons, New York.

Gill, J. O. 1978. *Gill's Index to Journals, Articles and Books Relating to Gems and Jewelry*. Gemological Institute of America, Santa Monica, CA, U.S.

Green, T. 1981. *The World of Diamonds*. Weidenfield and Nicolson, London.

Henry, D. J. 1952. *Gem Trail Journal*. Long Beach, CA, U.S.

Jahns, R. H. 1975. "Gem Materials" in *Industrial Minerals and Rocks*. 4th ed. A.I.M.E. New York.

Kraus, E. H., and Slawson, C. B. 1947. *Gems and Gem Materials*. McGraw-Hill, New York.

Lewis, D. 1977. *Practical Gem Testing*. Northwood, London.

Liddicoat, R.T., Jr., 1989. *Handbook of Gemstone Identification*. Gemological Institute of America, Santa Monica, CA, U.S.

McIver, J. R. 1967. *Gems, Minerals and Rocks in Southern Africa*. Elsevier (U.S.), New York.

Read, P. G. 1991. *Gemmology*. Butterworth-Heinemann Ltd., Oxford, UK.

Rouse, J. D. 1986. *Garnet*. Butterworths, London.

Shaub, B. M. 1975. *Treasures from the Earth*. Crown Publishers, New York.

Shipley, R. M. 1974. *Dictionary of Gems and Gemology*. Gemological Institute of America, Santa Monica, CA, U.S.

Sinkankas, J. 1970. *Gemstones of North America*. D. Van Nostrand, New York.

Sinkakas, J. 1972. *Gemstone and Mineral Data Book*. New York.

Smith, G. F. H., and Phillips, F. C. 1962. *Gemstones*. 13th ed. Methuen & Co., London.

U.S. Geological Survey (annual). Gemstones: ch. in Minerals Yearbook, U.S.G.S., Reston, VA, U.S.

Van Landingham, S. L. 1985. *Geology of World Gem Deposits*. Van Nostrand Reinhold, New York.

Webster, R., and Anderson, B. W. 1983. *Gems—Their Sources, Descriptions, and Identification*. Butterworths, London.

Yaverbaum, L. H. (ed.). 1980. *Synthetic Gems Production Techniques*. Noyes Data Corp., Park Ridge, NJ, U.S.

Gems and Gemology. Gemological Institute of America. Los Angeles.

Gems and Minerals. Mentone, CA, U.S.

Journal of Gemmology. Gemological Institute of Great Britain, London.

Journal of the German Gemmological Association. Idar-Oberstein, Germany.

Lapidary Journal. San Diego, CA, U.S.

The Mineralogical Record. Tucson, AZ, U.S.

Schweizer Strahler. Journal of the Swiss Association of Mineral Collectors and Polishers.

Glossary

accessory minor and nonessential constituents in rocks

accompanying mineral sharing the same paragenesis (see below)

acidic rocks rich in silica, at least 65%

adularescence bluish or milky sheen when cut en cabochon

amorphous minerals without a definite crystalline structure

arid climate in a region where moisture evaporates faster than can be replaced by precipitation

asterism reflection of light on parallel fibers which results in a star-shaped figure of light.

atoll coral island consisting of a reef surrounding a lagoon

aventurescence leaf-like inclusions whose metallic reflections create a play of color

basic rocks containing less than 52% silica

bituminous mass consisting of naturally occurring hydrocarbons (coal) or their derivatives (petroleum)

botryoidal resembling a cluster of grapes

cabochon jewel or gemstone with roundish cut

carat measure of weight used for gemstones. Equal to 0.2 g. International abbreviation is ct.

cat's eye effect narrow streak of light suggesting the shape of a cat's eye. Also called *chatoyancy* (*chatoyant*)

chatoyancy *See* cat's eye effect

cleavage the angle created between cleavage faces when a mineral is split

concretion spheroidal or tuberous body of mineral aggregate formed in sedimentary rocks

covering crystallized minerals forming a crust-like cover

crevice open or mineral-filled space in rock

crust thick covering of minerals

crystal a homogenous solid with regular atomic inner structure

crystal lattice a geometric arrangement of the smallest structural elements of a crystal

crystalline designation for minerals with crystal structure

crystallography the science of crystals

crystal system one of seven categories to which all crystals can be classified according to their crystal axes

cubic system one of the crystal systems

cut one-sided cutting

dense mineral aggregates whose individual components are so small that they cannot be detected with the naked eye

dendritic moss- and branch-like shapes or markings; developed during crystallization of ore and manganese compounds

deposit a particular layer of rocks within a rock formation

dike rock formation that infiltrates adjacent rocks like a foreign body substance, usually with contours. Usually igneous, but also sandstone

distortion deviation of a naturally grown crystal from its ideal shape

double refraction splitting of one light ray into two as it enters a crystal

drusy cavities hollow spaces within a rock, such as volcanics, that are filled with a collection of secondary minerals

dusting extremely thin, sometimes crust-like mineral occurrence that appears as if the mineral were sprinkled as dust across its host

emery a mixture of finely granulated corundum, magnetite, hematite, ilmenite, and quartz

epitaxy intergrowth of several well-developed crystals

facet small surface displayed by a crystal either naturally occurring from growth, as in crystal faces, or cut, as on a precious stone

fahlerz group of olive-grey-yellowish (pale luster) sulfide minerals comprising the series tetrahedrite-tennantite

feldspars a group of rock-forming silicate minerals with the subgroups orthoclase and plagioclase

fluorescence characteristic of minerals to glow when exposed to ultraviolet light (often in a different color)

fluvial belonging to or produced by a stream or river

fossil remnant, impression, or trace of animals or plants of past geological ages that has been preserved in the earth's crust

fracture breaking a mineral into irregular planes due to an external force

foyaite a kind of syenite first described in Foya, Portugal. Related to Eläolite

fumarole volcanic vent of various gases with temperature of 200-800° C

gangue the relatively worthless rock or vein material in which valuable metals or minerals occur

gemology the science of gemstones

geode cavity within a rock that has been filled with a collection of minerals

geology the science of the earth's crust, its composition and active forces

glass bead–shaped reniform-botryoidal mineral aggregate with smooth, shiny surface

gneiss foliated metamorphic rock corresponding in composition to feldspathic plutonic rocks

goniometer an instrument for measuring crystal angles

gravel small pieces of rock, with edges rounded and surfaces smoothed through water movement

guano phosphate-rich bird droppings found especially on Pacific islands that receive little rainfall

hardness usually refers to the Mohs' hardness (scratch hardness) with minerals

heat-treated subjected to a process of heating (especially precious stones) to change the color

hexagonal system one of the crystal systems

hook-shaped angular fracture, particularly in metallic minerals

host minerals that make up the bulk of a rock

hygroscopic readily taking up and retaining water

ideal crystal ideal crystal shape usually constructed according to the real crystal found in nature

imitation replication of natural gemstones

impregnation diffusely disseminated mineral in the pores of a rock

inclusion defect or foreign object, gas, or liquid contained within a mineral or rock

intermediate rocks with a 52-60% silica content

iridescence play of color that changes with the angle of the incident light

iridescent rainbow-like display of color of some minerals due to the breakdown of light in cracks and fissures

kimberlite pipe volcanic, pipe-shaped structure filled with kimberlite rock that might contain diamonds

knitted resembling knitted material

labradorescence play of color in metallic hues with labradorite

law of constant angles universally valid law stating that the angles between faces remain always constant

luster shiny appearance caused by the reflected light on the surface of the stone as on a pearl

magmatite rocks, also called igneous, created from the molten substance of the earth (magma). Those developing in the earth's crust are plutonic rocks, those on the earth's surface are volcanic rocks.

metamorphic rocks rocks that have developed into new rocks due to changes in condition in the earth's crust; well-known examples are quartzite, gneiss, phyllite, marble, slate, schist, serpentinites, amphibolites.

metamorphosis intensive transformation of rock due to great pressure and/or high temperatures. What results are metamorphic rocks (metamorphites)

meteorite a firm mass of matter from outer space that hits the earth's surface

microcrystalline designation for the smallest crystals visible only under a microscope

micromount smallest size up to approximately the size of a fingernail

mineral a naturally occurring and homogenous component of the earth's crust.

mineral aggregate mineral mixture resembling rock

mineralogy the study of minerals

mixed crystal mineral in which individual elementary components of the crystal are replaced by related substances of a similar mineral.

Mohs' hardness hardness scale for minerals with 10 degrees named after Friedrich Mohs

monoclinic system one of the crystal systems

multiple twinning twinning of many individual intergrown crystals

nodule rounded or almond-shaped lump of mineral or aggregate, typically in siliceous volcanic rocks

nugget clumps of gold or platinum in alluvial deposits

ochre yellow-to-brown-colored mixture of different iron compounds such as hematitie and limonite

oolite sedimentary rocks made up of very small spheroidal granules often of calcium carbonate cemented together

opaque impenetrable by light

opalescence the milky blue or pearly appearance of a common opal

opalization a play of color in metallic hues which produces a sheen with some opal varieties

ore mineral material with usable mineral content; in petrology all metallic minerals

orthoclase group of potash feldspar minerals

orthorhombic system one of the crystal systems

oxidized zone layers in ore deposits close to the surface, where weathering produces secondary minerals

paragenesis the formation of minerals in contact in such a manner as to affect one another's development

pegmatite magmatites with large, individual crystals

petrification the process by which the outer structure of plant or animal material buried in fine-grained sediments can be preserved as the organic material is replaced by mineral crystallization

petrography more descriptive study of rocks. Synonymous with *petrology*.

petrology the study of rocks

phosphorescence designation for the condition in which substances continue to glow even after energy-rich light has been removed

piezoelectric characteristic of some crystals that become electrically charged when mechanically altered

pisolite rocks that look like a conglomeration of small pea-shaped spheres

placer accumulation of heavy, robust minerals in a sedimentary deposit, especially of fluvial origin

plagioclase a group of triclinic feldspars

pleochroism the property of some minerals to exhibit different colors and depth of colors when viewed from different directions

plutonic rocks igneous rocks within the earth's crust that were crystallized from magma; well-known examples are: greisen, granite, granodiorite, syenite, gabbro, peridotite.

polymorphism the ability of a chemical substance to crystallize in more than one form

pore space open or subsequently mineral-filled space between grains or crystals in a rock

powder color less common designation for streak or streak color

powdery ground into powder form or having the appearance of powder

precious stone mineral or mineral aggregate with special characteristics, such as hardness, color, luster; therefore considered particularly precious for gemstones

pseudomorph mineral or mineral group displaying a strange crystal shape on the outside

pure metallic minerals in their basic elemental condition

pyroelectric a characteristic of some minerals that become electrically charged when heated or cooled

real crystal a crystal grown in nature with all its imperfections

refraction of light the bending of a ray of light when entering a crystal

rock natural mixture of different or even the same minerals in greater expansion

rock-forming significantly present in the formation of rocks

rough minerals or mineral aggregates which occur without a regular crystal surface

salt dome mushroom-shaped structure of salt contained within other rocks, usually diapiric

scattered or dispersed larger minerals (xenoliths) with typical distinct shapes scattered throughout a deposit or magmatite

secondary mineral formed subsequently to the host rock and usually derived from the host

sedimentary rocks rocks developed in the weathering process; well-known examples are: marl, shale, sandstone, greywacke, limestone, dolomite, gypsum, bauxite

silk silk-like appearance due to fine fibrous inclusions or thin channels

sinter mineral deposit in springs

space lattice less common designation for crystal lattice

sparlike aggregates having characteristically smooth, often shiny cleavage faces

stalactitic cone-like formations, similar to those suspended in dripstone caves

stalagmite column-shaped dripstone growing upwards from the ground or cave floor, or features resembling such columns

star effect *see* asterism

stratification the identifying, visible structure of a rock

sublimation transition from solid to a gas without passing through liquid phase

syenite hornblende, feldspar plutonic rock allied to granite, with or without quartz

synthetic artificially created crystal, often used as precious stone

tenacity resistance of a mineral to mechanical deformation. Sometimes synonymous with the term *toughness*

terrestrial referring to the earth's surface

tetragonal system one of the crystal systems

toughness in the more narrow sense: property of minerals to not be deformed or shattered. In the broader sense: synonymous with the term *tenacity*

transparency diaphaneity, i.e. light can pass through a medium.

trigonal system one of the crystal systems.

triclinic system one of the crystal systems

tufa porous rock formed as a deposit from springs or streams, including, among others, stalactites and stalagmites

tuff porous rock formed as a by-product of volcanic eruption

ultrabasic rocks with a silica content below 45%

variation variety of a mineral or a gemstone

vein refers to either a predominantly quartz hydrothermal crystallization or a usually horizontal, relatively narrow layer of minable mineral material — ore, lode

vent gas and steam exhalations of volcanic origin

volcanic rock igneous rocks developed from magma at or near the earth's surface, such as rhyolite, trachyte, phonolite, basalt, kimberlite

weathering the effect on rocks at the earth's surface under the influence of the elements

zeolite mineral group with more aqueous silicates

Index

Picture Credits

V. Betz: 155 br

M. Claye/Jacana: 31 al, 39 bl, 63 b, 79 bl, 83 br, 89 Mr, 107 al, 107 Mr, 107 br, 113 a, 117 bl, 119 M, 125 ar, 131 aM, 147 br, 165 a, 167 Ml, 179 Mr, 199 Ml, 201 M, 211 Ml, 211 b

W. Eisenreich/Schumann: 18a, 25, 28

H. Freese: 63 Ml, 85 a

K. Hartmann: 37 al, 69 a, 79 al, 83 al lower, 101 Mr, 103 al, 105 bl, 105 bM, 105 br, 109 br, 117 al, 119 br, 123 MM, 123 Mr, 123 br, 127 Ml, 129 al, 129 ar, 131 ar, 185 a, 193 b

R. Hochhleitner/Archive LAPIS: 31 Ml, 31 Mr, 31 b, 33 a, 35 ar, 35 Mr, 37 M, 41 Ml, 41 Mr, 53 bl, 55 Ml, 57 ar, 59 Ml, 61 ar, 63 Mr, 71 a, 71 Mr, 73 ar, 75 Ml, 91 Ml, 91 b, 93 Mr, 95 bl, 97 Mr, 105 Ml, 109 M, 113 Mr, 119 al, 133 al, 133 b, 137 Mr, 137 b, 139 Mr, 141 al, 143 a, 143 Ml, 143 Mr, 143 b, 145 ar, 145 M, 153 M, 153 br, 155 Mr, 155 bl, 157 al, 157 ar, 161 Ml, 163 al, 163 bl, 165 Ml, 169 ar, 169 Ml, 171 Mr, 173 al, 173 bl, 177 Mr, 179 Ml, 181 al, 183 Ml, 183 Mr, 189 al, 189 Ml, 191 bl, 197 a, 197 Ml, 197 Mr, 201 al, 205 al, 205 ar, 205 br, 207 a, 207 Ml, 211 Mr, 215 Mr, 217 Mr

U. Medenbach: 34 Ml, 35 Ml, 35 b, 37 al, 39 br, 43 ar, 43 bl, 47 al, 47 ar, 47 br, 49 Ml, 51 Mr, 53 al, 53 Ml, 55 a, 55 Mr, 57 al, 65 Mr, 73 al, 77 al, 81 Mr, 87 al, 87 ar, 87 bl, 89 Ml, 89 b, 97 Ml, 103 bl, 111 Mr, 115 a, 119 ar, 119 bl, 125 Ml, 125 br, 129 br, 131 bl, 135 ar, 135 bl, 139 a, 141 ar, 145 al, 149 Ml, 149 bl, 155

al, 157 M, 157 bl, 167 a, 167 Mr, 177 al, 179 a, 181 ar, 185 b, 187 Mr, 189 b, 197 br, 203 ar, 103 Ml, 209 a, 209 b, 213 Mr, 215 Ml

W. Schumann: 16

M. Viard/Jacana: 129 Ml

Weiss/Archive LAPIS: 37 br, 41 b, 45 a, 71 b, 75 al, 85 Ml, 87 br, 91 Mr, 93 a, 95 Mr, 107 Ml, 109 ar, 113 Ml, 137 Ml, 139 Ml, 141 M, 141 b, 155 Ml, 159 Ml, 165 b, 169 al, 171 Ml, 171 bl, 193 al, 201 ar, 211 a, 213 Ml, 215 b, 217 a, 217 Ml

Abbreviations:
a: above; b: below; al: above left; ar: above right; bl: below left; br: below right; M: middle; Mr: middle right; Ml: middle left; MM: center.

All other photos: H. Eisenbeiss

Photo of danburite on cover and page 119: U. Medenbach

Photo of mottramite on back cover and page 143: R. Hochleitner/Archive LAPIS

Photos pp. 2 and 3:
al (and p. 37): gypsum rose;
ar (and p. 70): pectolite;
bl (and p. 118): euclase;
M (and p. 176): pyrolusite;
r (and p. 50): hydrozincite

Drawings:
Helmute Hoffmann (except for those on pp. 11 and 12); Walter Schumann on pp. 11 and 12; from: *Knauers Buch der Erde (Knauers' Book of the Earth)*, Droemer Knauer, Munich.